Reforming Parliamentary Democracy

EDITED BY

F. LESLIE SEIDLE

AND DAVID C. DOCHERTY

McGill-Queen's University Press
Montreal & Kingston · London · Ithaca

ISBN 0-7735-2507-6 (cloth)
ISBN 0-7735-2508-4 (paper)

Legal deposit second quarter 2003
Bibliothèque nationale du Québec

Printed in Canada on acid-free paper that is 100% ancient forest free (100% post-consumer recycled), processed chlorine free.

This book has been published with the help of grants from the Canadian Study of Parliament Group and Wilfrid Laurier University.

McGill-Queen's University Press acknowledges the support of the Canada Council for the Arts for our publishing program. We also acknowledge the financial support of the Government of Canada through the Book Publishing Industry Development Program (BPIDP) for our publishing activities.

At the time of publication a French version of this publication was in progress. For information, see http://www.studyparliament.ca.

National Library of Canada Cataloguing in Publication

Reforming parliamentary democracy / edited by F. Leslie Seidle and David C. Docherty.

Includes bibliographical references and index.
ISBN 0-7735-2507-6 (bnd)
ISBN 0-7735-2508-4 (pbk)

1. Legislative bodies – Reform. 2. Legislative bodies – Canada – Reform. 3. Comparative government. I. Seidle, F. Leslie II. Docherty, David Campbell, 1961–

JF501.R43 2003 328.3'04 C2003-900023-0

Typeset in Sabon 10/12
by Caractéra inc., Quebec City

Contents

Acknowledgments

Like all edited books, this volume is the product of many people's efforts, and not just of those who contributed chapters. A number of other individuals and organizations played a major role in the process that led to its publication.

The Canadian Study of Parliament Group (CSPG) launched the project by sponsoring the original meeting of contributors. This provided an opportunity to share initial thoughts and review the thrust and direction of reforms to parliamentary democracy that had been carried out or were under discussion in the countries represented. Carmen DePape, then the secretary of the CSPG, was instrumental in arranging the schedule and itineraries of a truly international cast of scholars. Without her enormous effort this entire project would not have gotten off the ground. Robert Marleau, then Clerk of the House of Commons, was a huge supporter of this project, and arranged for logistical and financial support for the meeting. We very much appreciate all these contributions.

We would like to thank the anonymous reviewers who offered some very sound and helpful views on how to improve the consistency and quality of the volume. Many of their suggestions were reflected in revisions to the various chapters. The book has been strengthened as a result.

We appreciated the patience of the contributors who faced a few delays and many e-mails from the two of us. Their goodwill and willingness to strengthen their already high quality analyses were most encouraging.

The Canadian Study of Parliament Group and the Research Office at Wilfrid Laurier University provided financial assistance toward the publication of the book. We thank both for their continuing efforts to foster academic dialogue and public debate on parliamentary reform.

McGill-Queen's University Press demonstrated an early interest and keen support for this project. We would like to thank Aurèle Parisien, Joan McGilvray, David Schwinghamer, and Joanne Pisano for all the time they dedicated to this project.

Finally we would be remiss if we did not acknowledge the quiet encouragement of those personally close to us who provided the understanding and moral support necessary to complete the project. From Leslie to Henry, and David to Sarah, Angus, and Quinn, thank you.

REFORMING PARLIAMENTARY DEMOCRACY

Introduction

DAVID C. DOCHERTY
AND F. LESLIE SEIDLE

Parliamentary government is the most popular form of government in the democratic world. Its predominant feature is that the executive branch "derives its mandate from, and is responsible to, the legislature."[1] Yet this oldest surviving form of government, which links democratic representation and accountability of the executive to the legislature, is also the most dynamic. While countries have adopted their own style of parliamentary government to suit their societal needs, parliamentary institutions have also undergone dramatic changes within many of these states. The last decade of the twentieth century alone saw the establishment of legislatures in Scotland and Wales, a move to proportional representation in New Zealand, a referendum on the future of the monarchy in Australia, and the establishment of a new second chamber in South Africa. Parliamentary government may be old, but it is hardly stodgy.

The "mother" of parliamentary governments, the British Parliament (comprised of the House of Commons and House of Lords), has developed over several centuries and was highly influential throughout the British Empire. In consequence, the Canadian, Australian, New Zealand, and other parliaments are reflections of not only their unique histories and cultures but also the main features of the British Parliament as it was at the time of each country's founding. Questions of representation and governance – including those about how citizens and groups are represented, electoral systems, the existence of and role of second chambers, and the responsibilities of the various orders of government – are thus addressed differently in systems that originated from a shared set of principles. This volume examines the state of parliamentary democracy in Great Britain, Canada, Australia, New Zealand, and South Africa. Looking at these countries together, it is evident that in parliamentary states, as in almost all democracies, the rate of societal change outpaces the society's ability to alter its institutional arrangements. Some states (Great Britain, New Zealand, and South Africa) have recently experienced more rapid reform than others (Australia and Canada).

That said, one of the most remarkable traits of parliamentary governments since the late 1990s is how comfortable they have been in moving away from certain historic characteristics of Westminster-style democracy. The United Kingdom has not been afraid to let loose its children. In fact, it has followed them, also looking to other systems for new electoral rules and establishing devolved governments. South Africa turned to Germany as a model for its second chamber. New Zealand also turned to Germany when it devised a new electoral system. Although Australia has failed to change, it has nonetheless questioned certain traditional understandings of responsible government, notably the role of the Crown.

In many ways Canada stands alone in its adherence to the Westminster model, even as Westminster has begun to look elsewhere. That said, Canada has been active on other fronts in addressing changing understandings of representation and responsiveness in government. Yet Canada has much to learn from the ways that other Westminster systems have embraced reforms that stray from the classic conception of Westminster government.

In examining the current state of parliamentary government in the five countries mentioned above, we focus on three themes: representation, responsiveness, and multi-level governance. None of these themes is unique to parliamentary systems, but each interacts with the institutions and processes of parliamentary government as a country evolves. Just as important, how a state manages to channel representation, respond to citizens, and develop new channels for popular involvement strongly influences how people view the legitimacy of their democratic institutions and the contributions of the men and women who serve in them.

Representation, responsiveness, and multi-level governance are inextricably linked. Changes to make institutions more representative may reduce the capacity of the state to respond effectively to unforeseen crises. Increasing the number of levels of government may provide more avenues for citizens to be heard, but it may also encourage squabbles over jurisdiction, which reduce responsiveness. Additionally, the state that can offer the quickest response to societal or economic challenges might be the simplest in structure, but it might also be unrepresentative of the people it governs. The challenge for parliamentary democracies is first to find the right balance among representation, responsiveness, and effective governance, and, second, to try to ensure that changes to serve one objective do not weaken the service of others.

The countries examined in this volume share Westminster-style parliamentary government as a principal democratic feature. Beneath this canopy, however, each has developed its own way of responding to demands for change. In each country, change has been an amalgam of both incremental adjustments and more rapid and dramatic attempts at institutional renewal. We recognize that it is impossible to properly cover this evolution of democratic rule in a short section (let alone a book). As it is necessary, however, to establish a background for our examination of the themes of representation, responsiveness, and multilevel governance within these varied political systems, we begin with a cursory discussion of the development of parliamentary government.

THE ROOTS OF PARLIAMENTARY DEMOCRACY

Under the Westminster system of government, Parliament both allows the government to operate and serves as a watchdog over its actions.[2] Formally, Parliament includes the legislature, the executive, and the Crown. Although most can be excused for paying less attention to the formal role of the Crown, its importance should not be overlooked: the relationship between the monarchy and Parliament has been a central element in the evolution of Westminster governments.[3]

Originally, the House of Commons was the primary check on the power of the monarch. According to Philip Norton, the House had this role as long ago as the fourteenth century. Citizens had the right to seek "redress" through a petition to the King, but Parliament was charged with presenting it to the monarch.[4] At the same time, Parliament was also beginning to increase its authority to limit the King's spending and had the power to order an audit of government accounts.[5] (Of course at this time the monarchy was still supreme to a Parliament that consisted primarily of knights.)

The ascension of the Tudors to the throne brought the next dramatic change in the evolution of parliamentary governance. Needing parliamentary support for financing international confrontations, Tudor monarchs gradually ceded further spending authority to Parliament. It is more than a coincidence that service in Parliament became more prestigious as the power of Parliament increased in the sixteenth century. Historians disagree on the extent of the change, but most concur that it was during this period that the House of Commons began to replace the House of Lords as the primary legislative chamber.[6] That said, while parliamentary power increased and the role of Parliament began to be formalized, the Tudor period still marked an era of Crown dominance.

The most significant change in power and the eventual beginnings of parliamentary democracy came not with the English Civil War but well after when James II, angry at the Commons' refusal to grant him money, prorogued Parliament in 1685.[7] The result of the long struggle that ensued was not just a new monarchy but a Parliament that was more powerful than the monarch. As Anthony Birch notes, this "bloodless revolution" and the eventual coronation of William and Mary led to a Parliament that was no longer subservient to the monarchy, but in fact supreme over it.[8] The Bill of Rights, passed in 1689, firmly established the superiority of Parliament in law.

The subsequent development of a cabinet and first minister completed the evolution from traditional hereditary rule to the foundations of constitutional monarchy and representative government. David Judge reminds us that British government was representative long before it was democratic. Avenues to represent selected interests were available since the Magna Carta. Democratizing these processes was much longer in coming.[9]

The Reform Act of 1832 introduced the first significant expansion of the franchise (still open to only a minority of Britons) and began the process that was to result in the cabinet being held accountable to Parliament under the constitutional principle of responsible government.[10] This single move was to become the hallmark of parliamentary democracy. It also ushered in, albeit only briefly, an era of what C.E.S. Franks has termed "legislative-centred" government. While the British Parliament, like those that mirrored it, moved quickly to an era of executive-centred government (which is still with us), the notions of responsibility and accountability have endured.[11]

Most of the major developments of Westminster-style democracy had passed by the time parliamentary governments were being formed in the then British colonies. Yet the pattern of evolution, incremental change, and quick challenges to institutional equilibrium was to be repeated in many states that used parliamentary government as their model.

The experience of Canadian federalism has been one of ongoing change, most of it relatively slow, with bursts of reform (such as patriation in 1982) and sometimes tense periods of confrontation between the federal government and some of the provinces, notably Quebec. Constitutional challenges facing Canada have been more sustained in the past quarter century but are part of the pattern of continual struggle between the provinces and the federal state. Australia's recent referendum on the future of the monarchy is an example of a democratic and relatively quiet challenge to the traditional role of the Crown in parliamentary states.

By contrast, South Africa's movement to a state where all citizens are fully enfranchised captured the world's attention. Its continuing labours reflect a struggle that contrasts with the pattern of change in the United Kingdom and several other states in recent decades. New Zealand's adoption of proportional representation followed a period of economic and social turmoil. Feeling removed from a government that was elected under the plurality system, citizens were ready to embrace the recommendations of a royal commission that advocated a change to proportional representation.

The history of parliamentary democracy is thus one of change and stability. The changes are not complete, but represent a continued pattern of growth and development of parliamentary institutions and processes. Questions of representation, responsiveness, and multi-level governance lie at the heart of this ongoing evaluation.

THE THEORY OF PARLIAMENTARY DEMOCRACY

Given the evolution of parliamentary government in a wide range of countries, it is remarkable that the principles that underlie Westminster democracies have remained largely intact. Parliamentary government is, both in theory and practice, responsible government. The linkage of the executive and the legislature is the focus of political accountability. This feature of parliamentary democracy is present in all countries examined in this volume. As long ago as 1867, Walter Bagehot understated the linkage when he suggested that the cabinet is a "committee of the legislative body selected to be the executive body."[12] While he admitted that cabinet was in fact the pre-eminent committee, even such a qualification does not do justice to the power of the executive in parliamentary democracies.

The executive enjoys a degree of power that other members of the legislature can only envy. Yet with that power comes responsibility. At its most basic level, the theory of responsible government is simple. The executive is responsible *for* the actions and activities of the ministries and departments they oversee. Franks has argued that the increased complexity and sheer size of government in the latter half of the twentieth century have made this "front end" of responsibility difficult to monitor. Ministers have a difficult time keeping on top all the activities of their departments.[13]

At the same time, the executive is responsible *to* all members of the legislature for the actions and activities of the government. This is the second half of the responsibility function. Ministers must answer for their actions (or in some instances inaction) to all members of the legislature. As Mitchell and Sutherland point out, the most attractive feature of this system is to make the "bureaucracy subservient" to the legislature, albeit indirectly.[14]

From the vantage point of legislators, this doctrine of responsibility is often referred to as accountability or scrutiny. This latter activity is done both by Opposition members and by members of the governing party who are not in cabinet – so called government backbenchers. In bicameral states such as Australia, Canada, South Africa, and the United Kingdom, the second chamber can also play an effective scrutiny role – though the ability to do so varies by jurisdiction. There are many vehicles at the disposal of members for performing the accountability function, some of which are based on the standing orders of the legislature and others on the individual talents of members. In most parliamentary democracies the principal methods of accountability or scrutiny include question period, debates on the budget and Throne Speech, committees and, in the case of the governing party, the caucus.

In order to ensure that the government of the day can in fact govern, prime ministers must be secure that they constantly enjoy the confidence of the legislature. A prime minister cannot effectively lead an executive that sits in a legislature without that body's majority support. This means that a governing executive is not only responsible to the members of the legislature but must continually earn their confidence. It is this aspect of parliamentary government that Jennifer Smith refers to when she praises Westminster systems as being the most sensitive democratic systems.[15]

The role of the Crown, the third element in the triumvirate of Crown, legislature, and executive, has been altered more considerably. Reflecting the conceptual role of the monarchy in parliamentary government, when Bagehot wrote his famous treatise on parliamentary democracy in 1867 the Crown followed the cabinet in terms of importance. The House of Commons was in fourth place, below the House of Lords. As indicated earlier, the Crown continues to play an important role in the practice of parliamentary democracy. However, David Smith is correct in stating that the key relationship is between the Crown and the advisors to the Crown, namely the cabinet. The cabinet alone enjoys access to the Crown, not the legislature.[16]

In practice, this relationship provides the cabinet with additional advantages over the legislature. In Canada, for example, it means that order-in-council, or Crown, appointments are made not with the approval of the legislature, but by the governor general on the advice of the cabinet (in practice the prime minister). The prime minister – in the name of the Crown – makes thousands of appointments. Some of these have limited impact on questions of governance. But many, including ambassadorships, senior level judicial appointments, and even royal commissions, have profound public policy consequences.

Yet it is clear that there remains a disjuncture between the theory and practice of parliamentary government. In each jurisdiction the effectiveness of responsible government is justifiably open to question. However, the inability of governments to meet citizens' expectations of them transcends the quality of the men and women who are elected to serve. Instead, many of the contemporary problems that face parliamentary governments, and the attempts by countries to ameliorate these difficulties, result from additional institutional and social strains placed on parliamentary systems. These are discussed in several chapters in this volume, particularly those in the section on responsiveness.

The challenges for parliamentary governments today do not only entail getting theory to fit reality. As they face questions of representation, responsiveness, and multi-level governance, countries are also challenged by institutional barriers to reform. According to Stephen Krasner, institutions have both breadth (linkages to other institutions) and depth (long histories).[17] The more breadth and depth institutions have, the more difficult it is to alter existing arrangements. The relationship between democratic institutions and citizens' attachment to instruments of democracy can act like a web, entangling those who attempt to refashion structures. Untangling the web can be difficult, yet it has not stopped some of the countries examined in this volume from making the attempt and, in some cases, bringing about significant changes to make parliamentary democracy more responsive to current challenges.

REPRESENTATION

Parliamentary government is representative government. Members of legislative bodies are elected to Parliament to represent both specific and general interests. We traditionally think of the members as popularly chosen representatives who speak on behalf of their constituents during debates. Birch categorizes individuals who fit this style as "elected officials."[18] With this view, elected men and women are charged with protecting local interests in the national (or provincial/state) legislature.

In Canada this form of representation is assumed to be very important. In practice, elected officials act as both agents of the electors who vote for them and as representatives of the political party under whose banner they successfully sought office. A cause of some cynicism in Canada is the perception of many Canadians that members place constituency views second to party loyalty and do not fully represent local interests when they are forced to choose between the two.[19] Canadians are not alone in finding this fault with their legislators: strength of party discipline is a concern in Australia and to a lesser extent in Great Britain and New Zealand.

Concern over the ability of members to place constituency concerns ahead of party loyalty is not the result of the method used to select representatives. Canada and Australia have very strong party discipline, but the members of their lower houses are chosen by different electoral rules. Although Westminster-style parliamentary systems have traditionally relied on the single-member plurality system, of the countries examined in this volume only Canada and Great Britain still employ this system for their lower house at the national level. Australia uses a proportional representation (PR) system for senators and the alternative vote for members of the House of Representatives. There is little incentive in Canada, at least among the governing class, to experiment with a change to the electoral system. The result has been a series of majority elections where the winning party arrives with a much larger percentage of seats than votes. In addition, the governing party can often win a majority while being virtually shut out of some provinces and regions.

Great Britain has been far more willing than Canada to adapt its electoral system. After yet another long period of slow adaptation, perhaps the time was ripe for Britain to embrace fast-paced reforms. In Scotland, the move to institute a system of proportional representation produced election results that would not have occurred under the national system, namely a coalition government between the Scottish Labour and Liberal Democrats. The attempts by Labour in Westminster to control events in Wales had disastrous results. The first two leaders of the Welsh assembly, the choice of London, were gone in less than eighteen months.

While New Zealand did not tackle change on as many fronts, the adoption of a multi-member proportional system in 1996 was a major departure. As Jonathan Boston notes in his chapter, the move to PR was one of many options New Zealand's Labour Party considered in the mid-1980s to try to address citizen detachment from the state. Of the primary options on the table, PR was chosen over an entrenched constitution (with a charter of rights) and the re-establishment of a second chamber. Among other reasons for deciding to adopt PR was the view that PR would result in a diffusion of power from the executive to the legislature.

Unlike the British experiment, where PR was adopted for new legislatures, the New Zealand move affected an existing assembly. The inevitable threats to majority governments and a stable two-party system (the Labour and National parties) suggest that embracing PR was a brave move for the governing National Party (it is hard to imagine a sitting government instituting changes it knows will compromise its ability to maintain power). As Boston cautions, it is too early to dissect all the ramifications of New Zealand's experiment with electoral reform. Certainly the power that was once enjoyed by a single party in power (and the front bench of the governing party) has been dispersed. Yet, according to Boston, the surge in public confidence that was hoped for has yet to materialize. As with other nations with PR systems, the increased power accorded minor parties may be responsible for public sentiment that still largely distrusts those in, and those seeking, political power.

That New Zealand chose not to reinstate a second chamber is perhaps not surprising. In a unitary country with a more homogeneous population, it is not altogether clear who, or what, members of a second chamber represent. The question of representation can also be a problem for many second chambers in parliamentary democracies, particularly in states such as Canada and Great Britain, where their members are not popularly elected.

Unless representatives are elected, some may view their legitimacy as suspect. That is one reason the members of Canada's Senate are often seen as less critical to the representative function of Canada's Parliament than members of the House of Commons.[20] Proposals for a more "representative" upper chamber (at least in the sense of being elected) have long been discussed in Canada[21] and have made some progress in Great Britain. In Australia, where senators are elected, this shadow of supposed illegitimacy is not present.

But representation also means representing groups or segments of society that might not be restricted to a particular geographical area. Members elected from specific territorial units often find themselves representing a group that is not limited to any one geographic location. Representing individuals based on shared characteristics is a form of mirror representation, where the legislature should be seen to reflect the society it represents writ large.[22] In their most obvious form, cabinet ministers often represent specific interests. For example, the minister of agriculture is seen to speak on behalf of all farmers. This form of group representation also applies to individuals who are not members of the executive. Female members are often assumed to speak on behalf of all women; elected members of minority groups are expected to represent all members of their group, even if the member does not have a government portfolio or even a shadow cabinet role.

In nations with two chambers, this second type of representative function can be, and often is, performed by members of both bodies.

In Canada, the Senate was conceived of as an institution that would provide representation for the regions within Parliament. Today's Senate is at best a very weak mechanism of intrastate federalism,[23] although senators are still appointed to represent the provinces and territories. The perceived lack of legitimacy of non-elected representatives has nowhere been more topical than in Great Britain. The combination of life (appointed) and hereditary peers produced a House of Lords with over 1,250 peers. By effectively removing the right of hereditary peers to sit and vote in the House of Lords, in 1999 the Labour Party decreased this total to approximately 700. The Wakeham report on reform of the House of Lords argued that an unelected House should not "even attempt to compete with the House of Commons in terms of electoral legitimacy."[24]

However, the report did suggest that one of the primary goals of a reformed House of Lords should be able to "provide council from a range of sources" and be a voice different from that of the House of Commons.[25] It was believed that this would serve the representative purpose of democratic government by providing different voices in the legislative assemblies. In this and other ways the reformed House of Lords was meant to find popular support while distinguishing itself from the House of Commons. Lord Wakeham's chapter highlights the process adopted by the royal commission he chaired and what the commission hoped to achieve through reform. In sum, the commissioners envisaged a second chamber that would be broadly reflective of British society and representative of all parts of the nation. The Blair government shares the commissioners' goals of a more representative body and has indicated that it is committed to the second stage of House of Lords reform.

RESPONSIVENESS

Parliamentary government is not just representative but responsive. Governments must have the ability to meet the changing needs of, and demands from, different segments of society. At the same time, they must be sensitive to the interests of the majority. But while parliamentary government does have the capacity to react to meet its obligations to citizens, governments often fail to do so. When this happens it is often not the fault of the state, but of the men and women who have been elected to govern.[26]

As Smith demonstrates in her chapter on the Canadian Parliament, calls for the adoption of direct democracy measures and major parliamentary reform have been driven by the objectives of diminishing party discipline, particularly among members of the governing party, and of allowing citizens' views to be registered and counted on their own. It is fair to say that the overall goal is to bring about greater responsiveness within the system of governance as a whole. However, the desire to enhance responsiveness may in fact be diverting attention from an underlying problem. What many citizens (and a few elected officials) term responsiveness might better be viewed as an easy fix for an unwillingness on the part of voters to make difficult decisions in the first place by giving serious consideration to issues prior to casting a ballot. In some senses, the push in North America and abroad for such reforms as recalling members and term limits are a reflection of this desire for quick solutions. Recall of sitting members might provide increased opportunities for citizens, but it can be used improperly and lessen the importance of the vote at general elections. Term limits might decrease the continued rule of some legislators. However, at least in the nations covered in this volume, turnover rates are such that the problem of career politicians is minimal.[27]

Some see referendums as part of the same push for increased participation from citizens. When used for many issues, referendums raise concerns about who writes the questions, who (or which groups) are funding the various sides, and the lack of alternatives to a yes/no decision. Parliamentary democracies have been less inclined than congressional systems (such as the United States) to use referendums on a regular basis.[28] In Canada, referendums have been used nationally only sparingly, on the issues of prohibition (1898), conscription (1942), and major constitutional reform (1992 Charlottetown Accord). While the result of the 1942 referendum favoured the government's position and that of 1992 did not, in both instances the country was split and the aftershocks were felt for quite some time.

While the state can try to minimize concerns associated with the wording of referendum questions and the funding of the two sides, it cannot eliminate them. In her examination of the referendum on the future of the monarchy in Australia, Cheryl Saunders demonstrates that even the best planned and cautious of approaches to direct democracy can encounter significant roadblocks. Saunders suggests that the move towards a republican government can be seen as the logical development for Australia, where, as in Canada, the ties to the United Kingdom have loosened over time. Although the view that Australia should sever its monarchical connection had been around for some time, it was only in 1993 that the government began to move more seriously on the issue. The Constitutional Convention, composed of a combination of elected and appointed officials, subsequently met to determine the nature of the question to be put before the public. Yet, as Saunders indicates, even the most carefully crafted question, sensitive to the gravity of the issue, can have its flaws. The question was lost not because the majority were opposed to a republic, but because there was no agreement on the form of a republic. Despite a failed referendum, however, few in Australia believe the issue is resolved.

Being responsive also requires parliamentary democracies to acknowledge actions and, if necessary, take redress on the actions of previous governments. This includes meeting responsibilities to indigenous peoples. Canada, Australia, and New Zealand have all had less than noble pasts when it comes to recognizing Aboriginal peoples and their rights, cultures, and approaches to government. During the past two decades, the three countries have attempted, with mixed success, to make progress on Aboriginal issues.

The New Zealand experience offers some telling comparisons to Canada's historic relations with first peoples. Compared to the many First Nations of Canada, the Mäori are a homogeneous nation. Covered under the single Treaty of Waitangi, the Mäori's constitutional place in New Zealand's government is in certain respects clearer than that of the Aboriginal peoples in Canada. As Mason Durie takes us through the history of Mäori participation in New Zealand society and government, it becomes clear that the notion of dedicated seats in Parliament has had both advantages and drawbacks. Just as the move to change the electoral system produced the opportunity for broad discussion on representation in New Zealand, it also put the question of how best to respond to Mäori calls for economic and political equality back on the table.

Durie argues that Mäori influence goes beyond representation in Parliament and includes a recognition of the need to promote Mäori culture and language in all areas of government. Most importantly, there has been a public acknowledgment that the Crown must meet its obligations under the Treaty of Waitangi to respect and protect Mäori interests and denounce the historic goal of assimilation.

In Canada, many Aboriginal peoples are not covered by a treaty. The varied arrangements mean the Canadian state and native peoples face a much different set of problems. Native Canadians are also burdened with negotiating with two levels of government whose goals are seldom complementary. This adds additional impediments to recognizing the role and place of Aboriginal people in Canadian society. In his chapter, Paul Chartrand persuasively argues for a new approach to dealing with First Nations. Doing so would require a type of national forum that could establish principles which recognize the First Nations' constitutional and democratic place. As Chartrand argues, doing so would move Canada further from its dominion past to a nation of shared power and responsibility, or a condominium.

It is worth noting one common trait of the Mäori and Canadian Aboriginal populations. Both are growing as a percentage of their country's population.[29] This may act as an encouragement for governments to pay more immediate attention to their concerns. That said, in neither nation have the living standards of first peoples improved dramatically. Addressing economic conditions remains an important aspect of the responsiveness dynamic.

The Durie and Chartrand chapters illustrate that unique solutions must be found within each state to address past injustices to indigenous people. The chapters also sadly remind us that the problems facing the Mäori and Canada's Aboriginal peoples are all too similar. Both face an uphill struggle for acceptance into the broader community while striving to protect their cultural, linguistic, and economic distinctiveness.

MULTI-LEVEL GOVERNANCE

A number of countries combine parliamentary government and multiple-level government (beyond a national government and local councils). Some have a large population and others a large territory. Canada and Australia, both longstanding federations, share the latter, while for South Africa the former is true. A third characteristic of some federal states is the presence of a significant minority or minorities. In Canada, the French-speaking population, which constitutes a majority within the province of Quebec, is the most obvious but not the only example of this aspect of federalism. In light of its highly diverse population, it is not surprising that federal principles are reflected in the constitutional structure of post-apartheid South Africa.

Federations provide avenues for legislative representation at both the national and subnational levels. Processes and institutional structures vary in response to factors such as the degree of diversity of the population, history, and political culture. A further issue is the role legislatures play, or do not play, with regard to interdependence among governments. Even in federations (such as Canada) where the founders developed what they believed was a relatively clear distinction between the powers of the national and regional governments, as opposed to those with a number of concurrent powers (Germany, South Africa), effective public policy and governance require cooperation among governments. In some federations, notably Germany, the second chamber plays an important role in accommodating national and constituent unit interests. In others, including the United States and Australia, senators represent their electors above all, not state governments.

The Canadian Senate does not fit into either of these categories. Its members, appointed by the federal prime minister until age seventy-five, do not have sufficient authority to play a significant role in accommodating the interests of a highly diverse country. This is one reason, as Stéphane Dion points out in his chapter "The Interdependence of Governments in Canada," that the network of intergovernmental negotiations and meetings referred to as "executive federalism" has acquired such prominence. Literally hundreds of meetings a year, covering a wide range of fields, bring together the prime minister and premiers (first ministers), ministers, and senior officials. Intergovernmental relations, Dion adds, are conducted between strong governments: the latter are most often formed by a single party (a tendency encouraged by the first-past-the-post electoral system). This also means that governments can usually act effectively to implement the agreements reached – some of which, as Dion reminds us in relation to health, are highly significant.

The South African second chamber, the National Council of Provinces (NCOP), was modelled after the German Bundesrat and was thus intended as a forum for representation of the constituent units within the national government. Each province sends a ten-member delegation to the NCOP; however, in contrast to the German second chamber, the members are appointed by the provincial legislature (not government). In her chapter, "Designing Parliament for Cooperative Federalism," Christina Murray explains that, by giving the provinces substantial power in Parliament, the NCOP was intended to compensate for the limited powers of the provinces under the constitution and thus become the central institution for the realization of cooperative federalism. During its relatively brief life, the NCOP has encountered certain problems, among them the provinces' lack of resources to deal with a large volume of legislation. Even so, Murray concludes that the NCOP has asserted itself in the "national arena." Its evolution will bear watching as South Africa consolidates its experience with democracy and multi-level governance.

Taken together, the chapters in this volume demonstrate that one strength of Westminster-style parliamentary systems is their provision of a stable foundation for representation and governance. Evolution, rather than revolution, has almost always been the order of the day, and there has thus been a strong measure of continuity over the centuries. At the heart of these arrangements have been the enduring principles of responsible government and accountability to the legislature. However, the capacity of these same legislatures to be representative and responsive has often been called into question by the prevalence of single-party governments (often underpinned by strong party discipline). In some of the countries under review, this critique has led to significant changes in electoral arrangements, while in others calls for reform of the composition and rules of various parliamentary institutions continue or have become more prevalent.

This volume should also provide valuable lessons for those interested in questions of representation and government responsiveness in Canada. We have expended great energies addressing issues through the processes of multi-level governance, often with fruitful results for public policy. But with the exception of the most significant constitutional changes in our history – the 1982 patriation of the constitution and adoption of the Charter of Rights and Freedoms – we have failed to move away from the Westminster model. The reasons for this and its implications are explored in our conclusion to the volume.

While it would be rash to predict the outcome in the individual cases examined in this collection, it is clear that the story of major change and lesser adaptation will continue. The obstacles to significant reform are not small. Changes to one aspect of parliamentary democracy will have subsequent, and often unintended consequences for other branches of government. As countries confront the challenges of representation, responsiveness, and multi-level governance they do so with the understanding that altering institutional arrangements will have significant implications for the practice of parliamentary democracy.

The countries reviewed here, and others as well, have a great deal to learn from changes adopted elsewhere, particularly as to the degree they helped meet the objectives of their proponents. It is hoped that this volume will enrich both this process of mutual learning and future debate about how to preserve the enduring qualities of parliamentary institutions while adapting them to the needs of increasingly diverse societies and the expectations of their citizens.

NOTES

1 Michael Laver and Kenneth Shepsle, "Cabinet Ministers and Government Formation in Parliamentary Democracies," in *Cabinet Ministers and Parliamentary Government*, ed. Laver and Shepsle (Cambridge: Cambridge University Press, 1994), 3.
2 C.E.S. Franks, *The Parliament of Canada* (Toronto: University of Toronto Press, 1987), 5–7.
3 David Smith, "Bagehot, the Crown and the Canadian Constitution," *Canadian Journal of Political Science* 28, no. 4 (1995): 624.
4 Philip Norton, *Does Parliament Matter?* (London: Harvester Wheatsheaf, 1993), 14.
5 Norton, *Does Parliament Matter?*, 14–15.
6 Michael Graves, *The Tudor Parliaments: Crown, Lords and Commons, 1485–1603* (London: Longman Press, 1985), 4.
7 Norton, *Does Parliament Matter?*, 16.
8 Anthony Birch, *The British System of Government,* 4th ed. (London: George Allan and Unwin, 1980), 31.

9 D. Judge, *Representation: Theory and Practice in Britain* (London: Routledge Press, 1999), 17–20.
10 Birch, *The British System of Government*, 35.
11 See Franks, *The Parliament of Canada*, chap. 1.
12 Walter Bagehot, *The English Constitution* (London: Oxford University Press, 1961), 9.
13 Franks, *The Parliament of Canada*, 227.
14 James R. Mitchell and S.L. Sutherland. "Ministerial Responsibility: the Submission of Politics and Administration to the Electorate" in *Public Administration and Policy: Governing in Challenging Times*, ed. Martin Westmacott and Hugh Mellon (Scarborough: Prentice Hall, 1999), 21.
15 Jennifer Smith, "Responsive Government and Democracy," in *Taking Stock of 150 Years of Responsible Government in Canada*, ed. F. Leslie Seidle and Louis Massicotte (Ottawa: Canadian Study of Parliament Group), 40.
16 David Smith, "Bagehot, the Crown and the Canadian Constitution," 625.
17 Stephen Krasner, "Sovereignty: An Institutional Perspective," *Comparative Political Studies* 21, no. 1 (1988): 66–94.
18 Anthony Birch, *Representative and Responsible Government* (Toronto: University of Toronto Press, 1965).
19 See David C. Docherty, "Citizens and Legislators: Different Views on Representation," in *Value Change in Canada,* ed. Neil Nevitte (Toronto: University of Toronto Press, 2002) 165–206.
20 John Stewart, "Parliamentary Democracy in Canada," *Isuma* 1, no. 2 (2000), 107–9.
21 F. Leslie Seidle, "Senate Reform and the Constitutional Agenda: Conundrum or Solution?" in *Canadian Constitutionalism, 1791–1991,* ed. J. Ajzenstat (Ottawa: Canadian Study of Parliament Group, 1992), 91–122.
22 See for example, Hanna Pitkin, *The Concept of Representation* (London: University of California Press, 1967), 81–2.
23 Donald V. Smiley and Ronald L. Watts, *Intrastate Federalism in Canada* (Toronto: University of Toronto Press, 1985), 4.
24 United Kingdom, Royal Commission on the Reform of the House of Lords, *A House for the Future*, 14.
25 *A House for the Future*, 28.
26 Michael M. Atkinson and David C. Docherty, "Parliamentary Government in Canada," in *Canadian Politics 2000,* ed. Michael Whittington and Glen Williams (Scarborough: Nelson Canada, 2000).
27 David C. Docherty, "Taking the Fall: The Electoral Fates of Cabinet v. Private Members in Three Westminster Systems," (paper delivered at the Fourth Annual Conference of Parliamentary Scholars and Parliamentarians, Wroxton College, Oxfordshire, June 2000).

28 Use of referendums and initiatives in the United States has been restricted to the state level, but even there not uniformly. California, for example, has initiatives on the ballot at every election, while other states, such as Vermont, never use such measures.

29 Kathy Brock, "Finding Answers in Difference: Canadian and American Aboriginal Policy Compared," in *Canada and the United States: Differences that Count,* ed. David Thomas (Peterborough: Broadview Press, 2000), 338–58.

Representation

Parliamentary democracies constitute a diverse set of political systems that nevertheless share a number of traits. Central among these are the principles and institutional practices of representative government. Members are seen to represent the interests of the constituencies where they are elected. Through political parties, other interests – including those of the country as a whole – find expression. The representation of constituency and larger interests can entail tensions, and accommodating such mdifferences is one of the functions of the legislature and cabinet. In those federal systems where citizens are also represented in parliamentary institutions at the provincial or state levels, the channels for accommodation are more complex. While second chambers are sometimes part of this dynamic, intergovernmental institutions and processes often have important functions (examples of these, and their evolution, are addressed in the chapters of the section "Multi-level Governance").

Inherent in the development of representative government is what Hanna Pitkin (in *The Concept of Representation*) labels "acting for": elected members are expected to give voice to, protect, and further the interests of those they represent. The evolution of parliamentary institutions has shown that these members, who belong to relatively disciplined political parties, face significant limits on their capacity to act independently in representing their constituents. However, the function of "acting for" must be seen in a broader perspective. The government that sits in and is accountable to Parliament represents and responds to a much broader range of interests. Whether or not governments, most often composed of ministers from a single political party, do this with sufficient sensitivity is a matter for constant public debate. For some, the capacity of governments to act in a relatively decisive manner is one of the strengths of the Westminster model; others see the absence of significant constraints on the power of the cabinet and prime minister as flaws within the democratic system that, among other things, diminish the contribution individual members could make to the work of Parliament and, more broadly, decrease responsiveness within government (Jennifer Smith's chapter addresses this in the next section).

A further aspect of representation within parliamentary systems, as within other forms of government, is what Pitkin calls "descriptive representation." In this context, the presumption is that a legislative body will correspond relatively closely to the population it is meant to represent. Westminster institutions are frequently scrutinized on this basis and often found wanting. They have long been criticized as reflecting only certain economic and social classes. More recently, attention has turned to the under-representation of women and minorities such as indigenous peoples.

Although the ongoing debate about representation focuses mostly on the first chamber in the countries surveyed in this volume, other institutions have been criticized. With the exception of New Zealand, which abolished its senate in 1950, all the countries surveyed in this volume have second chambers. The roles they play, or are intended play, range from taking a careful second look at legislation adopted by the first chamber (a function they all claim to carry out) to representing the people or governments of the country's constituent units (the case, at least in theory, in Canada, Australia, and South Africa). As with the various lower houses, these second chambers have evolved. However, the generally slower pace of that evolution has often led to calls for fundamental change.

Finally, the Crown is part of Parliament in all the countries reviewed in this volume except for South Africa. The Crown's representational function, at least in relation to citizens, is more limited. However, some continue to see the Crown as a symbol of continuity that transcends political party and other differences. There is ongoing debate, notably in Australia, whether continuity – notably the function of choosing a prime minister – could be provided by an office filled by one of the country's citizens through a method other than hereditary succession.

The first chapter in this section illustrates the links between issues of representation and government responsiveness. As Jonathan

Boston recounts, in the 1980s New Zealand's single-member plurality (SMP) electoral system was increasingly criticized because of marked distortions in party representation relative to the popular vote – most notably, that the party with the most votes in 1978 and 1981 (Labour) did not win the most seats and therefore did not form the government. After Labour assumed power in 1984 and enacted a significant program of government spending cuts and structural reform, arguments about government responsiveness, reflected in accusations of an "elective dictatorship," gained ground. This helped fuel support for proportional representation, which was instituted for the 1996 election following the report of a royal commission and popular endorsement of electoral reform in two referendums. Boston recounts that the mixed-member proportional system (MMP) has led to improved representation for women, Mäori and other minorities. Multi-party coalition government has become the rule in what he labels a "negotiation democracy," and Parliament is playing a somewhat greater role. However, in Boston's assessment, governments are not necessarily less effective. At the same time, MMP, though initially controversial, is no longer much contested. In its 2001 report, a parliamentary committee that reviewed the system recommended no significant change. After completion of Boston's chapter, New Zealand held its third election under MMP (July 2002). A post-election poll demonstrated that public opinion is solidly behind MMP.

Unlike New Zealand and Canada, Australia has witnessed a vigorous public debate, with roots in the 1920s, about the Crown (as head of state) and its position within parliamentary government. As Cheryl Saunders recounts in the second chapter in this section, political pressure in response to the diminished relevance of British symbols to many Australians led to the convening of a constitutional convention in 1998. However, instead of endorsing direct election of a future president, which had strong support among Australians, the convention proposed an indirect election model: a president would be appointed following a two-thirds majority vote of both houses of Parliament on a motion from the prime minister. According to Saunders, the proposal was intended to avoid disturbing Australia's "constitutional calm." However, the role of politicians in the appointment process prompted considerable criticism and led to division among supporters of a republic. Although the constitutional proposal was rejected by a majority of 55 percent in the 1999 referendum, the question of how to adapt the office of head of state to a society that has changed considerably since Australia's founding remains very much alive.

In the final chapter in this section, we turn our attention to the role, composition, and powers of parliamentary second chambers. Although Lord Wakeham's chapter is principally concerned with the British House of Lords, it raises considerations that apply to second chambers elsewhere. For example, what should be the overall role and specific powers of a second chamber that distinguish it from those of the lower house, with its constitutionally superior position within parliamentary government? Once that is set, how should the members of the second chamber be chosen and whom should they represent? As Lord Wakeham recounts, the royal commission he chaired concluded that transforming the House of Lords into a fully elected second chamber would lead it to compete with the House of Commons as to legitimacy. The commission therefore recommended that only a minority of the members of a reformed second chamber be directly elected for fifteen-year terms. The vast majority would be appointed, on the recommendation of an appointments commission, also for fifteen-year terms. This was meant to ensure that the reformed House of Lords would reflect a broad range of expertise and experience, be free from party domination, and have the ability to take a long-term view. Lord Wakeham concludes that the commission's recommendations "go with the grain of the traditional British evolutionary approach to constitutional development." However, the Blair government has adopted a cautious approach to the royal commission's report, particularly because of criticism of the small proportion of second chamber members who would be elected. In the wake of the various constitutional changes instituted by Labour since 1997, it seems the British public would prefer a bolder approach than the one advocated by the Wakeham commission.

Institutional Change in a Small Democracy: New Zealand's Experience of Electoral Reform

JONATHAN BOSTON

In a referendum held with the general election of 6 November 1993, New Zealanders voted to replace the existing first-past-the-post (FPP) electoral system with a form of proportional representation (PR) based largely on the German model.[1] The first election under the new system – known in New Zealand as the mixed-member proportional (MMP) system, but often referred to elsewhere as the additional-member system (AMS) – was held on 12 October 1996 and the second on 27 November 1999. The operation of the new electoral system was reviewed during 2000–01 by a multi-party parliamentary committee chaired by the Speaker, Jonathan Hunt.

This chapter explores the impact of PR on New Zealand's political system and assesses the extent to which the new system has fulfilled the aims of its architects. The chapter is structured as follows: First, it considers the constitutional and political context within which the move to PR took place. Second, it outlines the major recommendations of the 1986 Royal Commission on the Electoral System and summarizes the main features of the MMP system as adopted via the Electoral Act 1993. Third, it considers how the political elites expected PR to affect, both favourably and unfavourably, the operation of the country's political system. Fourth, drawing on the results of the first two elections under MMP and a range of other relevant data, the chapter examines the extent to which these expectations have been realized in practice and summarizes the main behavioural and institutional consequences of PR.

In a relatively brief analysis of this nature, it is obviously impossible to explore all the relevant issues.[2] Accordingly, some matters are seen only fleetingly. These include the circumstances under which MMP was introduced,[3] the process of government formation following the elections of 1996 and 1999, the art and craft of coalition management, changes to the policy process, and the management of Parliament under minority government. Equally important, this chapter does not explore in detail the methodological problems which arise in any evaluation of important constitutional changes – like electoral reform – such as the difficulties of establishing appropriate counterfactuals, distinguishing between transitional and continuing effects, and determining causation.[4]

THE CONTEXT OF ELECTORAL REFORM

In the mid-1980s, in his celebrated analysis of majoritarian and consensus democracies, the distinguished political scientist Arend Lijphart described New Zealand as being "a virtually perfect example of the Westminster model of democracy."[5] This "perfection," he argued, was founded upon nine specific attributes of the country's political system: a concentration of executive power in one-party bare-majority cabinets; cabinet dominance over the legislature; unicameralism; a two-party system; a one-dimensional party system; a simple plurality electoral system; a unitary and centralized system of government; a tradition of parliamentary sovereignty in the context of an unentrenched and flexible constitution; and a system of representative (rather than direct) democracy.[6]

But at the very time that Lijphart was characterizing New Zealand's governmental system as an exemplar of the Westminster model, support for this model among the country's citizens was rapidly waning.[7] Of fundamental concern was the extraordinary concentration of political power within the executive – the product of a small, unicameral Parliament, single-party majoritarian governments, and a rigid system of party discipline.[8] Such was the subordination of Parliament to the dictates of the cabinet, and such was the capacity for power to be concentrated within a few hands (graphically exemplified during the prime ministership of Sir Robert Muldoon), that Richard Mulgan – one of New Zealand's leading political scientists – was prompted to describe the country's governmental system as an "elected dictatorship."[9]

As in other Westminster-type systems there were, of course, a variety of related constitutional concerns. In the New Zealand context these included the lack of effective constitutional constraints (or veto points) on government action; the long-standing failure to give proper constitutional recognition to the rights and interests of the indigenous Mäori population; the increasing readiness of governments to ignore important manifesto commitments; and the growing unwillingness of ministers to take responsibility for administrative and policy failures within their portfolios.[10]

Aside from these wider constitutional concerns, there was also mounting dissatisfaction with the highly disproportional nature of the results generated by the FPP electoral system. Indeed, on every measure of disproportionality New Zealand's system ranked "near the bottom."[11] This was particularly evident at the general elections of 1978 and 1981. In both instances, a third party – Social Credit – secured a relatively high proportion of votes (16 per cent and 20 per cent respectively for each election). Yet it managed to win only one seat in 1978 and two in 1981. Likewise, at both elections the Labour Party won more votes than its major rival – the National party – but secured fewer seats and thus remained in opposition. Inevitably, such results called into question the fairness and legitimacy of the FPP system and generated increasing pressure for reform.

Against this background of mounting constitutional unease, and in the context of serious economic difficulties and a major program of economic liberalization and public sector restructuring, various proposals for constitutional reform were advanced within political circles. Three in particular deserve mention here.

The first involved the introduction of a constitutionally-entrenched Bill of Rights modeled upon the Canadian Charter of Rights and Freedoms, 1982. Under this option – which was strongly promoted by Geoffrey Palmer (a constitutional lawyer and the deputy prime minister in the fourth Labour government of the mid-to-late 1980s) – Parliament would cease to be sovereign and the courts would secure the power to declare unconstitutional any legislation that breached the Bill of Rights. In the end Palmer's proposal received little support – whether from the public, the legal fraternity, or his parliamentary colleagues – and the idea of an entrenched Bill of Rights was abandoned. However, a Bill of Rights Act – similar to the Canadian Bill of Rights, 1960 – was enacted in 1990 as an ordinary statute.[12]

A second reform proposal, which was advanced primarily during the late 1980s and early 1990s by Jim Bolger (the leader of the opposition at that time), was to establish a second parliamentary chamber. New Zealand had in fact maintained an upper house – the Legislative Council – for almost a century. But it had been abolished rather abruptly in 1950 on the grounds that it had few powers and was largely ineffective. While a replacement for the Legislative Council had been promised at the time of its abolition, the National governments of the 1950s and 1960s delayed any action, and political support for establishing a new upper house gradually waned. Bolger's attempt to rekindle interest in the idea attracted little backing from either his parliamentary colleagues or the wider political community. No doubt this lack of support reflects the unitary nature of New Zealand's governmental system, and hence the absence of states or provinces which might be attracted to the idea of a Senate as an instrument for protecting their interests. Equally, however, the establishment of an upper house was not regarded by critics of the existing constitutional arrangements as an effective solution to their particular concerns. After all, unless such a chamber had significant powers to veto legislation or block supply, it would not be able to exercise much control over the executive. Yet there was unlikely to be support within the political community for an upper house with powers of this kind.

The third option for constitutional reform – the one that ultimately secured political support – was to replace FPP with a form of PR. Advocates of this proposal argued that such a change would not merely enhance the fairness of the electoral system, but would also bring an end to single-party majority government, thereby encouraging greater interparty cooperation, increasing the influence of Parliament in the policy process, and reducing the capacity of governments to act in an arbitrary and unrestrained fashion. Furthermore, it was contended – at least by some – that PR would foster a more consensual and less adversarial approach to the conduct of parliamentary affairs, increase public confidence and trust in the nation's political institutions, and encourage greater citizen engagement in political life.

As one might expect, such contentions were not readily accepted by the country's existing political elites. Proportional representation, after all, represented a significant threat to the dominance of the two major parties – Labour and National. However, as a result of strong public pressure – founded upon widespread anger at the willingness of successive governments to break major campaign promises, and assisted by a carefully-crafted Royal Commission report recommending electoral reform – the National government in the early 1990s eventually agreed to allow the country's citizens to determine the future of the electoral system. In a vigorously contested binding referendum held concurrently with the general election of 6 November 1993, a majority of voters (54 per cent to 46 per cent) opted to endorse the Royal Commission's preference for a form of PR similar to that used in Germany.

Given the importance of the Royal Commission in the events leading up to the introduction of MMP, the next section of this chapter provides a brief account of the commission's key arguments and recommendations.

THE ROYAL COMMISSION ON THE ELECTORAL SYSTEM

Prompted by the growing concerns over New Zealand's constitutional arrangements, the Labour Party included a number of reform proposals in its 1984 election manifesto. Among these was a commitment to appoint a Royal Commission to examine the electoral system and to consider "whether proportional representation or some other variant from the existing first-past-the-post system should be introduced."[13] On winning the snap election, Labour duly established a five-member commission; this body consulted widely, evaluated a range of electoral systems, and in December 1986 produced a major report – *Towards a Better Democracy* – recommending the introduction of MMP.[14]

In arriving at its decision in favour of a radical reform, the Royal Commission identified ten criteria for judging the merits of electoral systems:[15]

- fairness between political parties
- effective representation of minority and special interest groups
- effective Mäori representation
- political integration
- effective representation of constituents
- effective voter participation
- effective government
- effective Parliament
- effective parties
- legitimacy

The Commission acknowledged that "no voting system can fully meet the ideal standards set by the criteria."[16] It also recognized that the criteria it had identified were not "all of equal weight" and in some cases were "mutually incompatible."[17] In its view, "the best voting system for any country will not be one which meets any of the criteria completely but will be one which provides the most satisfactory overall balance between them, taking into account that country's history and current circumstances."[18] Having said this, the Commission undoubtedly placed significant weight on the criterion of "fairness between political parties." This almost inevitably led it to favour systems of PR over the existing simple plurality system.

In applying its chosen criteria, the Commission examined a variety of alternatives to FPP, including MMP, a single transferable vote (STV) system, a supplementary-member system, and a preferential system. Its eventual preference for the German system was based on the judgment that MMP satisfied more of the relevant criteria than the other available options. For instance, the Commission argued that MMP was "clearly superior" to STV on at least three counts: it was expected to generate more proportional results and was thus more likely to satisfy the criterion of "fairness between political parties"; it was more compatible with New Zealand's tradition of single-member constituencies and would ensure more "effective representation of constituents"; and it would avoid the intraparty conflicts which STV systems tended to encourage (and was thereby more likely to satisfy the criteria of "effective political parties" and "effective Parliament").[19]

The Royal Commission conceded that under a proportional system like MMP both coalition and minority governments were more likely. Nevertheless, it questioned whether such outcomes would undermine the achievement of "effective government." Indeed, it argued that "where there is a reasonable threshold which prevents the proliferation of minor parties, governments remain at least as effective, and possibly more so if proportionality results in the adoption of more consistent, consultative and broadly supported policies."[20]

While preferring MMP to alternative systems of PR, the Royal Commission's proposal differed in some respects from the system used in Germany.[21] Under its preferred approach, Parliament would have 120 members, with 60 constituency seats and 60 party (or list) seats. As in Germany, each elector would have two votes, one for a party list and the other for a constituency representative. Once the winners of the constituency contests were known, the 60 list seats would be allocated so as to achieve overall proportionality. The party lists, as in Germany, would be closed (i.e., voters would not be able to alter the order of the candidates on the lists). However, unlike the situation in Germany, the party lists would be nationwide rather than regional. The Commission also recommended that there be two thresholds for achieving representation in Parliament: either a party would need to secure a combined list vote of at least 4 per cent of all list votes or it would need to win at least one constituency seat. In Germany, by contrast, the thresholds are 5 per cent and three seats within a region.

On the controversial and sensitive issue of separate Mäori representation (which had been introduced in 1867), the Commission argued that under MMP it would be possible for Mäori interests to be properly, effectively, and fairly represented under a common roll (albeit in the context where Mäori parties would be exempt from the proposed party vote threshold).[22] Accordingly, its preferred approach was for the separate Mäori seats and Mäori roll to be abolished. At the same time, it argued that if MMP were not adopted, then a system of separate Mäori representation (and thus dual constituencies) should be retained

– at least until such time as there had been appropriate constitutional discussions with a wide range of representatives of the Mäori people on how their rights and interests should be protected.

THE KEY FEATURES OF NEW ZEALAND'S MMP SYSTEM

The recommendations of the Royal Commission were the subject of vigorous and protracted debate.[23] As matters transpired, the form of MMP ultimately put to voters in the 1993 referendum, and subsequently implemented, was somewhat different from that recommended by the Royal Commission. In the interests of clarity, the main features of New Zealand's MMP system, as codified in the Electoral Act 1993, are outlined below.[24]

In keeping with the Commission's proposals, the new system is "mixed" in the sense that there are two different kinds of MPs: those elected to represent single-member constituencies and those elected via closed, nationwide party lists. It is also "mixed" in another sense: electors have two votes – a party (or list) vote and an electorate (or constituency) vote. The party vote under the New Zealand version of MMP is compensatory rather than supplementary. That is to say, it is the party vote which determines the overall share of the seats won by each party in Parliament. In this regard, the system conforms to the German model rather than the mixed systems in countries like Japan and Russia. Thus, if a party wins 20 per cent of the party vote, it is entitled to a similar share of the seats. Where a party secures constituency seats, these are deducted before the list seats are allocated. Hence, if a party that is entitled to 30 seats (in accordance with its party vote) wins 10 constituency seats, it will be allocated 20 list seats.

Under New Zealand's version of MMP, a party must win either 5 per cent of the party vote or at least one constituency seat in order to be eligible to receive list seats. This means that a party which wins a constituency seat but secures only, say, 2.5 per cent of the party vote is still entitled to its appropriate share of list seats (i.e., probably two or three seats, depending on the level of "wasted" party votes). Equally, however, a party that secures 4.9 per cent of the party vote but fails to win a constituency seat is not entitled to representation in Parliament. Such arrangements not only have the potential to generate results that are widely perceived to be unfair but also have a tendency to encourage parties to engage in strategic electoral cooperation in the interests of helping (or preventing) a smaller party to secure a constituency seat.[25]

Immediately prior to the introduction of MMP, there were 99 seats in the New Zealand Parliament. Under the system of dual constituencies,

4 seats were set aside for the indigenous Mäori population (who were able to choose whether to register on the general electoral roll or the separate Mäori electoral roll). Of the general seats, a fixed number (25) were allocated to the South Island, with the number of North Island seats adjusted every five years according to the relative size of the population of the two islands. In 1993, there were 70 North Island seats, an increase of 19 since the early-1960s (reflecting the North Island's more rapid population growth).

Under MMP, the number of seats increased to 120 in line with the Commission's recommendations. The main anchor in the new system (as under the previous FPP regime) is provided by the allocation of a fixed number of general seats to the South Island. This has been set at 16, 9 fewer than under FPP (reflecting the reduced number of constituency seats under MMP). On this basis there were 44 general seats in the North Island in 1996 and 45 in 1999.

Contrary to the Commission's recommendations, it was decided to retain separate Mäori seats.[26] However, the number of these seats is no longer fixed at 4 but instead varies according to how many voters choose to register on the Mäori electoral roll. For a variety of reasons, there has been a trend since the mid-1990s for more Mäori to opt for the separate roll: the result has been a gradual increase in the number of Mäori seats – to 5 in 1996, 6 in 1999, and 7 in 2002.

As should be evident, the number of party (or list) seats under the new electoral system is not fixed. Instead, it depends on the total number of general and Mäori constituencies. At the first MMP election there were 65 constituency seats; this increased to 67 in 1999. Accordingly, there were 55 party seats in 1996 and 53 three years later. If current population trends continue and there is no reduction in the South Island quota, the number of constituency seats will gradually increase. While this presents no major problems in the near future, at some stage the number of party seats will fall to a point where it will be increasingly difficult to ensure that the parties receive their proportionate share of parliamentary seats.

EXPECTATIONS CONCERNING THE IMPACT OF MMP ON THE POLITICAL SYSTEM

The introduction of MMP was accompanied by numerous, and often sharply conflicting, expectations and predictions.[27] On some matters there was relatively little controversy. For instance, it was widely expected – given the experience of other countries with PR (especially of some of the smaller European states with constitutional arrangements and political traditions similar to those in New Zealand) – that the introduction of MMP would generate a somewhat higher voter turnout, reduce the level of disproportionality, increase the number of parliamentary parties, and contribute to a more representative Parliament (with a higher proportion of women and people from minority backgrounds). Among opinion leaders there were also widespread expectations that:

- the formation of governments was likely to be more difficult and protracted
- single-party majority governments were most unlikely, with most governments being (minority or majority) coalitions of two or more parties
- the size of the cabinet would be little altered but the convention of collective responsibility would be weakened
- the composition of governments would probably be subject to more regular changes
- the pace of policy making would be slower
- interest groups would have a larger role in the policy process
- the role and influence of Parliament would increase relative to that of the cabinet, with somewhat weaker party discipline, more opportunities for opposition parties to contribute to the policy process, and more independent-minded select committees[28]

On many other matters, however, expectations differed. For instance, there was considerable disagreement over how MMP would affect the role and influence of the public service, the degree of policy stability, the overall direction of public policy (especially economic policy), and the size and role of the state. There was also uncertainty about the long-term impact of MMP on the configuration of the party system.[29] There were, for example, conflicting views as to whether proportional representation would give rise to a two-bloc approach (with a relatively clear political divide in Parliament between the parties of the centre-left and those of the centre-right) or a balancing-centre approach (under which one or more parties would occupy the centre of the political spectrum and thus be in a position to determine whether the government was of the centre-left or the centre-right).

Furthermore, whereas supporters of electoral reform regarded most of the expected changes as improvements to the political system, critics were much less sanguine. Opponents of MMP were particularly concerned that PR would give a small party (or parties) a disproportionate influence over public policy, that the list system would enable the party leadership to exercise undue influence over parliamentary colleagues, and that governments were likely to be both less stable and less effective. There were also concerns that the transition to the new electoral system could be politically destabilizing, especially given the need to reduce the number of electorate seats from ninety-nine to sixty-five and the disruptive effects which this would have for many parliamentary careers.

THE IMPACT OF MMP ON THE POLITICAL SYSTEM

It will be many more years before the long-term impact of electoral reform in New Zealand can be systematically and comprehensively assessed. Nonetheless, with more than eight years having passed since the electoral referendum in late 1993 and with two elections having been held under MMP, it is certainly possible to evaluate the short-to-medium-term consequences of the new electoral system and to consider the extent to which the expectations of opinion leaders have been fulfilled. Of course, not all of the political changes and developments since the electoral referendum in 1993 can be attributed directly, or even indirectly, to the introduction of MMP. While acknowledging the problems of determining causality, there can be little doubt, however, that MMP has had some significant institutional, behavioural, and policy consequences. Hence, to quote Lijphart's more recent analysis, "New Zealand is no longer a good, let alone the best, example of the 'true British system.'"[30]

Anticipatory Behaviour and the Transition to MMP

As many political observers expected, the move to MMP began to affect New Zealand's political system not in late 1996 but almost immediately after the referendum decision three years earlier. Of the initial consequences of the vote in favour of electoral reform, the most politically significant was an increase in party fragmentation within Parliament and the impact this had on the durability, composition, and parliamentary base of the government.[31]

As Table 1 shows, four parties secured parliamentary seats at the 1993 general election: the two large parties, National and Labour; a grouping of five left-leaning parties under the banner of the Alliance and led by Jim Anderton (a former president of the Labour Party); and a new populist-cum-centrist party, New Zealand First (NZF), founded by Winston Peters (a former National MP and minister of Mäori Affairs). During the 1993–96 parliamentary term, nine National MPs and four Labour MPs left their parties for another party, and four new parliamentary parties were formed: Future New Zealand (which quickly merged with United); United (a liberal centrist party with seven

Table 1: Results of the 1993, 1996, and 1999 New Zealand general elections

	1993		*1996*						*1999*					
	Votes	*Seats*	*Party votes*	*Total seats in Parliament*		*Electorate votes seats*		*List seats*	*Party votes*	*Total seats in Parliament*		*Electorate votes seats*		*List seats*
Party	%	No.	%	No.	%	%	No.	No.	%	No.	%	%	No.	No.
National	35.1	50	33.8	44	36.7	33.9	30	14	30.5	39	32.5	31.3	22	17
Labour	34.7	45	28.2	37	30.8	31.1	26	11	38.7	49	40.9	41.8	41	8
New Zealand First	8.4	2	13.4	17	14.2	13.5	6	11	4.3	5	4.2	4.2	1	4
Alliance	18.2	2	10.1	13	10.8	11.3	1	12	7.7	10	8.3	6.9	1	9
ACT	–	–	6.1	8	6.7	3.7	1	7	7.0	9	7.5	4.5	0	9
United	–	–	0.9	1	0.8	2.1	1	0	0.5	1	0.8	1.1	1	0
Green	–	–	–	–	–	–	–	–	5.2	7	5.8	4.2	1	6
Christian Heritage	2.0	0	–	–	–	–	–	–	2.4	0	0.0	2.2	0	0
Christian Coalition	–	–	4.3	0	0.0	1.5	0	0	–	–	–	–	–	–
Legalise Cannabis	–	–	1.7	0	0.0	0.2	0	0	1.1	0	0.0	0.3	0	0
Future New Zealand	–	–	–	–	–	–	–	–	1.1	0	0.0	0.9	0	0
Others	1.6	0	1.5	0	0.0	2.7	0	0	1.5	0	0.0	2.6	0	0
Total	100.0	99	100.0	120	100.0	100.0	65	55	100.0	120	100.0	100.0	67	53
Turnout of those enrolled:	85.2%				88.2%						84.8%			

Source: Chief Electoral Office, *The General Election and Electoral Referendum 1993* (1994); *The General Election 1996* (1997); *The General Election 1999* (2000).

Note: Parties that obtained at least 1 per cent of the vote or at least one seat in any of the three general elections are included in this table.

In 1996, the Christian Heritage Party was part of the Christian Coalition.

Table 2: Governments in New Zealand Since 1990

Prime Minister	*Dates*	*Parties*	*Parliamentary Basis*
Bolger 1	Oct 1990-Nov 1993	National	Majority
Bolger 2	Nov 1993-Sept 1994	National	Majority
Bolger 3	Sept 1994-May 1995	National-ROC	Majority
Bolger 4	May 1995-Aug 1995	National-ROC	Minority
Bolger 5	Aug 1995-Feb 1996	National	Minority
Bolger 6	Feb 1996-Dec 1996	National-United	Minority
Bolger 7	Dec 1996-Dec 1997	National-NZF	Majority
Shipley 1	Dec 1997-July 1998	National-NZF	Majority
Shipley 2	July 1998-Aug 1998	National-NZF	Minority
Shipley 3	Aug 1998-Dec 1999	National-Independents	Minority
Clark 1	Dec 1999–	Labour-Alliance	Minority

Source: Jonathan Boston, *Governing Under Proportional Representation: Lessons from Europe* (Wellington: Institute for Policy Studies, 1998), 96.

Abbreviations: ROC = Right-of-Centre Party
NZF = New Zealand First Party

MPs); the Christian Democrats (a centre-right, religiously-oriented party with one MP); and the Right-of-Centre party, subsequently renamed the Conservatives (a rural-oriented party with two MPs for a brief period). Such a high rate of defections was unprecedented in New Zealand's political history, as was the large number of new parliamentary parties founded during these years.

With the National government under the leadership of Jim Bolger having been returned to office in 1993 with a majority of only one seat, it was not long, given the volatile parliamentary situation, before it was unable to govern alone. Indeed, during the 1993–96 parliamentary term, National was forced to build alliances of various kinds with all of the new parties and held office as a majority coalition government, a minority single-party government, and a minority coalition government (see Table 2). While the increase in party fragmentation and the high defection rate during the transitional Parliament generated considerable political uncertainty, it also yielded a number of important benefits. First, it helped prepare New Zealand's political elites (including parliamentarians, senior public servants, and interest group leaders) for the new era of PR, including the conduct of interparty negotiations and the management of parliamentary business under minority government. Second, National's loss of a secure parliamentary majority created an environment more conducive to reforming Parliament's Standing Orders, thereby enabling new rules and procedures to be crafted to accommodate the requirements of proportionality and a multi-party chamber.[32]

Political Participation

Countries with PR systems tend to have higher voter turnout at general elections than those with FPP systems.[33] The reasons for this have been the subject of continuing scholarly debate. One possibility is that FPP systems discourage participation on the part of minor party supporters because their votes tend to be "wasted," thus giving rise to a diminished sense of efficacy and feelings of alienation. PR systems, by contrast, tend to reduce the number of "wasted" votes and are generally perceived to be fairer. This may enhance citizens' "attachment to and trust in a political system ... and motivate more people to vote."[34] Additionally, under PR there are generally more parties and there is greater incentive for parties to distinguish themselves as this may increase their share of the vote. This, in turn, provides citizens with a wider, and often clearer, choice and may also encourage stronger party attachments.[35] Such factors are likely to produce higher voter participation.

Under FPP, turnout at general elections in New Zealand (as a percentage of the estimated population of voting age) averaged about 82 per cent during the 1980s and fell to an average of 78.6 per cent in the elections of 1990 and 1993.[36] Such figures placed New Zealand near the average among Western democracies. In keeping with international trends, turnout had been falling for many decades (apart from the elections in 1975 and 1984). This decline was attributed by Vowles to partisan dealignment and an increase in disproportionality.[37]

As expected, the introduction of PR has boosted the average level of voter turnout, but only to a very modest degree. In the 1996 election, turnout as a percentage of the estimated population of voting age rose from 78.9 per cent to 80.8 per cent; as a percentage of those enrolled, it increased from 85.2 per cent to 88.2 per cent (see Table 1). In the 1999 election, however, the upward trend was reversed. Turnout as a percentage of the estimated population of voting age declined to 77.2 per cent, while as a percentage of those enrolled it fell to 84.8 per cent. If the results of the two elections are averaged, turnout as a percentage of the estimated population of voting age increased marginally from 78.6 per cent (for the two FPP elections in the early 1990s) to 79 per cent, while as a percentage of those enrolled it rose from 85.2 per cent to 86 per cent. But if voter turnout has increased marginally under MMP, it is notable that the proportion of the population of voting age choosing to enroll has declined from 92.6 per cent in 1993 to 91.6 per cent in 1996 and 91.1 per cent in 1999. This is not an encouraging trend. Against this, participation rates among certain minority groups, including Mäori and those on the left of the ideological spectrum, increased significantly in 1996, no doubt reflecting perceptions on the part of such electors that voting would be more efficacious under PR than FPP.[38]

It is not entirely clear why voter turnout fell in 1999. One possibility lies in the failure of the 1996 election, and the subsequent 1996–99 parliamentary term, to generate the kinds of political changes that many had hoped PR would bring. The lacklustre nature of the 1999 election campaign, together with the apparent inevitability (given the results of opinion polls) of a change of government, may also have contributed to a lower turnout. It remains to be seen whether subsequent PR elections encourage higher voter participation or whether the introduction of MMP merely provided a temporary interruption to a long-term trend towards lower turnout. What is abundantly plain, however, is that the positive effects of PR on political efficacy and electoral participation have so far been less than many had anticipated (perhaps because turnout was relatively high prior to the introduction of MMP).

Proportionality, the Party System, and Political Power

In general, the impact of MMP on the proportionality of party representation and the character of the party system has been in line with expectations.[39] Compared with the previous FPP system, MMP has delivered a marked reduction in the degree of disproportionality. For instance, on the basis of the Gallagher/Lijphart index, the disproportionality effect of the electoral system declined from an average of 11.1 per cent between 1946 and 1993 to 4.36 per cent in 1996; it declined again to 3.01 per cent in 1999.[40] Alternatively, as measured by the Loosemore-Hanby index, the degree of disproportionality fell from 26.2 per cent in 1993 to 7.6 per cent in 1996 and 6.2 per cent in 1999.[41] The levels of disproportionality in 1996 and 1999 were near the average for countries with PR.

A significant increase in the number of political parties has occurred since 1993 – whether measured by the number of parties contesting elections, the number of parties represented in Parliament, the effective number of elective parties (ENEP), or the effective number of parliamentary parties (ENPP). For instance, whereas twenty-six parties contested the last FPP election in 1993, thirty-four parties (twenty-two registered and twelve unregistered) stood candidates in 1996, and thirty-six parties (twenty-four registered and twelve unregistered) contested the 1999 election.[42] Similarly, whereas under FPP it was usual for only two or three parties to secure parliamentary seats, in 1996 six parties achieved parliamentary representation, while in 1999 seven were successful (see Table 1). These outcomes were broadly in line with predictions based on an analysis of the dimensionality of New Zealand politics and the thresholds which parties are required to meet under MMP.[43]

In relation to the ENEPs, the average increased from 2.01 during the immediate post-war years (1946–51) to 2.91 during the immediate pre-MMP years (1984–93). In the 1996 election, the figure rose steeply to 4.36, and then fell slightly in 1999 to 3.86.[44] Likewise, whereas the ENPP averaged 1.97 between 1946 and 1993, it almost doubled to 3.76 in 1996 before declining modestly to 3.45 in 1999.[45] Thus, whereas New Zealand ranked among those democracies with the lowest ENPPs under FPP, it now ranks closer to the average, with a number of ENPPs similar to that of countries like Norway and Sweden.[46] At the same time, the results of the 1999 election mean that the fractionalization of the party system has decreased somewhat since 1996, with the two major parties (Labour and National) having a slightly larger proportion of seats.

Thus, the introduction of MMP has resulted in the replacement of the two-party system that dominated New Zealand politics for sixty years – between 1936 and 1996 – with a multi-party system. But it is a multi-party system of a particular kind.[47] As expected, party competition has continued to be structured in accordance with the dominant socio-economic (or left-right) dimension, with relatively little competition being generated by other dimensions (such as ethnicity, religion, or the materialism/post-materialism cleavage). Accordingly, most of the parties that won seats in the first two MMP elections competed with each other primarily on socio-economic issues. The main exception was the Green Party (formerly a constituent part of the Alliance, between 1993 and 1999) which successfully crossed the 5 per cent threshold in the 1999 election on an essentially post-materialist policy platform.

In keeping with the predominantly one-dimensional character of New Zealand politics, party competition under MMP has remained largely "bipolar and centripetal";[48] this has left little policy space for ostensibly centrist parties like United and NZF. Indeed, thus far, United has only survived under MMP through the capacity of its leader, Peter Dunne, to secure an electorate seat. Similarly, NZF would have lost its parliamentary representation following the 1999 election had its leader not retained his seat of Tauranga (albeit by a mere sixty-three votes). Unless these parties are able to repeat their success at the electorate level in subsequent MMP elections, or find another issue along which to build sufficient electoral support to cross the 5 per cent threshold, neither party has a secure long-term parliamentary future.[49] Accordingly, it would not be surprising if the number of parliamentary parties were to fall from the current seven to around five. Having said this, electoral volatility, as measured by the Pedersen index, has remained relatively high – at about twice the average level for Western European democracies.[50] In these circumstances, there is a real prospect of further major shifts in the level of support for the current parliamentary parties. Equally, the emergence of new parliamentary parties cannot be ruled out.

In fact, one of the more significant, if not somewhat surprising, features of the first MMP Parliament was the continuing process of party fragmentation and the defection of MPs to other parties. Whereas six parties secured parliamentary representation in 1996, by mid-1999 the legislature contained ten parties and three independents. The new parties emerged from the two least cohesive parties – the Alliance and NZF – and included Mauri Pacific (with five MPs), the Greens (with two MPs), Mana Wahine (with one MP) and Christian Heritage (with one MP).[51] The three independents were all former NZF MPs. While further party fragmentation cannot be ruled out, a repeat of the high number of defections that occurred between 1994 and 1999 is most unlikely.

The greater proportionality of seats to votes under MMP has not resulted in political power being proportionately distributed among the parliamentary parties. In fact, as many critics of MMP predicted, the move to PR has given rise to situations in which small pivotal parties have been able to exert a disproportionate influence over the formulation of public policy. The most graphic example of this occurred in the wake of the first MMP election.[52] In this instance, NZF (with 13.4 per cent of the party vote and seventeen seats) held the balance of power between the centre-right bloc (comprising ACT, National, and United, with a total of fifty-three seats) and the centre-left bloc (comprising the Alliance and Labour, with a total of fifty seats) (see Table 1). Given the unwillingness of the two major parties to cooperate and the likely electoral penalties associated with the formation of ideologically disconnected coalitions, NZF was in effect able to determine the composition of the first MMP government and exercise a significant influence over the new government's policy program.[53]

But if New Zealand's experience under MMP confirms the possibility of small, pivotal parties securing disproportionate power, it also provides another salutary lesson: in a competitive electoral marketplace, parties that are perceived to have misused their power are subject to substantial, and swiftly inflicted, political penalties. In the case of NZF, the electoral consequences of its behaviour following the 1996 election were severe indeed: in 1999 it lost more than two-thirds of its votes and seats (see Table 1) and is no longer in a position to exercise sustained or substantial political influence. There were at least five reasons for NZF's fall from grace: the inherent difficulties and tensions which populist parties face upon entering office; public irritation over the way its leader, Winston Peters, conducted the coalition negotiations in late 1996 and the fact that it took two months to form the first MMP government; the party's decision to enter a coalition with National rather than Labour, contrary to the preferences of the overwhelming majority of NZF's supporters; the imprudent and aggressive behaviour of some its new MPs; and the incapacity of Peters to fashion his ethnically and ideologically disparate caucus into a stable, disciplined, and cohesive team.[54]

Representation and Political Recruitment

As expected, the introduction of MMP, coupled with an increase in the size of Parliament from 99 to 120 MPs, brought a substantial influx of new people – of varying backgrounds, experience, and expertise – into the legislature. In the first MMP election, 42.5 per cent of the MPs were new, the highest percentage recorded during the post-war era.[55] The overwhelming majority of these (76.1 per cent) were list MPs.[56] Despite the collapse in support for NZF and the failure of any of the defectors to retain their seats, turnover in 1999 was a more moderate 26.7 per cent.[57]

MMP has undoubtedly produced a more representative Parliament (see Table 3 below).[58] The representation of women has improved significantly, from 21.2 per cent after the last FPP election to 29.1 per cent after the first MMP election, and 30.8 per cent after the second. The majority of women MPs since 1996 have been elected via their respective party lists; also, twenty-five of the thirty-seven women MPs elected in 1999 were members of centre-left parties. Not insignificantly, the prime minister (Helen Clark) and the leader of the opposition (Jenny Shipley) are both women. Moreover, of the twenty-five members of the Labour-Alliance ministerial team appointed in December 1999, no fewer than eleven (or 44 per cent) are women. The representation of women in New Zealand's key political institutions is thus relatively high by international standards, and not far behind the pattern in Scandinavia.

Mäori representation in Parliament has also improved markedly.[59] Whereas there were only six Mäori MPs in 1993, there were sixteen (or 13.3 per cent) in both 1996 and 1999. With Mäori comprising about 15 per cent of New Zealand's population, Mäori representation is at last approaching more equitable levels. Importantly, too, four

Table 3: The social composition of the House of Representatives under FPP and MMP

	MPs 1945	*MPs 1993*	*MPs 1996*	*MPs 1999*
Women	2.5	21.2	29.1	30.8
Mäori	5.0	6.0	13.3	13.3
Pacific Islanders	–	1.0	2.5	2.5
Asian	–	–	0.8	0.8

Source: Elizabeth McLeay, "The New Parliament," in *Left Turn: The New Zealand General Election of 1999*, ed. Jonathan Boston et al. (Wellington, Victoria University Press, 2000), 220.

Mäori were appointed to the Labour-Alliance ministerial team – a record number. At the same time, Mäori representation remains low among the parties of the centre-right: National and ACT have only one Mäori MP each. By contrast, Labour has ten and the Alliance two. A return to centre-right administrations, therefore, is likely to witness a reduction in the representation of Mäori within the cabinet.

MMP has generated a more representative Parliament in other respects.[60] For instance, there are now three MPs with Pacific Island backgrounds and one MP with a Chinese background. The 1999 Parliament also contains two openly gay MPs and a transsexual MP. Quite apart from this, Parliaments under MMP have been more socially representative. The average age of MPs has declined and the occupational backgrounds are more varied.

Government Formation and Durability

As widely predicted, the move to MMP has resulted in no single party securing an overall parliamentary majority. Inevitably, this has altered the process of government formation and the nature of interparty relationships.[61] It has also affected the kinds of governments formed and their durability (see Table 2, p. 36).

Under FPP, certainly since the mid-1930s, it was usually clear on election night whether Labour or National would form the next government. Regardless of whether the incumbent government had been defeated, a new government was typically sworn in by the governor general within two weeks of the election. No doubt the period of time would have been even shorter had there been no requirement to await the writs from the returning officers in each electorate before a new ministry could be formed.[62]

Following the first MMP election, it took two months to form a government. This is roughly twice as long as the average in other countries with PR systems.[63] There were three main reasons for the lengthy delay: First, there are no statutory limitations on how long the process of government formation can take (although there is a requirement, under Section 19 of the Constitution Act 1986, for Parliament to meet within six weeks of the return of the writs). Second, neither the centre-left bloc nor the centre-right bloc had an overall majority. Third, NZF – which, as already noted, held the balance of power – decided to negotiate detailed coalition agreements with both Labour and National, and then choose the best deal – a process which inevitably took considerable time.[64]

By contrast, the process of government formation following the 1999 general election was remarkably swift and uncomplicated.[65] A coalition agreement between Labour and the Alliance was negotiated within nine days, and the ministers in the new centre-left government were sworn in within two weeks of the election. The speed of the process was greatly assisted by the fact that the election delivered the three centre-left parties (the Alliance, Labour, and the Greens) a comfortable parliamentary majority (notwithstanding a ten-day period of uncertainty over the fate of the Greens). Moreover, for more than a year prior to the election Labour and the Alliance had been forging a cooperative relationship and discussing how they would manage a coalition government if they had the opportunity to form one.[66] As part of this process, it had been agreed that lengthy, highly specific, policy-oriented coalition agreements (of the kind concluded between National and NZF) should be eschewed. Given this situation, it was not difficult for the two parties to act quickly after the 1999 election to finalize a brief agreement and negotiate the composition of a new ministry. Of course, events might have been rather different if NZF had again held the balance of power or if the Greens had expressed a clear wish to be part of the government rather than serve as a support party for the minority Labour-Alliance coalition. It should not be assumed, therefore, that the rapid process of government formation in late 1999 will become the norm under MMP.

As highlighted by Table 2, there have been a significant number of different governments since the 1993 referendum. The precise count, of course, depends on the criteria selected for determining what constitutes a change of government.[67] If the sole criterion is a change in the parties represented within the cabinet, then there have been seven governments since late 1993, and three since the first MMP election. If, however, other criteria are included, such as a change of prime minister and a change in the parliamentary support for the government (e.g., from majority to minority status), then the number of different governments since late 1993 rises to ten. Either way, this represents a dramatic change from the norm under FPP. In short, the durability of governments has fallen sharply.

Yet the implications of this should not be exaggerated. To be sure, rapid changes of government and the collapse of coalitions (as happened, for instance, in August 1998) can generate considerable political uncertainty. But this doesn't necessarily have a major impact on policy outcomes or governmental effectiveness. Moreover, it is important to recognize that between 1990 and 1999 the National Party was always in office and all of the governments formed during these years were of the centre-right. From the perspective of most citizens, there has only been one real change of government since 1990 (i.e., in late 1999 when the National-led government was replaced by the Labour-Alliance coalition).

Significantly, since the process of party fragmentation commenced in mid-1994, there has been only one single-party government: the National minority government between August 1995 and February 1996. Under MMP, therefore, New Zealand has moved into an era of coalition politics. Moreover, minority government has increasingly become the norm. In this respect, New Zealand appears to be following the pattern in Scandinavia rather than in continental Europe. This early prevalence of minority governments is doubtless the product of a number of influences, including the rules surrounding the process of government formation,[68] the mathematics of the election results (including the number and relative size of the parliamentary parties), and the preference of some of the smaller parties, like ACT and the Greens, not to enter office. But whatever the reasons, the move to minority government represents a decisive break from New Zealand's long tradition of majoritarianism.

The Impact of MMP on Parliament

Significantly, no government since 1993 has enjoyed more than a bare parliamentary majority, with minority coalitions increasingly the norm. Necessarily, therefore, governments have been less able than under FPP to impose their will on Parliament and its committees, and have been forced to take greater notice of the views of their support party (or parties) and, in some cases, opposition parties.[69] This has meant, for instance, that it has been more difficult for governments to rush legislation through the House under urgency or to prevent members' bills that are controversial from being sent to parliamentary committees for consideration.

The impact of MMP on the role and operation of select committees has been especially marked. In keeping with the proportionate allocation of committee places and the removal of the casting vote from chairpersons (following the changes to standing orders in 1996), governments are now rarely in a position to control select committee agendas and deliberations. As a result, there have been a number of important changes in the way such committees have operated. These include a greater willingness to recommend substantial changes to government bills; to initiate in-depth policy inquiries; to scrutinize, and criticize, the operations of public agencies; and to challenge or embarrass individual ministers. In short, as was widely expected, MMP has led to select committees becoming more independent of the executive. Of course, this does not mean that governments have always followed the advice of select committees; where they have enjoyed a clear (albeit small) parliamentary majority, they have not hesitated to override committee recommendations during debates in the House (or to prevent issues from being referred to committees for consideration).[70]

But if MMP has brought some notable changes to parliamentary processes and procedures, it has not produced a marked improvement in the quality or tone of parliamentary debates. Nor has it ushered in a new era of multi-party cooperation and consensus.[71] On the contrary, party competition in the House has remained intense, and governments have rarely pursued the practice, as in some other countries with PR, of seeking the support of the main opposition parties on major policy issues (in the interests of long-term policy stability).

Governmental Effectiveness

Prior to the introduction of MMP, many critics of electoral reform argued that PR would impair governmental effectiveness and that this, in turn, would have detrimental economic consequences. Any attempt to assess such claims, however, raises numerous methodological problems, not least of which is the difficulty of measuring "effectiveness."[72] Furthermore, it is too early to assess the long-term economic consequences, if any, of the move to MMP. Having said this, a number of brief observations can be made.

First, while governments under MMP have been less cohesive and durable than under FPP, and while the policy process has tended to be more uncertain and protracted, governments have continued to pass large volumes of legislation and regulations, including many bills of a highly controversial nature. Admittedly, not all legislation introduced into the House has received parliamentary endorsement; in many cases ministers have been forced to negotiate amendments with support parties (and occasionally with opposition parties). Second, governments have had little difficulty, to date, in winning parliamentary support for their major budgetary initiatives. So far there have been only a few instances (not connected to budgetary legislation) in which ministers have felt obliged to use their financial veto (to prevent the passage of legislative amendments with significant fiscal implications). Third, the Labour-Alliance coalition, notwithstanding its minority status, is in the process of implementing a major package of reforms, some of which involve significant departures from the neo-liberal orthodoxy which has dominated the policy agenda since the mid-1980s. Finally, governments have continued to pursue policy initiatives which impose financial losses (both in real or relative terms) on powerful lobby groups, such as pensioners and employers. They have also demonstrated a continuing capacity to act decisively – including actions to reduce public expenditure and break electoral commitments, as for instance occurred in 1998 in response to the Asian financial crisis. While such actions, whether individually or collectively, do not provide conclusive evidence that governmental effectiveness has been unaffected by MMP, they certainly cast serious doubt on any suggestions that effectiveness has been substantially impaired.

Public Support for MMP

So far, this chapter has considered some of the behavioural, institutional, and policy implications of MMP. But how do citizens regard the new electoral system? Has it fulfilled their hopes and expectations? Opinion poll data indicate that the initial public reaction to MMP was characterized by a degree of disappointment, if not hostility, with support for the new system falling sharply in the immediate aftermath of the first PR election. For instance, in April 1997 only 31 per cent of those questioned said that they supported MMP while 53 per cent favoured FPP.[73] Similar results were reported during much of the remainder of the first MMP Parliament. There is also survey evidence to suggest that citizens became less satisfied with the democratic process and increasingly cynical about their capacity to influence the actions of policy-makers.[74] Having said this, surveys conducted during and immediately following the 1999 election campaign demonstrated a resurgence in support for MMP, but not to the levels achieved during the early-to-mid 1990s.[75]

The reasons for the initial negativity towards the new electoral system are not difficult to discern.[76] They include the behaviour of NZF immediately following the 1996 election, and in particular its decision to forge a coalition with National; the questionable behaviour of various new MPs; the acrimony and uncertainty surrounding the collapse of the National-NZF coalition in August 1998; the sluggish rate of economic growth during the mid-to-late 1990s; anger over the high number of MPs defecting to other parties (and the consequent undermining of the principle that parliamentary seats should be allocated on a proportional basis); and the failure of MMP to generate a more harmonious, consensual style of politics. In short, during its early years, MMP failed to fulfil the public's hopes and expectations.

The initial dissatisfaction with the new electoral system had at least three direct consequences. First, it led to the holding of a referendum on the size of Parliament initiated by citizens (in conjunction with the 1999 general election) in which 81.5 per cent of voters supported a reduction in the number of MPs from 120 to 99 (the same number as in 1993).[77] Second, it has given rise to legislation – the Electoral (Integrity) Amendment Bill – which, if passed, will require MPs who leave their political parties to resign from Parliament. Third, it prompted repeated calls for the holding of a further binding referendum in which voters would have the opportunity to choose between MMP and an alternative voting system.

As noted, public support for MMP rebounded somewhat in late 1999. There are various possible reasons for this, including the electoral defeat of the unpopular National-led government, the rapid formation of a new administration, and the swift implementation of a set of policies, most of which appear to have the support of the majority of the population. Also, it should not be forgotten that the cause of electoral reform secured substantially greater support from those on the left of the political spectrum than those on the right; the centre-left's victory in 1999 doubtless brought comfort to those who hoped that MMP might temper, if not halt, New Zealand's radical neoliberal experiments. If the centre-left government proves to be relatively effective and stable, support for MMP is likely to consolidate over the next few years. The pressure for holding another electoral referendum will also probably diminish.

The Parliamentary Review of MMP

In accordance with section 264 of the Electoral Act 1993, a special parliamentary committee – the MMP Review Committee – was established in April 2000 to examine the operation of the new electoral system. The committee commissioned research on public attitudes to

MMP, invited and heard submissions, and considered a range of possible changes to the Electoral Act. These included the abolition of separate Mäori seats, a reduction in the number of MPs, an increase in the term of Parliament to four years, the holding of a referendum on the future of MMP, and various modifications to the nature of MMP (such as a reduction in the party vote threshold).

In the event, the committee's report, which was released in August 2001, contained few recommendations.[78] The main reason for this was procedural: the committee had agreed at the outset of its deliberations that, because of the constitutional significance of the matters under investigation, it would only make recommendations to the government when there was unanimity or near-unanimity. Given that the six parties represented on the committee were divided (for strategic, ideological, and other reasons) on most of the key issues, including the pivotal question of whether there should be a binding referendum on the future of MMP, unanimity or near-unanimity was achieved on only a limited number of relatively minor matters.[79] Accordingly, the committee did not recommend any changes to the basic features of MMP, the number of MPs, the issue of Mäori representation, or the mechanics and operation of the electoral system. This outcome, not surprisingly, was of considerable disappointment not merely to the opponents of PR, but also to those who had championed significant modifications to aspects of the MMP system.

In early November 2001, the Labour-Alliance government announced that it would not make any changes to the voting system or the number of MPs and that no referendum would be held. In support of this decision it argued that electoral reforms should not be made "lightly or too frequently."[80] "Changing any major constitutional arrangements would require a higher level of consensus from the public than currently appears to exist. In the absence of that high degree of consensus, the Government is of the view that ... it would not be appropriate to recommend any significant amendments at this time."[81] Plainly, a number of other considerations influenced the government's decision to resist pressure for changes to the Electoral Act and the holding of a further referendum on the voting system. Among these were, first, the widely-held view that it is still too early to judge the merits of MMP and thus too soon to hold another referendum; second, the internal tensions that any reform proposals would generate within the coalition; and third, the difficulties of reaching a multi-party agreement on the wording of any binding referendum. No doubt the latter two issues will remain ongoing constraints on the capacity of any future coalition government to promote significant changes to the current electoral arrangements.

CONCLUSION

For political scientists, major electoral reforms of the kind introduced in New Zealand in the mid-1990s provide a seemingly ideal laboratory for testing and refining theories about the relationship between institutions and political behaviour. In New Zealand's case, the move to PR has generated outcomes that are largely consistent with the predictions of the relevant literature: the former two-party "majoritarian democracy" has been replaced with a multi-party "negotiation democracy";[82] single-party majority governments have been replaced with coalitions, mostly of a minority nature; the coalitions which have been formed have been ideologically connected rather than disconnected; government formation has been more complex, and in one case, substantially more protracted; governments have become less durable, but not necessarily less effective; the representation of women, Mäori, and minorities in Parliament has significantly improved; and the balance of power between Parliament and the executive has shifted, albeit only slightly, in Parliament's favour. Also, as many expected, there were significant political growing pains associated with the introduction of MMP – although their magnitude (especially the degree of party fragmentation following the first MMP election) was greater than most informed observers had thought likely.

Equally important, New Zealand's experience under PR has highlighted that securing greater proportionality between votes and seats does not guarantee greater proportionality between seats and power. Against this, of course, the move to MMP has thus far prevented any single party from obtaining an absolute monopoly of power, as was the norm under FPP. Accordingly, it has achieved one of the crucial aims of its supporters, namely to distribute executive power more widely and thus render it more difficult for a single, cohesive party to operate as an "elected dictatorship."

But if most of the results of PR in New Zealand have been consistent with the predictions of the political science literature, this has not of course guaranteed a ready public acceptance of the outcomes. Nor has it thus far restored public confidence and trust in the nation's political institutions, encouraged substantially greater electoral participation, or led to a widespread perception that the quality of New Zealand's democracy has improved. In fact, in the short term, the introduction of MMP probably served to increase concerns about the integrity and efficacy of the country's constitutional arrangements. Any suggestion, therefore, that electoral reform will provide a cure for the constitutional discontent that currently afflicts many democracies can be quickly dismissed. Indeed, there is a risk that it might simply make matters worse.

Finally, a word of caution: as New Zealand's experience under MMP is still young, some of the consequences remain to be fully felt. Accordingly, any conclusions concerning its institutional, behavioural, and policy implications must remain tentative and incomplete. Similarly, care is needed in applying any lessons from New Zealand's experience to other countries which might be toying with the idea of electoral reform. After all, New Zealand has many distinctive institutional arrangements and a unique political history and culture. Such factors have undoubtedly influenced how PR has operated thus far (particularly the nature of the party system which has emerged) and will continue to shape its future political impact. Any serious analysis of the implications of PR for a country such as Canada would require a detailed exploration of the experience of a range of countries, including those with long histories of PR and those with greater ethnic, linguistic, or geographical cleavages than New Zealand.

NOTES

1 This analysis draws heavily on research conducted since 1995 by the New Zealand Political Change Project, of which the author is a member. The Project, based at Victoria University of Wellington, is funded by the New Zealand Foundation for Research, Science and Technology, and is concerned with the institutional, behavioural, and policy implications of the introduction of MMP. The author would like to thank the other members of the Project (Stephen Church, Stephen Levine, Elizabeth McLeay, and Nigel S. Roberts) for their assistance with the preparation of this analysis.

2 There is now a reasonably extensive literature exploring the consequences of New Zealand's move to PR. Important sources include Fiona Barker et al., "The Consequences of MMP: An Initial Assessment," Proceedings of the Joint Conference of the Australasian Political Science Association and European Union Studies Association of New Zealand, Christchurch, NZ, 27–30 September 1998; Fiona Barker et al., "An Initial Assessment of the Consequences of MMP in New Zealand," in *Mixed-Member Electoral Systems: The Best of Both Worlds?* ed. Matthew Shugart and Martin Wattenberg (Oxford: Oxford University Press, 2001); Jonathan Boston et al., eds, *From Campaign to Coalition: The 1996 MMP Election* (Palmerston North, NZ: Dunmore Press, 1997); Jonathan Boston et al., eds, *Left Turn: New Zealand's General Election of 1999* (Wellington: Victoria University Press, 2000); Jack Vowles et al., eds, *Voters' Victory? New Zealand's First Election Under Proportional Representation* (Auckland: Auckland University Press, 1998).

3 The best analysis of why New Zealand adopted PR can be found in Keith Jackson and Alan McRobie, *New Zealand Adopts Proportional Representation* (Aldershot, NZ: Ashgate, 1998).

4 A brief exploration of these issues can be found in Elizabeth McLeay, "Analysing the Impact of MMP," (speech given at the Wallace Awards Annual Dinner, Wellington Club, Wellington, 9 July 1999).

5 Arend Lijphart, *Democracies: Patterns of Majoritarian and Consensus Government in Twenty-One Countries* (New Haven: Yale University Press, 1984), 16. Lijphart is of course well aware that the political system in New Zealand has undergone profound change since the mid-1990s; see his *Patterns of Democracy: Government Forms and Performance in Thirty-Six Countries* (New Haven: Yale University Press, 1999), 21.

6 Lijphart, *Democracies*, 16–20.

7 For a fuller analysis of the operation of the Westminster model in New Zealand during these years see Hyam Gold, ed., *New Zealand Politics in Perspective* (Auckland: Longman Paul, 1985); Keith Jackson, *The Politics of Change* (Christchurch, NZ: Reed Education, 1973); Geoffrey Palmer, *Unbridled Power?* (Auckland: Oxford University Press, 1979).

8 See Keith Jackson, "Caucus: The Anti-Parliament System?" *The Parliamentarian* 59, no. 2 (1977): 159–64.

9 Richard Mulgan, "New Zealand – An Elected Dictatorship," in *New Zealand Politics in Perspective*, 2d ed., ed. Hyam Gold (Auckland: Longman Paul, 1989), 446–56. Mulgan's choice of the phrase "elected dictatorship" was no doubt influenced by Lord Hailsham, who had described the democratic process in the United Kingdom in similar terms more than a decade earlier.

10 Good analyses of these issues can be found in Richard Mulgan, *Mäori, Pakeha and Democracy* (Auckland: Oxford University Press, 1989); Richard Mulgan, *Politics in New Zealand* (Auckland: Auckland University Press, 1994); and Richard Mulgan, "The Democratic Failure of Single-Party Government: The New Zealand Experience," *Australian Journal of Political Science* 30, Special Issue (1995): 82–96.

11 Michael Gallagher, "Proportionality, Disproportionality and Electoral Systems," *Electoral Studies* 10, no. 2 (1992): 45.

12 See Therese Arseneau, "A Bill of Rights," in *The Fourth Labour Government: Politics and Policy in New Zealand,* ed. Martin Holland and Jonathan Boston (Auckland: Oxford University Press, 1990), 22–40.

13 Quoted in Jonathan Boston et al., "Why did New Zealand Adopt German-Style Proportional Representation?" *Representation* 33, no. 4 (1995): 135–6.

14 See Royal Commission on the Electoral System, *Report of the Royal Commission on the Electoral System: Towards a Better Democracy* (Wellington: Government Printer, 1986).

15 Ibid., 11–12.

16 Ibid., 11.

17 Ibid.
18 Ibid.
19 Ibid., 45–64.
20 Ibid., 64.
21 Ibid., 43–4. See also Boston et al., "Why did New Zealand?"
22 Royal Commission, *Report*, 113.
23 See Jackson and McRobie, *New Zealand Adopts Proportional Representation*, esp. 125–201.
24 A fuller account of the MMP electoral system can be found in Electoral Commission, *New Zealand Electoral Compendium*, 2d ed. (Wellington: Electoral Commission, 2000).
25 For an analysis of the impact of MMP on interparty cooperation and competition prior to, and during, election campaigns, see Jonathan Boston and Stephen Church, "Pre-Election Wheeling and Dealing: Theory and Practice," in Jonathan Boston et al., eds, *Left Turn: New Zealand's General Election of 1999* (Wellington: Victoria University Press, 2000).
26 Ibid., 202–31.
27 In late 1995, the New Zealand Political Change Project conducted a survey of around 1,600 opinion leaders (including parliamentarians, senior public servants, business leaders, interest group representatives, etc.). The results of this survey are reported in Jonathan Boston et al., *New Zealand Under MMP: A New Politics* (Auckland: Auckland University Press, 1996), 27–42. For another perspective in relation to public expectations of MMP see Jack Nagel, "The Defects of Its Virtues: New Zealand's Experience with MMP," in *Making Every Vote Count: Reassessing Canada's Electoral System*, ed. Henry Milner (Peterborough: Broadview Press, 1999), 157–69.
28 Boston et al., *New Zealand Under MMP*, 30–6.
29 For a more detailed analysis, see Jack Nagel, "How Many Parties Will New Zealand Have Under MMP?" *Political Science* 46, no. 2 (1994): 139–60.
30 Lijphart, *Patterns of Democracy*, 27.
31 For a fuller account of these developments, see Jonathan Boston et al., "Experimenting with Coalition Government: Preparing to Manage Under Proportional Representation," *Journal of Commonwealth and Comparative Politics* 35, no. 3: 108–26.
32 For an account of the changes to standing orders see Boston et al., *New Zealand Under MMP*, 71–86.
33 See Jeffrey Karp and Susan Banducci, "The Impact of Proportional Representation on Turnout: Evidence from New Zealand," *Australian Journal of Political Science* 34, no. 3 (1999): 363–77; and Lijphart, *Patterns of Democracy*, 284–5.

34 Karp and Banducci, "The Impact," 363–4.
35 Ibid., 364.
36 Ibid.
37 Jack Vowles, "Dealignment and Demobilisation? Non-voting in New Zealand 1938–90," *Australian Journal of Political Science* 29, no. 1 (1994): 96–114.
38 Karp and Banducci, "The Impact," 375.
39 For a detailed analysis of the impact of MMP on the party system, see Fiona Barker and Elizabeth McLeay, "How Much Change? An Analysis of the Initial Impact of Proportional Representation on the New Zealand Parliamentary Party System," *Party Politics* 6, no. 2 (2000): 131–54.
40 Barker et al., "An Initial Assessment."
41 Ibid., 300.
42 Electoral Commission, *New Zealand Electoral Compendium*, 1st ed. (Wellington: Electoral Commission, 1997), 18–19; and Electoral Commission, *New Zealand Electoral Compendium*, 2nd ed. (Wellington: Electoral Commission, 2000), 60–1. In order to register, and thus have an opportunity to submit a party list at an election, parties must have at least 500 current financial members who are eligible to register as electors.
43 Nagel, "How Many Parties," 157.
44 Barker et al., "An Initial Assessment." See also André Kaiser and Thomas Brechtel, "Party System, Bargaining Power and Coalition Formation after the 1999 New Zealand General Election," *Political Science* 51, no. 2 (1999): 182–6.
45 Barker et al., "An Initial Assessment."
46 Barker et al., "The Consequences," 51.
47 Kaiser and Brechtel, "Party System," 182.
48 Ibid.
49 Note that the capacity of small parties to win constituency seats under MMP has been one of the surprising features of the new system.
50 Kaiser and Brechtel, "The Party System," 183.
51 The Christian Heritage party had contested elections since the early 1990s but had not won any parliamentary seats.
52 Nagel, "The Defects," 162–5. See also Jonathan Boston and Elizabeth McLeay, "Forming the First MMP Government: Theory, Practice and Prospects," in *From Campaign to Coalition: the 1996 MMP Election* (Palmerston North, NZ: Dunmore Press, 1997), 207–46.
53 On the Banzhaf scale (calculated on the basis of the number of potential ideologically-connected minimum winning coalitions to which a party's membership is crucial for victory), NZF held 40 per cent of the power, twice that of Labour, National, and the Alliance.
54 See Jonathan Boston, Stephen Church, and Hilary Pearse, "The Termination of New Zealand's First Coalition Government Under MMP: Testing

Theories of Cabinet Durability," (paper presented to a joint conference of the Third Wellington Conference on World Affairs, the European Union Studies Association of New Zealand, and the New Zealand Political Studies Association, Wellington, 1–3 December 1999).

55 Elizabeth McLeay, "The New Parliament," in Boston et al., *Left Turn*. See also Helena Catt, "Women, Mäori and Minorities: Microrepresentation and MMP," in *From Campaign to Coalition*, 199–206.

56 McLeay, "The New Parliament," 206.

57 Ibid., 205.

58 Bear in mind that Parliament has become more representative in a number of important respects over many decades (e.g., in relation to the proportion of women securing seats). Hence, part of the impact of PR has simply been to speed up certain trends and processes that have long been in evidence.

59 McLeay, "The New Parliament"; and Catt, "Women, Mäori and Minorities."

60 Ibid.

61 See Boston and McLeay, "Forming the First"; and Jonathan Boston, "Forming the Coalition Between Labour and the Alliance," in Boston et al., *Left Turn*.

62 Under current arrangements, a period a ten days is allowed after the election for the counting of "special votes." This inevitably delays the return of the writs.

63 Jonathan Boston, *Governing Under Proportional Representation: Lessons from Europe* (Wellington: Institute of Policy Studies, 1998), 25.

64 The simultaneous parallel negotiations between NZF and its potential coalition partners is relatively unusual by international standards. See Boston and McLeay, "Forming the First," esp. 220–33.

65 Boston, "Forming the Coalition."

66 Boston and Church, "Pre-Election Wheeling and Dealing," in Boston et al., *Left Turn*.

67 See Boston and Church, "The Termination"; and Eric Damgaard, "Termination of Danish Government Coalitions: Theoretical and Empirical Aspects," *Scandinavian Political Studies* 17, no. 3 (1994): 193–211.

68 Note that New Zealand has a system of freestyle bargaining and no requirement for an investiture vote. See Boston, *Governing Under*, 20–6.

69 Barker et al., "The Consequences," 49–50.

70 See Michael Taggart, "Deja vu all over again," *New Zealand Law Journal* (July 1998), 234–6.

71 The suggestion that proportional representation would give rise to a greater measure of consensus among the political parties was almost certainly connected to Lijphart's distinction between majoritarian and consensus democracies. As Kaiser correctly argues, however, a degree of

consensus is vital for the successful functioning of all democratic systems. Moreover, if consensus is equated with unanimity or harmony, then such outcomes cannot be expected in any democratic system. Kaiser suggests that Lijphart's "consensus democracy" would be better termed "negotiation democracy." See André Kaiser, "Types of Democracy: From Classical to New Institutionalism," *Journal of Theoretical Politics* 9, no. 4 (1997): 419–44.

72 The issues surrounding the measurement of governmental effectiveness are examined by Kaare Strom, *Minority Government and Majority Rule* (Cambridge: Cambridge University Press, 1990), 113–123; and Kent Weaver and Bert Rockman, eds, *Do Institutions Matter? Government Capabilities in the United States and Abroad* (Washington, D.C.: The Brookings Institution, 1993). The impact of institutional rules on policy outcomes, including economic performance, is considered in Lijphart, *Patterns of Democracy*, 258–300.

73 Jeffrey Karp and Shaun Bowler, "Coalition Government and Satisfaction with Democracy: An Analysis of New Zealand's Reaction to Proportional Representation," *Proceedings of the 1999 Conference of the Australasian Political Studies Association, Volume 2*, (Sydney: University of Sydney, 26–29 September 1999).

74 See the results of the major survey of New Zealanders' values conducted in October 1998: Paul Perry and Alan Webster, *New Zealand Politics at the Turn of the Millennium: Attitudes and Values about Politics and Government* (Auckland: Alpha Publications, 1999).

75 See New Zealand Election Study, "Submission to the MMP Review Committee on the Inquiry into MMP," 25 July 2000, 53.

76 See Karp and Bowler, "Coalition Government," 406–13; Nagel, "The Defects."

77 See Stephen Church, "Crime and Punishment: The Citizens' Initiated Referenda to Reform the Criminal Justice System and Reduce the Size of Parliament," in Boston et al., *Left Turn*.

78 Report of the MMP Review Committee, *Inquiry into the Review of* MMP (Wellington: New Zealand House of Representatives, August 2001).

79 The New Zealand First Party, by its own decision, was the only party not represented on the MMP Review Committee.

80 Tracy Watkins, "Government rules out MMP change and MP cuts," *The Dominion*, 7 November 2001.

81 Ibid.

82 Kaiser, "Types of Democracy," 434.

The Australian Republic: Act I

CHERYL SAUNDERS

Like most countries, Australia has a constitution and system of government borrowed in part from elsewhere. The United States was one important influence that shaped the Australian federation and, to a degree, the framework for the federal judicature.[1] From Switzerland, Australia adapted the referendum as a requirement for constitutional change.[2] For the rest, however, Australia drew on Britain, either directly, or indirectly through the filter of the experience of the six colonies that came together in a federation in 1901. The colonies' systems of government had been designed almost exclusively on the British model, but modified as needed to meet local circumstances and to recognize the supreme authority of the imperial Parliament[3] and government. In these circumstances, it was natural for the new national government and Parliament of the Commonwealth of Australia also to be broadly established along Westminster lines.

On the threshold of the twentieth century, Australia still has a range of institutions, principles, and attitudes shared with other countries derived from the Westminster tradition. Many of these relate, in one way or another, to the nature and form of representative government. Importantly, they include a popularly elected chamber – the Australian House of Representatives – in which the government is based and on which it depends for its legitimacy. Naturally there are other points on which the Australian system diverges from others, due both to its mixed constitutional heritage and the distinctive Australian context in which it operates. One such difference is the composition and operation of the Senate, the powerful elected second chamber of the Australian

Parliament. It is relevant here both for its effect on the operation of representative government in Australia and for the influence of its actions on the design of an Australian republic.

The most recent phase of the Australian republican movement began in 1992, with an eye to the symbolism of the constitutional centenary in 2001. It ended in 1999, with the rejection of a referendum that would have altered the constitution and established a republic. This chapter seeks to explain how the idea of a republic arose and was handled and why it failed. It suggests that the referendum's rejection can be explained in part by the dissatisfaction with parliamentary representation that is common throughout the Western world. At the very least, the result was a form of protest vote against the model of republic that politicians seemed to want and which depended on politicians for its efficacy. In one view, the public debate on the referendum model also showed support for a different or additional form of representation. If this is correct, when the issue of the republic is raised again in Australia, there may be pressure for it to be the vehicle of more substantial change. The response will determine whether Australia will diverge even further from the original Westminster model than at present.

PARLIAMENTARY GOVERNMENT IN AUSTRALIA

Superficially at least, the Australian parliamentary system is organized and operates along familiar Westminster lines. Members of the lower house of Parliament, the House of Representatives, are elected from single-member constituencies. Thanks to preferential voting, which eliminates the most obvious excesses of first-past-the-post, there is no pressure for change to the electoral system of the kind there was in New Zealand. Governments are formed by reference to the confidence of the House of Representatives. All ministers must be members of Parliament. Executive power is formally vested in the Crown[4] but exercised in almost all cases on government advice, which in general is delivered formally through the Executive Council.[5] Executive power is defined consistently with common law principles and includes the conduct of international relations and the ratification of international agreements.[6] In commissioning a government after an election and in summoning, proroguing, and dissolving Parliament, the Crown plays a role that is the product of the long evolution of the relationship between the Crown and Parliament in the United Kingdom. The Australian Parliament is bicameral. In general, legislation must be passed by both houses and receive the Royal Assent before it becomes law.[7]

Conceptually, the Australian approach to representation is also similar to that of other Westminster systems. Members of Parliament are acknowledged to have both constituency and parliamentary functions. They do not regard themselves as delegates of their electors and there are no procedures to encourage or enable voter control of representatives beyond periodic elections. In theory, the responsibility of members of Parliament is to exercise their own judgment and to make decisions in the collective interest. In practice, members of Parliament in Australia, as elsewhere, are bound by decisions of the party to which they belong and on whose platform they were elected.[8]

In addition, the role of Parliament is the same in Australia as in other Westminster systems. The complication of judicial review aside, all new law must be made by or with the authority of Parliament.[9] Taxation and expenditure also require the approval of Parliament. In exercising these functions, however, the role of Parliament tends to be passive rather than creative. Essentially, Parliament provides a public forum in which government proposals of new legislation and public expenditure are approved in a context where the opposition also has a voice. The Parliament also provides the formal mechanism for enforcing the accountability and responsibility of the government collectively, and of ministers individually, with all the ambiguities that attend these rules, given the strict discipline of the parties.

The product of these institutions, principles, and practices is a political culture that places great weight on periodic elections, which in Australia take place at least every three years.[10] Popular sovereignty is certainly acknowledged in political theory, but it is for the most part manifest through elections. Between elections parliamentary sovereignty holds sway, within the limits of the constitution. The rhetoric assumes the right of governments to govern and the responsibility of members of Parliament to their parties, but influenced by voters to the extent that pragmatism suggests necessary.[11] These arrangements are the result of a long evolutionary process in which incremental change takes place in response to opportunities or pressures. Rarely, if ever, is it driven by symbols or visions of an ultimate goal.

This limited view of representation in Australia has ironically been reinforced by observations of the High Court. These observations were made when considering whether and to what extent the bare bones of the Australian constitution imply a protection for important incidents of representative democracy.[12] Over a series of cases,[13] in which the Court became increasingly divided, the justices began to draw a distinction between representative government, some elements of which are constitutionally protected, and representative democracy which, for the most part, is not protected. The most determined exponent of this view was Justice McHugh:

> Representative democracy is commonly used to describe a society which provides for equality of rights and privileges ... The essence of representative government, on the other hand, is a political system where the people in free elections elect their representatives to the political chamber which occupies the most powerful position in the political system ... Even if representative democracy is given the narrow meaning that it had in Athenian times of "government by the people" it is still wider than the concept of representative government which the makers of the Constitution probably had in mind ... The absence of a Bill of Rights or any guarantee of universal suffrage or political equality in the Constitution is also consistent with the view that the ... Constitution does not give effect to any general doctrine of representative democracy.[14]

The significance of one point on which Australian democracy differs from that of almost every other Westminster jurisdiction is still being worked out. Colonial status notwithstanding, the Australian constitution was drawn up by an elected constitutional convention and approved by popular vote – of an admittedly limited electorate – before being sent to the United Kingdom for enactment.[15] This fact has become increasingly important in explaining the overriding legal status of the Australian constitution and the decline of the British Parliament's authority.[16] The historical use of a convention for achieving consensus on a constitution also influenced the decision to establish a convention for the republican question, with consequences that will be seen below.

The manner in which the constitution was originally approved also affected the procedure for its alteration. The requirement for constitutional change by referendum[17] was a natural and perhaps necessary feature of a constitution that had been approved by a direct vote in the first place. The Australian constitutional referendum is passive, however, relying on the initiative of the Commonwealth Parliament.[18] I have suggested elsewhere that one reason for the high failure rate of Australian referendums is that the country's elected representatives in Parliament and government have not adapted their own decision-making procedures sufficiently to the very different imperatives of the referendum.[19] Only eight of forty-four proposals put to the people since federation have been approved, and at least half of those were minor. In the wake of the failure of the republican referendum, there is renewed interest in finding ways to make the referendum process work effectively. If it succeeds, Australia may have a contribution to make to the experimentation with direct democracy that seems likely to be a feature of the early twenty-first century. If it does not, Australia will continue to be portrayed, rightly or wrongly, as an object lesson in the problems that direct democracy may cause.

One other respect in which Australia departs from the traditional Westminster model is the Senate. It is considered in greater detail next.

THE SENATE

The upper house of the Australian Parliament, the Senate, draws on the two founding constitutional traditions of the common law from which the constitution was derived. Most obviously, it is a federal institution modelled loosely on the United States Senate and with some important differences. Even in the absence of a federal system, however, it is likely that the Australian Parliament would have had an upper house of some kind. The British Parliament is bicameral. Each of the Australian colonies also had a bicameral Parliament when the constitution was written. The influence of the colonial example can be seen in how the framers of the constitution resolved their differences over the extent of the Senate's powers in relation to money bills. The solution adopted – and which enabled the federal movement to proceed – was based on a mechanism that helped regulate relations between the two houses of the Parliament of South Australia.

As in the United States, the original states of the Australian federation have equal representation in the Senate. In a departure from the United States model, in deference to the smaller number of states, each state has a larger number of senators, with the possibility of further increase as long as the equality rule is preserved.[20] In a greater departure still, reflecting the democratic temper of Australia, the constitution required senators to be elected directly by the people of their state, using the state as a single electorate.[21] The constitution, however, did not prescribe the electoral system for the Senate. In 1949, proportional representation was introduced, in response to the largely party character of Senate politics, with the effect of ensuring that governments based in the House of Representatives would not face a large non-government Senate majority. One consequence of proportional representation has been, however, that governments rarely enjoy a Senate majority either, a development that has had profound implications for the role the Senate has crafted for itself in the Australian parliamentary system as a whole.

A Senate with substantial power was a key element in the federal bargain, without which federation would not have taken place as and when it did. The Australian Senate has almost co-equal power with the House of Representatives, with the exception of the power to introduce money bills and to amend their key categories.[22] The Senate can reject all bills. There is a procedure to resolve deadlocks,[23] but it is so cumbersome that it is rarely used, and almost never as it was originally intended.[24] The procedure involves dissolution of the whole Senate and no doubt plays an important role in the power struggle between governments and the Senate. In this respect, the Australian arrangements differ from those in the United States, where deadlocks can be resolved only by negotiation, if at all. Nor does the Australian Senate have power to advise and consent in relation to high appointments and treaties, which adds to the authority of the Senate in the United States.[25]

Some of the framers of the Australian constitution worried about the compatibility of responsible government and federalism, if the latter required a Senate with extensive powers of this kind. They were right. The two are indeed incompatible, if as an essential element responsible government requires relative harmony between the legislative and executive branches for speed and certainty in the implementation of policy. In fact, with the exception of the dismissal of the government in 1975, the tension between responsible government and federalism, represented by the Senate, has not led to major conflict. It is a source of continuing controversy, however, reflecting the tension between competing values.

The strong two-party system associated with parliamentary responsible government caused the Senate to become a chamber that votes almost exclusively on party lines. In consequence, it is questionable whether the Senate plays any role as a federal institution at all, apart from providing the smaller states a vehicle for greater numerical representation in Parliament than the size of their populations otherwise would suggest. To this extent, responsible government has modified federalism. In turn, however, the Senate has had an impact on responsible government. The emergence of the Senate as a party house caused the introduction of proportional representation, which in time enabled the Senate to craft a distinctive role. Proportional representation also encouraged the formation of minor parties and enabled the election of their candidates and of independents, who more often than not hold the balance of power. Lack of government control over the majority in the Senate, coupled with the long fixed term of senators and the rotation of Senate elections, ultimately created a chamber with a will distinct from that of the government of the day.

The infrastructure to support a more powerful Senate began to be put in place in the early 1970s, in the form of a system of Senate committees. These became increasingly powerful as they came to perceive their own potential and develop their own traditions. The committees enabled the Senate to probe government conduct, evaluate proposed legislation, measure delegated legislation against its own prescribed standards, determine whether to exercise power to disallow delegated legislative instruments, scrutinize government expenditure, and engage in a measure of public consultation over proposed new laws. The existence of the Senate committee system ultimately caused the House to establish mirror committees and led to the introduction of at least one new, significant joint committee which considers treaties that Australia may become a party to.

Thanks to the Senate, the Australian Parliament performs a distinctive role. In one respect at least, moreover, the Senate has enhanced the quality of responsible government in Australia by extending the real capacity of the Parliament to scrutinize the executive. In other respects the Senate detracts from the operation of responsible government, as generally understood. Legislation proposed by the government is not guaranteed passage through the Australian Parliament, even if it is for an item in the government's election platform. In rejecting or forcing the modification of proposed laws, as well as in exercising its scrutiny function, the Senate operates as a check and balance in a system of government that otherwise tends to concentrate power. It lends some credibility to a view that has long since been judicial doctrine, namely that there is a three-way separation of powers at the level of the Commonwealth government.[26]

When the Senate rejects legislation, the incumbent government always criticizes the action as contrary to the basic tenets of the Australian system of government. There is no difference between the two main sides of politics in this regard. To the extent that the activism of the Senate is due to the effects of proportional representation, a solution also lies in the hands of the major parties. Proportional representation is the result of legislation, not constitutional prescription. If the major parties were prepared to do so, they could use their combined numbers in the Senate to change the electoral system and reduce the influence of minor parties and independents. Despite occasional threats, however, it seems unlikely that this will happen. There appears to be public support for the Senate as a check on government and there would likely be opposition to substantial change. Even in the states, upper houses tend to be perceived favourably for having a potential to check government action.[27]

With one qualification, the Senate has not caused the essential principles and structures of responsible government to change. After an election, the numbers in the House of Representatives alone are relevant to the formation of a government. While senators may be appointed as ministers, passage of a motion of no confidence in the Senate against an individual minister or against the government as a whole would not bring down the government nor, of itself, cause the resignation of the minister. The qualification relates to the circumstances that attended the dismissal of the government in 1975, an event with repercussions that are still being felt.

The occasion for the dismissal was the refusal of the government to resign or advise an election after the Senate blocked key money bills. The Senate in turn claimed to have been provoked by the "reprehensible" behaviour of the government, although most commentators were inclined to attribute the Senate's action to political expediency. In dismissing the government, the governor-general referred to a principle stating that a prime minister who cannot obtain supply *from the Parliament* must resign – a significant variation of the traditional association of rejection of supply with a loss of confidence in the government on the part of the popular House. The dismissed government was resoundingly defeated in the election that followed. By inference at least, therefore, both the action of the governor-general and the rationale on which it was based became accepted as part of the Australian constitutional fabric. The events of 1975 remain highly controversial between the parties. It is far from certain, however, that the Australian public would support change.

The constitutional and legal issues raised by the dismissal of the government in 1975 were complicated by the constitution's lack of specificity on matters of this kind. As written, the constitution confers all executive power on the Crown. Both the general requirement for the executive power to be exercised on advice and the so-called "reserve" powers which qualify this general rule depend on constitutional conventions that are unwritten, unclear, and disputed. Twenty-five years after the dismissal, this emerged as one of the major impediments to the development of an acceptable model for an Australian republic.

THE DEBATE ON A REPUBLIC

Constitutional Background

The terms of the Australian constitution suggest that the monarch has a significant role. The preamble to the Commonwealth of Australia Constitution Act describes the Australian federation as "established under the Crown of Great Britain and Ireland." The Queen is a component of the tripartite Parliament[28] and the "Queen's assent" is required before bills can become law.[29] All executive power is vested in the Queen. Section 61 describes this power as "exercisable by the Governor-General"; the governor-general in turn, however, is introduced as the representative of the Queen who holds office during her "pleasure."[30] A range of powers in relation to the Parliament is conferred on the governor-general who also is described as Commander-in-Chief of the armed forces.[31] Even in 1901, it was assumed that most of the powers of the Crown would be exercised on government advice and that in most cases the advice would come from Australia. There are few signs of this in the constitution, however, although there are some for those who know where to look. A similar situation prevails in each of the states, with a governor, appointed by the Queen, exercising powers and functions under a state constitution that in most cases is even less explicit than the constitution of the Commonwealth.

Australia was a colony when the constitution came into effect. Thereafter it became independent over a relatively long period of time, with little outward manifestation or public debate. With hindsight, the process was clearly well underway by the end of the First World War. It was effectively over by 1942 at the latest, when Australia adopted the Statute of Westminster, backdated to 1939.[32] But the process of tidying up loose ends continued for another forty years. Appeals to the Privy Council in federal jurisdiction were abolished in two stages, in 1968 and 1975. As a matter of form as opposed to substance, the states remained subject to British law of paramount force until the passage of the Australia Acts in 1986. Until 1986, also, it remained possible for the United Kingdom Parliament to legislate for the Commonwealth as well, albeit with the request and consent of the Commonwealth Parliament.

In one view, the monarchy is merely another residual sign of colonial status which survived the transition to independence because, being entrenched in the constitution, it could not be removed without considerable disturbance. That view is complicated by changes to the institution of the monarchy itself, which were made during this same period in partial response to Australian independence.[33] By 1926[34] it was accepted that the monarch would act only on Australian advice in relation to Australian affairs and this notion was reinforced in 1930.[35] In 1953 the monarch began to use the title "Queen of Australia";[36] by 1973 this was the only title she used in relation to Australia.[37] During the constitutional crisis of 1975, it became clear that the governor-general had emerged as an actor in his own right when the Queen refused to intervene, at the instance of the Speaker, in decisions which the constitution "clearly places in the hands of the Governor-General."[38] In 1986 the Australia Acts specifically stated that the only functions that the Queen could now perform in relation to a state were to appoint and if necessary to dismiss the governor of the state unless, perhaps, she was physically present in the state concerned.[39] In the short interval between 1986 and the start of the debate on an Australian republic, it became apparent that the functions of the Queen in relation to the Commonwealth were assumed to be similarly limited. One issue underlying the debate on an Australian republic was whether these changes rendered the monarchy sufficiently indigenous or whether they merely postponed inevitable change.

Consideration of an Australian republic began in 1992, with an eye to the symbolism of the constitutional centenary in 2001. From the outset it was encouraged by the Australian Labor Party, then in office at the national level, and by Prime Minister Keating himself. The National Conference of the Australian Labor Party held on 25 June 1991 called on the government to take action "to enable Australia to become an independent Republic" on 1 January 2001. At his policy launch address for the 1993 federal election, on 24 February 1993, Prime Minister Keating made the proposal more concrete. He committed his government to the creation of a "committee of eminent Australians" that would develop a discussion paper setting out options for a Federal Republic of Australia, with a view to a referendum in time for the constitutional centenary. The Labor Party won the election and the Republic Advisory Committee was established soon after.

From the perspective of the Opposition at that time, the republic was thus a Labor Party initiative. Inevitably, this affected the debate and contributed to the failure of the proposal. Unusually, however, the issue of a republic in fact split the non-Labor side of the political spectrum and the Labor Party also ultimately divided over the details of the model. Also unusual in the Australian context, the main driving force for change came from outside the Parliament. The principal republican grouping was the Australian Republican Movement (ARM), the head of which was appointed to chair the Republic Advisory Committee. Its counterpart was another extra-parliamentary body, Australians for a Constitutional Monarchy (ACM). These two groups exercised an extraordinary influence over the manner in which the republican issue was handled, the proposal that was put to referendum, and the official information that was distributed to the public.

There had been relatively little debate on the monarchy before the decade began. Nevertheless, the idea attracted respectable levels of public support quite quickly.[40] A possible explanation is that, unlike Canada, Australia never went through a process of patriation of the constitution. There was no imperative to do so because, from the outset, the Australian constitution incorporated its own amendment procedure. The nearest Australian equivalent was the passage of the Australia Acts 1986; this was, however, essentially a technical, lawyers' exercise.

Seeking a Minimalist Model

From the outset, the degree of public support for the idea of a republic caused the debate to focus on what should be done and how, rather than on whether Australia should become a republic at all.

Both the ARM and the government assumed that the changes should be minimal whether to the constitution or to the system of government as a whole.[41] This meant that the scope of the movement and the concept of a republic should be confined to breaking the links with the Crown as Australia's head of state. Even so, two issues of principle were involved: whether the highest public office should be hereditary; and whether the incumbent should be a person who is not Australian.

In one view, minimalism was a pragmatic choice, driven by the largely negative results of proposals to change the constitution in the past.[42] But it also reflected some complacency about existing constitutional arrangements on the part of the leaders of the debate, including the ARM and most of the politicians involved. With hindsight, it appears that this satisfaction was not shared by the voters; and herein lies one of the dilemmas for the Australian process of constitutional change. Proposals for change must both pass through the Parliament and be approved by the voters at referendum. Representative government assumes that the views of representatives will be similar to those of the represented, albeit better informed and less self-interested. At least in relation to constitutional change, the Australian experience suggests that this is not necessarily so. The challenge for advocates of change, especially those outside the Parliament, is to persuade both the public and Parliament at the same time.

The corollary of minimalism was that no extraneous changes unrelated to the republic, narrowly conceived, should be made to the constitution. In all views, however, some change was required. At the very least, the constitution needed to provide for a new office of Head of State. During most of the course of the debate it was assumed that the incumbent would be called a President, in the absence of any better, more generally accepted term, although there was some support also for retaining the term "Governor-General." It was also necessary to specify the qualifications for appointment as president and the length of the president's term of office. Importantly, creation of such an office also required a method for the selection and appointment of a president and, for extreme cases, his or her removal. A surprisingly large number of references to the Queen or the governor-general needed to be removed from the constitution as well. Many of them were cosmetic and no replacement was required. A few, however, raised tricky issues of their own.[43]

A move to a republic requires at least consideration of the powers of the head of state and the nature of the role. Questions of principle were largely avoided during the Australian debate by the assumption of the prevailing minimalist view that the powers of the president would be broadly the same as those of the governor-general. This did not come close to solving the problem, however. The formal written powers of the governor-general are extensive under the Australian constitution. They are tempered by constitutional conventions, the precise scope of which is not clear. The position is complicated further by the events of 1975, which remained contentious between politicians. Those events also had demonstrated to Australians more generally that the reserve powers could be significant, for good or ill.

In the circumstances, there was some incentive to avoid dealing with the question of powers. It was not clear, however, how this could be done. There was some small danger in simply assuming that the same conventions that had applied to the governor-general in the conditions of constitutional monarchy would apply to the formal powers of a president under a republic. In any event, such an approach was unsatisfactory for other reasons. The apparent breadth of the powers of the president could unsettle and confuse voters, who might be unpersuaded by arguments about conventions. The exercise of all or some of those extensive formal powers might also prove tempting to a president whose legitimacy would be viewed by all as greater than that of the monarch or her representative in Australia. On the other hand, to attempt to articulate the powers of the president by codifying the conventions might invite opposition and difficulty on other obvious fronts.

There was also the question of how to handle the position of the states. Each state has a governor, appointed by the Queen as her representative in the state.[44] If Australia broke the links with the Crown at the national level, clearly it would be desirable for links also to be broken between the Crown and the states. The problem concerned the method. Should republicanism be forced on the states by national constitutional change?[45] Or should the decision be left to each state, at the possible risk that some states might retain the Crown, or choose to deal with the matter more slowly?[46] This had all the makings of a states' rights issue. The Australian constitution says very little about the constitutional arrangements of the states. Historically, the states have been unwilling to allow the Commonwealth to act as intermediary in their own relations with the United Kingdom, which typically has been perceived as less of a threat to state power and autonomy than the Commonwealth itself. History is full of precedents for the Commonwealth and the states proceeding at different speeds on such matters.[47] On the other hand, the prospect of some states retaining the monarchy, even in the short term, was undignified. It also complicated continuation of the existing practice by which state governors act as deputies to the governor-general.

As the debate unfolded, the principal focus was on the method of selecting the president, the most creative decision to be made. Under current arrangements, the prime minister chooses the governor-general, although the Queen formally makes the appointment, acting on the prime minister's advice. It was assumed that this procedure could not continue under a republic, because the real authority of the prime minister would be evident and would likely be unacceptable. Some ingenuity therefore was needed to design a method of appointment that was more inclusive, without conferring undue legitimacy on the office of president. This was seen to be all the more important if, as was possible, the powers of the office were not codified. One option was to have both houses of the Parliament involved in appointing the president, possibly by special majority on a motion of the prime minister and supported by the opposition in some way. The support of the opposition would be necessary to secure acceptance of the motion and to ensure that the president was not perceived as partisan.

There was little focus on the manner of removal of the president until the debate was well advanced. No Australian governor-general has been removed before the end of the agreed term. The possibility of removal was an underlying theme in the events of 1975, however. Arguably, the speed and secrecy with which the governor-general had moved to dismiss the prime minister was pre-emptive. Had the prime minister had advance warning, so the argument goes, he might have been able to contact the Queen to cause the removal of the governor-general instead. This scenario assumed that, consistent with the principles of constitutional monarchy, the Queen would remove a governor-general on the advice of a prime minister, if the occasion arose.

To the extent that it was considered at all, early proposals for a republican model treated the issue of the manner of early removal of a president as incidental. The tendency was to assume that the process used to appoint a president could be used for removal as well. Midway through the debate, this view was challenged by a former governor of Victoria, Richard McGarvie.[48]

The underlying premise of the McGarvie position was that the governor-general and prime minister (and their counterparts at state level) are kept in a state of perpetual check by the power of the other. The events of 1975 had shown that the governor-general could dismiss a prime minister. What prevented the governor-general from exercising this and other powers inappropriately was not convention alone, but the threat of removal by the Queen at the instance of the prime minister. The prime minister could not act pre-emptively either, to cause the removal of a governor-general who was acting within conventional limits, because of the delay inherent in the Queen receiving and acting on such advice. These checks were particularly important where the scope of real power depended on constitutional convention. The solution did not lie in codifying the powers, because they were too subtle and nuanced and value would be lost. Instead, the solution was to mirror existing arrangements as nearly as possible under a republic. This meant that the prime minister should continue, in effect, to appoint and remove the president. But the formal act should be that of a Constitutional Council, comprising the three most recent previous presidents or governors-general,[49] simulating the Queen. The council would make the appointment on the advice of the prime minister. It would dismiss the president on the advice of the prime minister also, but only after an interval of two weeks during which the propriety of the prime minister's own actions could be judged and the president could dismiss the prime minister if circumstances called for that to be done.

The McGarvie analysis apparently was intended as an endorsement of Australia's current democratic arrangements, which it claimed to preserve, in the transition to a republic. It offered a bleak view of the political process. It was unexpectedly persuasive, however, for different reasons. First, it focused attention on the mechanism for removal of a president and raised some difficult questions about how a republican model would work in the unlikely event that there was a repeat of the events of 1975. Second, McGarvie offered an argument for even more minimal constitutional change, which was attractive in conservative quarters. Ultimately, it did not prevail and McGarvie himself advocated a "No" vote at the referendum. Nevertheless, his views had some influence on the final model, which contributed to its rejection.

Process

The process to be followed was as important as the model itself, particularly in view of the need for a referendum. On this matter, the two main federal parliamentary parties had different views, which may in part reflect their different attitudes at the time to the issue of a republic itself.

Following his re-election in 1993, Prime Minister Keating established the promised Republic Advisory Committee, to develop options for a republican model. The committee was required to consult broadly, but on somewhat confined issues.[50] His intention was to put the question of a republic to the voters as a non-binding plebiscite. If the vote were positive, the final model would be designed by a parliamentary committee and would be put to referendum as a proposal for constitutional change.[51]

This process was contested by the federal Opposition, at this stage also officially hostile to the notion of a republic. The Opposition suggested an alternative process, drawing loosely on the manner in which the original constitution had been written and approved.[52] Instead of a plebiscite, it suggested the establishment of a constitutional convention, half of whose delegates would be elected. The convention would advise on a republic and develop a model, which would be put to referendum if need be.

The Keating government was defeated at the general election in 1996. Incoming Prime Minister Howard was a known supporter of the monarchy and the question was whether he would abide by the election commitment to hold a convention at all. In time, however, a decision was made to proceed.

It is no simple matter to design a constitutional convention in the political conditions of the end of the twentieth century. The essential features of the Australian Constitutional Convention were as follows. There were 152 delegates. Half were elected, using a state or a territory as a single electorate. Each state's share of the total number of elected delegates was proportionate to its total representation in Parliament, including its Senate representation.[53] Serving politicians were precluded by legislation from standing for election.[54] Voting was by post and was voluntary, breaking with the long-established Australian practice of compulsory voting.

The other 76 delegates were appointed. There were 20 members of the federal Parliament,[55] and another 20 from the Parliaments of the states and territories. The government appointed the remaining 36, following a consultative process. In the end, delegates in this category included representatives of business, unions, religious groups, youth, and indigenous Australians.

The convention took place over a two-week period in February 1998. The terms of reference required delegates to answer three questions: whether Australia should become a republic, when it should do so, if at all, and what the model for the republic should be. The prime minister agreed to put to referendum any proposal that had clear support.[56] Failing clear support, there was a somewhat vague commitment to hold a plebiscite on the issue.[57]

Superficially, the convention was a great success. It attracted tremendous public interest, bordering on emotion, during the two weeks it met. Even those who had been sceptical about the idea of a convention were impressed by the experience and by public reaction to it. By the end of the fortnight, the delegates had crafted a compromise between competing views. The compromise, known at the time as the "bipartisan appointment of the President model," attracted more support than any other. However, this fell short of majority support. In the closing stages of the convention, the prime minister agreed to put the proposal to referendum.

On more sober assessment, the convention was flawed.[58] Only approximately 50 per cent of electors voted for the 50 per cent of delegates who were to be elected. While most candidates stood for election as part of a group of some kind, there was no clear view of how the representative process was to work. The answer was most obvious in the cases of the ARM and the ACM, which had clear positions worked out over a period of years. Even in relation to the ARM, however, there was a question about the extent to which elected delegates could properly deviate from their original policy position. All other groups were smaller and less organized, and had had only general policy positions from the start, complicating the notion of representation even further.

These difficulties would be inherent in any elected constitutional convention. But there were other problems. The process was rushed, from the passage of the enabling legislation[59] in August to the meeting of the convention at the beginning of the following February.[60] The result was that the opportunity the convention presented to encourage voters to understand the issues was lost. The smaller groupings were insufficiently prepared by the time the delegates met. The agenda for the convention, already constrained by the terms of reference,[61] was restricted further by details of how the convention would be organized, settled largely between the government and representatives of the ARM and the ACM. Most important of all, there was no opportunity for reflection on the model after the end of the two-week period, to refine it or adjust it in light of public opinion. When the convention ended, it was assumed and accepted that the details of the model were settled. The only task of the Parliament was to put convention recommendations into draft form[62] and to supply any details that the delegates had omitted. While the Parliament established a joint select committee that deliberated on the details of the legislation, it had no opportunity to change the proposal in matters of substance, however, even when the weight of criticism suggested that the model could be improved.

The Bogey of Direct Election

The delegates encountered, but failed to deal adequately with an issue that had been bubbling under the surface of the republican debate for some time: the public seemed to prefer direct election of the president.

Well before the convention, opinion polls suggested that a large proportion of voters wanted a republican model under which the president was elected by popular vote. For the most part, the prospect was not taken seriously by the leaders of the republican movement and was dismissed. With a few notable exceptions, direct election is anathema to politicians of all persuasions. Direct election might change the moral, if not the legal relationship between head of state and head of government, if the former was chosen by popular vote. It made it almost inevitable, as was frequently pointed out, that the president would be a politician of some kind, or at least endorsed by political forces. Maintenance of the impartiality of the office of head of state would be more difficult in these circumstances. In practical terms, an elected presidency also demanded codification of the powers the president could use as long, at least, as the office was intended to remain non-executive in character.

Despite these objections, support for direct election was unwavering. Even now, the explanation for it is unclear. No doubt it had a connection of some kind with the increases in populism and discontent with established political processes. This was manifested in another way at about the same time, with the rise of the maverick "One Nation" party and its grassroots approach. Support for direct election was a much more general phenomenon, however, which seems to have been the product of a number of different influences. There is a perception that the Queen and the governor-general are above politics and to that extent broadly representative, replaceable only by someone who is the direct choice of the voters themselves. The focus on elections as the principal moment at which voters have a say may have fuelled support for another opportunity to vote, of a different kind. Levels of satisfaction with existing constitutional arrangements may not have been as high as the leaders of the republican movement originally supposed. The republic may have been the only opportunity for voters to make this point and thus force a measure of change. In this regard, there may be some parallel with the results of the referendums on the electoral system in New Zealand.[63]

Signs that the issue of direct election would need to be dealt with at the convention were obvious as soon as the results of the election for delegates were known. A significant number of delegates were elected on platforms of support for greater rather than less constitutional change which included, but was not confined to, direct election of the president. These delegates faced a difficult task in the convention, however. Direct election of a president required a model that was substantially more complex than the other "minimalist" proposals. The organization of the convention did not encourage deliberation on wider issues, and the principal republican group, the ARM, was opposed to broadening the debate to include direct election or any other matter.

The issue came to a head early, when the delegates voted against codification of the powers of the president. It was generally understood that this made direct election impossible. In the face of the outcry that followed, within the convention and outside it, the delegates chose the somewhat odd course of allowing proposals that had attracted a minimum level of support, but had fallen short of majority support, to remain on the table for consideration. In this way, both the direct election option and some other minority positions remained theoretically open until the final votes were taken. At no stage, however, was the direct election model crafted with sufficient care to be adopted by the delegates had they intended to do so. In this respect, the lack of prior organization on the part of delegates who supported direct election seems to have been crucial.

The leaders of the ARM had a difficult task also. Their firm and longstanding view was that the president should be appointed by Parliament in some way. To attract sufficient votes in the convention, however, they had to win the support of at least some of the supporters either of direct election or of the McGarvie position. The McGarvie model had the support of some of the key government delegates, including both the attorney general, and the treasurer and deputy Liberal Party leader. The prime minister was known to prefer this model, if Australia was to become a republic at all. On the other hand, from the standpoint of the voters it was likely to be even less acceptable than appointment of the president by the Parliament.

The model that finally emerged from the convention[64] had something for everyone. It dealt only with the republic at the national level, leaving the states to make their own arrangements. The final step in the appointment of a president required a two-thirds majority vote in a joint sitting of both houses of the Parliament. To that end, however, a single name would be put to the Parliament by the prime minister, in a motion seconded by the leader of the opposition. In settling the nominee, the prime minister was to take into account a short list compiled by a Presidential Nominations Committee, from suggestions put forward by members of the public. The committee in turn would be established by legislation and was supposed to be broadly representative. In the end, however, the prime minister would make community appointments and in this sense the composition of the committee was left to him.

The powers of the president would not be codified. The constitution, however, would give the president the same powers as the governor-general, to be exercised in accordance with the same constitutional conventions that applied to the governor-general. In this way, the delegates sought to avoid the questions that still rankled from 1975, while providing some assurance that the president's functions would be essentially ceremonial and symbolic. It was an ingenious if cumbersome compromise, which probably would have worked well enough. But it was vulnerable to the McGarvie view that a president could not be trusted to comply with the conventions, in the absence of the threat of removal from office. An associated difficulty was that, if the president retained the power to dismiss a prime minister in the circumstances of 1975, a procedure for removal of the president that involved the agreement of the Senate was likely to be wholly unacceptable to the Labor Party and its supporters.

In an attempt to respond to these difficulties, the model approved at the convention conferred power on the prime minister alone to remove the president from office. No grounds for removal were prescribed. In order to impose a measure of accountability on the prime minister, the House of Representatives was required to ratify the prime minister's action within thirty days, unless an election was to follow. In its final draft form, the Constitution Alteration (Establishment of Republic) Bill also provided that a state governor would take over as deputy if the president were removed, armed with the same powers and subject to the same conventions. In all probability, this would have been a more effective deterrent to abuse of the prime ministerial power than the requirement for a vote in the House.

The Referendum

In Australia, the government typically initiates proposals for constitutional change through the introduction of the necessary legislation into the Parliament.[65] In some cases, the proposal is drawn from recommendations of an inquiry established by the government or in which it has participated.[66] Almost invariably, however, referendum proposals represent government policy at some level. In many cases, they are opposed by the opposition. The Australian record of rejection of referendum proposals is often attributed to a failure to achieve bipartisanship, although bipartisanship itself is no guarantee of success.[67] The lack of it may reflect difficulties with a proposal or with the manner in which it came forward, and may be a cause of its defeat.

How the process is initiated typically affects the manner in which the electorate is informed of referendum proposals. Each voter is sent a text of the proposed changes. In addition, each voter receives statements of the arguments for and against the proposal, of up to 2,000 words each, prepared or approved by supporters and opponents in the Parliament.[68] If there is no contrary vote in the Parliament, no statement against the proposal is prepared. Over the decades, the cases for and against have become increasingly strident and argumentative,[69] and do relatively little to assist voter understanding and deliberation on the merits.

These typical behaviour patterns were altered by the nature of the republican issue, by the process of placing the issue before the people, and by the degree to which forces outside the Parliament conducted the debate. Two illustrations follow. The first concerns the lines of division over both the principle of monarchy or republic and over this particular model, which were complex both inside and outside the Parliament. The second concerns the range of additional mechanisms used on this occasion to inform the public, albeit with somewhat limited success.

The lines of division between supporters and opponents of a republic did not run neatly along party lines. Ostensibly, Labor members of Parliament and most of their supporters favoured a republic of some kind. The non-Labor parties and in particular the Liberal Party were divided, however. The prime minister himself favoured the status quo, as did the parliamentary secretary (later minister) Senator Minchin, who had principal responsibility for handling the logistics of the constitutional convention and the referendum process. Gradually, however, other senior ministers of the Commonwealth government declared themselves in favour of a republic in principle. Outside Parliament, most of the media favoured transition to a republic, as did some influential parts of the business community.

Supporters of a republic in principle were divided over the chosen model, however. The principal division was within the ranks of those who favoured direct election and were not persuaded by the device of a public nomination process to aid selection of a President. There were some supporters of direct election within senior Labor Party ranks, including at least two leaders of a parliamentary party. While most of those who held party positions publicly supported the bill, having earlier lost the debate about direct election, many Labor voters voted against the bill on this ground. Another possibly less significant group of disaffected republicans supported an even more minimalist republic, along the lines proposed and still actively promoted by former Governor McGarvie. A third group, who were republican in sympathy, worried about aspects of the model, including the somewhat peculiar proposal of allowing a prime minister to peremptorily dismiss a president, without requiring some justification for doing so.

In the result, during the referendum campaign supporters of the republican question came from various quarters. Those officially in favour of a "Yes" vote included the ARM and its supporters and the federal and state parliamentary Labor parties. Importantly, they also included substantial groups of influential non-Labor politicians, a little nervous about the company that they found themselves keeping. Among them were almost every state Liberal leader and senior ministers in the Commonwealth government, including the treasurer, the attorney general, and the minister for finance. They were ranged against an even more varied group of opponents with vastly different aims. The core group advocating a "No" vote was the ACM. Other prominent voices, however, comprised former governor McGarvie and, importantly, supporters of direct election around whom much of the "No" strategy was built.

The convention's delegates had endorsed the importance of public education in connection with the referendum. The government responded to this in several ways. First, it identified official "Yes" and "No" camps inside the Parliament, focused on the ARM and the ACM. Each of these was given $7.5 million in public funds for campaigns which, in effect, they could run as they pleased. Second, the usual parliamentary cases for and against the proposal were also published. In the circumstances, however, these inevitably reflected the strategies adopted by the external "Yes" and "No" campaigns. Third, the government funded a public information campaign.[70] Its effectiveness was diminished by the government's desire to ensure that the campaign was accepted as impartial by both warring sides, which overshadowed any commitment to the information needs of the public and the manner in which they are best served. An expert committee was appointed to oversee the process. It comprised Sir Ninian Stephen, as an impartial chair, and myself, as a representative of the Constitutional Centenary Foundation,[71] as well as members committed to either of the debate's two sides. Its role was limited to information distributed in printed form, however, and in the end this exercise was something of a disappointment.

One consequence of the composition of the group opposing the proposal was that the monarchy itself was barely mentioned during the campaign. Rather, opposition centred on the particular model, for two broad sets of reasons. First, it did not provide for popular election of the president. Second, it had some odd features, of which the mechanism for removal of the president was perceived to be the worst. The principal slogan for the "No" campaign was "Say no to the politicians' republic." A supporting tactic was confusion, which was easily achieved and which the official information campaigns did little to dispel. Arguments particularly effective for this purpose ranged from assertions that the governor-general already was Australia's head of state to claims that all Crown land would revert to native title under a republic.

The referendum was defeated, in all states and nationally, by a majority of 54.8 per cent.[72] Analysis of the voting by electorates shows that the proposal attracted high levels of support in electorates with higher education levels, including many Liberal electorates, and lost in rural areas and in many urban Labor electorates.[73] In the circumstances, however, the result was ambiguous. The principal arguments against the referendum were directed against the model rather than the principle of a republic. Labor electorates that opposed the proposal could be expected to support a different model at a future referendum; if the price is direct election, however, it may cost the support of at least some conservative voters who supported the proposal this time around. Levels of support for a republic remained high during the campaign and after it. The experience of the 1999 referendum demonstrates the difficulty of translating the principle into practice, now made worse by having failed to do so on the first attempt.

CONCLUSION

Despite the complication of federalism, Australia's constitutional arrangements are evidently in the Westminster mould. Australia enjoys the classical benefits of parliamentary government, Westminster-style, in terms of strong and stable but democratic government. For the most part the system works well, in the sense that the country is governed effectively, and in a manner generally consistent with constitutional principle. Superficially at least, there is no significant pressure for change.

The proposal to establish a republic was not intended to disturb Australia's constitutional calm. The changes initially sought were largely symbolic and it was assumed they could be confined. A move to a republic appeared merely to involve a continuation of the process of removing the signs of formal colonial status which, on this occasion, happened to involve formal constitutional change. In the event, the republic failed. But the system has been disturbed nevertheless, and on several fronts.

First, the debate suggested profound public distrust of the political process. This took the form of opposition to appointment of a president by the Parliament, visible in voter response to the destructive theme of the "No" campaign. More subtly, distrust can also be deduced from voter perceptions of the role the Crown plays in the Australian constitutional system. In some quarters at least, there seemed to be a view that the monarch and his or her representatives offer a genuine check and balance, tempering the power of both government and Parliament. There are echoes here of public support for the role the Senate plays. The role of the Senate is a reality, however. Public willingness to accept what essentially was a fiction during the debate on the republic – the Crown as a check and balance – was almost as disturbing as the distrust of the democratic process it suggests.

The debate on an Australian republic is not over. When it revives, the key issue will be the model. On this occasion, direct election of the president will need to be taken seriously. Whether, in the end, Australia goes down that path depends on negotiations still to come between supporters of direct election and those who are presently deeply concerned about the implications of direct election for the system of government as a whole.

NOTES

1 Australian Constitution, chap. III.
2 Constitution, s. 128.
3 In accordance with the Colonial Laws Validity Act 1865 and other principles and rules.
4 Constitution, s. 62.
5 Constitution, ss 62, 63.
6 See *Barton v. Commonwealth* (1974) 131 CLR 477.
7 Constitution, s. 58.
8 Cheryl Saunders, "Democracy: Representation and Participation," in *Essays on Law and Government,* ed. P. Finn (Sydney: Law Book Co., 1995), 51.
9 See *Brown v. West* (1990) 169 CLR 195.
10 Constitution, s. 28.
11 The attitude was neatly encapsulated in 1994 by then Prime Minister Keating: "First, in this country the electors get a chance to change the government every three years at least; secondly, the chamber is elected representatively; and thirdly, the government is drawn from the representative chamber and is subject to party public opinion and the ballot box three years hence"; *The Australian,* 4 March 1994.
12 In particular, freedom of political speech.
13 *Nationwide News v. Wills,* (1992) 177 CLR 1; *Australian Capital Television v. The Commonwealth,* (1992) 177 CLR 106; *Theophanous v. Herald and Weekly Times,* (1994) 182 CLR 104; *Stephens v. Western Australian Newspapers,* (1994) 182 CLR 211; *McGinty v. Western Australia,* (1996) 186 CLR 140; *Lange v. Australian Broadcasting Corporation,* (1997) 189 CLR 520; *Levy v. Victoria,* (1997) 189 CLR 579.

14 *Theophanous v. Herald and Weekly Times*, 199–201.

15 J. Quick and R.R. Garran, *Annotated Constitution of the Australian Commonwealth* (1901; reprint, Sydney: Legal Books, 1975).

16 *Australian Capital Television v. The Commonwealth*, (1992) 177 CLR 106.

17 Two majorities are required under section 128: a national majority and a majority in most states. At present there are six Australian states; majorities in at least four therefore must approve a referendum.

18 Markku Suksi, *Bringing in the People: A Comparison of Constitutional Forms and Practices of the Referendum* (Dordrecht: Martinus Nijhoff, 1993), 34–5.

19 Cheryl Saunders, "The Parliament as Partner: A Century of Constitutional Review," (paper prepared for *The Vision in Hindsight*, 2000 series of the Australian Parliament's Information and Research Services Department).

20 Constitution, s. 7. The present number of Senators for each state is twelve.

21 Direct election to the United States Senate was not provided until 1913, with the seventeenth amendment to the constitution.

22 Constitution, s. 53.

23 Constitution, s. 57

24 Cheryl Saunders, "The Constitutional Framework: Hybrid, Derivative but eventually Australian," in *Public Administration in Australia: A Watershed*, ed. John Power (Sydney: Hale and Iremonger, 1990), 106.

25 U.S. Const. art. II, s. 2.

26 See *Victorian Stevedoring and General Contracting Co. v Dignan* (1931) 46 CLR 83.

27 Only Queensland lacks an upper house.

28 Constitution, s. 1.

29 Constitution, s. 58. Assent is given, however, by the governor-general.

30 Constitution, s. 2.

31 Constitution, s. 68

32 Statute of Westminster Adoption Act 1942.

33 These modifications applied also to the operation of the monarchy in the other former dominions and, specifically, in Canada and New Zealand.

34 The acknowledgment was made in the Balfour Declaration of the Imperial Conference 1926, *Summary of Proceedings of the Imperial Conference 1926*, vol. 5 (CPP, 1926–8): 1049, 1059.

35 The catalyst was a dispute between the government and the monarch over an appointment of an Australian as governor-general: L. Crisp, "The Appointment of Sir Isaac Isaacs as Governor-General of Australia 1930," *Historical Studies* 11 (1964): 253.

36 Royal Style and Titles Act 1953.

37 Royal Style and Titles Act 1973.

38 The letters from the Speaker of the House of Representatives to the Queen and from the Queen's private secretary in reply are reproduced in Colin Howard and Cheryl Saunders, *Cases and Materials on Constitutional Law* (Sydney: Law Book Co., 1979), 124–5.

39 Australia Acts 1986, s. 7.

40 A Newspoll survey in late 1997 showed the changes in opinion over the decade. In October 1987, the total in favour of a republic was 21 per cent, with 64 per cent opposed. In 1997, 51 per cent were in favour with 35 per cent opposed and the remainder undecided: *The Australian*, 3 December 1997.

41 The terms of reference of the Republic Advisory Committee sought options for "the minimum constitutional changes necessary": Republic Advisory Committee, "An Australian Republic: The Options", (Canberra: AGPS, 1993), iv.

42 At the time the debate began, forty-two proposals had been put to referendum and eight had been approved, the most recent in 1977.

43 For example, the need to replace the reference to "subjects of the Queen" in section 117 of the Constitution as the beneficiaries of the rule against discrimination on grounds of state residence.

44 Australia Acts, s. 7.

45 Given the requirement for majorities in only four out of six states, it was possible that this could occur in the face of opposition from the state concerned.

46 This was made all the more likely by the need for state referendums to change the relevant part of state constitutions in four of the six states.

47 See, for example, the long delay in achieving the formal independence of the states that was the principal purpose of the Australia Acts.

48 Richard E. McGarvie, "Our Democracy in Peril: The safe way to a democratic republic," (a paper released to the Australian media on 1 May 1997 and widely distributed before the constitutional convention). For a published and refined version of his position, see Richard E. McGarvie, "The Timely Resolution of the Republic Issue," in *No Case Papers*, ed. Rick Brown (Sydney: Rozelle, 1999).

49 A modified version subsequently allowed for the most senior female ex–head of state to be included as one of the three for the first forty years of the operation of the procedure, after which it was assumed that the problem of gender balance would be overcome.

50 Republic Advisory Committee, *An Australian Republic: The Options*, (Canberra: AGPS, 1993).

51 Legal Information Access Centre, "A Republic?" *Hot Topics* no. 22, (1999): 5.

52 The proposal was originally made by Alexander Downer, as leader of the opposition. It was confirmed by his successor, John Howard: Liberal and National Parties of Australia, "Election Policy 1996."

53 The distribution of elected delegates between states was as follows: New South Wales (20), Victoria (16), Queensland (13), Western Australia (9), South Australia (8), Tasmania (6), and the Australian Capital Territory and Northern Territory (2 each).

54 Constitutional Convention (Election) Act 1997, s. 24.

55 The 20 Commonwealth members comprised 12 from the government, 6 from the opposition, one Australian Democrat, and one Independent.

56 Report of the Constitutional Convention, Old Parliament House, *Transcript of Proceedings,* (Canberra, 2–13 February 1998), 3.

57 This stemmed from the original government policy, which referred to a plebiscite if "no consensus" emerged from the convention: Liberal and National Parties of Australia, "Election Policy, 1996."

58 Cheryl Saunders, "How Important Was The Convention?" *University of New South Wales Law Journal* 21 (1998): 268.

59 Constitutional Convention (Election) Act 1997.

60 The Constitutional Convention (Election) Bill passed the Senate on 28 August 1997. The formal notice of the election for delegates was issued on 29 September. Nominations for election closed ten days later. Voting papers and associated material were posted to voters between 3 and 14 November 1997. The poll closed on 9 December. The Convention met on 2 February 1998.

61 The Convention was asked to consider three questions: Should Australia become a republic? In what timeframe and under what circumstances might any change be considered? Which republic model should be put to the voters to consider against the current system of government?

62 Constitution Alteration (Establishment of Republic) 1999; Presidential Nominations Committee Bill 1999.

63 See generally Alan Simpson, ed., *Referendums: Constitutional and Political Perspectives* (Wellington: Victoria University of Wellington, 1992); Alan McRobie, ed., *Taking it to the People?* (Christchurch: Hazard Press, 1993).

64 Report of the Constitutional Convention, Old Parliament House, Canberra, 2–13 February 1998, *Report of Proceedings.* See also Constitutional Centenary Foundation, *The Constitutional Convention: What Next?* (1998).

65 Constitution, s. 128.

66 There were four major, general inquiries in the first century of federation, at roughly quarterly intervals: in 1927, 1957, 1973–85, and 1988; Saunders, "The Parliament as Partner."

67 Some referendums have failed despite bipartisan support, notably the 1967 proposal to break the nexus between the numbers in the House of Representatives and the Senate.

68 Referendum (Machinery Provision) Act 1984, s. 11.

69 For a summary of each of the cases that had been used prior to the referendum on the republic, see House of Representatives Standing Committee on Legal and Constitutional Affairs, *Constitutional Change*, (February 1997), 62–114.

70 Damien Freeman, "Public Information Machinery and the 1999 Referenda," *Public Law Review* 10 (1999): 243.

71 The Constitutional Centenary Foundation was an independent body that operated during the decade leading to the constitutional centenary. Its purpose was to encourage an informed public debate on the constitution in general. It provided a great deal of additional public information during the referendum campaign. For an assessment of its experience, in this and other matters, see Constitutional Centenary Foundation, *Report on the Decade*, 2000.

72 The highest state "Yes" vote was in Victoria (49.84 per cent). The lowest state "Yes" vote was in Queensland (37.44 per cent). The national capital itself voted "Yes": 63.27 per cent; the territories are not included in the calculations of state majorities, although their votes are counted in the overall national total.

73 For example, the prime minister's own electorate of Bennelong voted in favour of the proposal with 54.62 per cent. For a breakdown of the referendum results, see <http://referendum.aec.gov.au>.

Solving the Conundrum of Second Chamber Reform in the United Kingdom

LORD WAKEHAM

Parliament at Westminster has been described as "the mother of Parliaments." I suppose that is because the bicameral system of parliamentary democracy which has operated in the United Kingdom over the past three hundred years is mirrored in the arrangements for governing the major countries in the Commonwealth.

One of the features of the United Kingdom's system of parliamentary democracy that certainly seems to have been exported to those countries is a sense of dissatisfaction with the operation of the second chamber. Even in countries that consciously modelled their parliamentary arrangements on those of the United Kingdom, the second chambers have developed in different ways. None even began by adopting the hereditary principle which was a defining feature of the House of Lords until 1999. But, like the House of Lords, most of those second chambers have been "contested" institutions, the subject of more or less virulent criticism and various proposals for reform, or even (as in the case of New Zealand) abolition.

I do not suggest that the Royal Commission I chaired has come up with recommendations that could be applied to other second chambers. Indeed, one of our early conclusions was that those second chambers around the world which seemed to work best were those that suited the history, traditions, and prevailing political culture of the country concerned; and that what worked in one country would not necessarily work in another.

We therefore concentrated on drawing up a blueprint for the reform of the second chamber of the national Parliament of the United

Kingdom, with all its unique circumstances and idiosyncrasies. It must be for others to judge whether general lessons could be drawn from our conclusions and applied to other second chambers around the world.

THE CONUNDRUM

Of course, reforming the House of Lords – reforming *any* second chamber – is not as easy as people like to think. If there is a second chamber, there must be a "first" chamber, and first chambers – in parliamentary democracies at least – are very powerful institutions. Typically they are directly elected on a universal adult franchise, with seats distributed on a population basis. They determine which party forms the government. They usually control finance and supply. In most cases they have the final word over proposed legislation. Because, by definition, governments in parliamentary democracies control the first, or "lower," chamber they end up in a very powerful position, with access to all the levers of power – executive, legislative, and financial.

This gives rise to several fundamental obstacles to reform of the second chamber. Why should any "first" chamber, or any government, in a parliamentary democracy want to initiate or support a process of reform which would be almost certain to cramp its own style? Why should the members of a "lower" chamber, having achieved victory in an often-bruising battle to represent their constituents, agree to any enhancement of the status of members of the second chamber who could become rivals for political influence?

Indeed, it is no accident that second chambers in parliamentary democracies tend to have features that call their legitimacy and authority into question. This ensures that they cannot challenge the pre-eminence of the lower chamber as the country's decisive political forum. The House of Lords, even after the 1999 reform, retains a substantial proportion of members who are there by virtue of being hereditary peers. Other second chambers may be wholly or largely appointed. Those which are elected usually use indirect election (as, for example, in France) or at least a different form of election from the system used to elect the lower chamber. In general, seats in the second chamber are not allocated on a population basis. As I have said, the formal powers of second chambers in parliamentary democracies are usually less than those of lower chambers. But this too is intimately bound up with and justified by the lower degree of political authority and legitimacy which arises from how the second chambers' members enter it. As Australia has discovered, it is less easy for a government based in the lower chamber to argue that the views of a directly-elected second chamber should be overridden.

That may or may not be a good thing. My point is simply that, given a free hand, governments and lower chambers around the world are unlikely to support proposals to reform their second chambers unless their own pre-eminence is secured, both formally and in practice. That is a political reality with which all reformers must deal.

THE HISTORY OF ATTEMPTS TO REFORM THE HOUSE OF LORDS

In retrospect, these factors contributed to the failure of successive attempts to reform the House of Lords throughout the twentieth century. The constitutional crisis of 1909–11 led ultimately to the Parliament Act 1911 under which any Commons bill passed by the House of Commons in three successive sessions of Parliament would become law whatever the House of Lords thought. The length of the House of Lords' suspensory veto was subsequently reduced by the Parliament Act 1949[1] and the resulting balance has survived without serious challenge up to the present day. But attempts to reform the *composition* of the House of Lords – especially in 1918, 1948, and 1968 – broke down largely because of the failure to identify a satisfactory alternative.

By the end of the twentieth century, however, the situation had changed in two very significant respects. First, the introduction of life peers under the Life Peerages Act 1958 was a conspicuous success. By the late 1990s the House of Lords contained well over 500 life peers, in addition to some 750 hereditary peers. The life peers were mostly people of great distinction and ability with a wide range of experience and expertise. Mainly due to their influence, the House had become more professional and effective, and played a larger role in revising legislation and scrutinizing the executive, especially in those areas which were of less immediate political impact.[2]

Second, the 1997 Labour Party manifesto committed the government to removing the right of hereditary peers to sit and vote in the House of Lords, and that commitment has now largely been given effect by the House of Lords Act 1999. That made it imperative to find a new basis for constituting the House of Lords while avoiding the difficulties which led to the failure of previous attempts at reform. That is the task which the Royal Commission was asked to undertake.

It was in any event timely to consider the role and functions of the second chamber in the light of other elements of the Labour Government's constitutional reform program, including devolution, the enactment of the Human Rights Act 1998, and the United Kingdom's developing relations with the European Union.

THE COMMISSION'S APPROACH

We began by determining the roles and functions which a reformed House of Lords should perform and the powers it would need to do an effective job. Only then did we review the characteristics which the House should possess and the methods of composition most likely to produce a second chamber with those characteristics.

Roles of the Reformed House of Lords

We concluded:

- that the reformed House of Lords should enable a range of perspectives to be brought to bear on the development of public policy
- that it should be broadly representative of British society
- that it should play a vital role in working with the House of Commons to hold the government more accountable
- that it should provide a formal voice at the centre of national affairs for the nations and regions of the United Kingdom[3]

Political life in the United Kingdom is becoming increasingly professional. Members of the House of Commons are now typically full-time public representatives with little direct experience of life outside the relatively narrow world of politics. One advantage of the old House of Lords was that the hereditary peers and especially the life peers had a very wide range of occupations and so could bring relevant personal experience and expertise to bear on the discussion of public policy issues. It seemed to us that this feature was worth preserving in the reformed House of Lords.

We also saw the opportunity to develop a second chamber which was more broadly representative of British society. Members of the House of Commons clearly represent their constituents' basic political choices, and their constituency needs, but they are not, as a group, at all representative of modern British society. The origin of the House of Lords, as with many other second chambers around the world, was as a place in which the aristocracy – one of the "estates of the realm" – was represented. The need for different sectors of society to be represented in that particular way has long passed. But there did seem to us to be advantage in aiming for a situation in which there were voices in Parliament for a whole range of different aspects of society.

A reformed House of Lords has a vital role to play as one of the key checks and balances in the British system of parliamentary democracy. The United Kingdom does not have a written constitution. There is no authority above Parliament to which people can appeal for a binding judgment. Even though the European Convention on Human Rights has now been effectively incorporated into UK domestic legislation, the most the courts can do if they find that an Act of Parliament breaches one or more convention rights is to issue a statement of noncompatibility. It is then for Parliament to decide whether to respond, and if so, how.

Parliament is therefore sovereign and within Parliament the House of Commons is pre-eminent – rightly so, because it represents the political will of the whole electorate as expressed in general elections.

Within that system, the government of the day is very powerful. It normally controls the House of Commons and has access to all the executive power of the state. As politics has become a more professional and full-time occupation, the party machines have extended their control over individual members of Parliament, all of whom are dependent on their party for their livelihood and for preferment. Political power in the United Kingdom is increasingly concentrated in the hands of a few people at the top of the respective party hierarchies, and there are very few formal constraints on what they can do. Most cabinet ministers, and the prime minister, can be held directly to account in the House of Commons, but they can usually rely on the partisan support of their party. The House of Commons can find it difficult to balance its twin responsibilities of sustaining the government in office and holding it to account.

A key role for the second chamber, therefore, is to act as a restraining influence within the system, challenging the government to justify or rethink its policies. This is where the conundrum to which I referred earlier really bites. What is the basis on which the second chamber should intervene in the political discourse and invite the government and House of Commons to think again?

One answer which is given is that the second chamber should have the authority of democratic election, perhaps on a different basis from that of the House of Commons. Such authority, it is argued, would give the second chamber real teeth and allow it to act as a powerful restraint on the government, even holding out against the clearly expressed will of the lower house.

But there is the rub. In that direction lies what I think Americans call "divided government." It may be a very good system. But it is alien to the British tradition of "strong government" and it is difficult to envisage circumstances in which any British government or House of Commons would vote to establish such a system.

The Royal Commission's answer to the conundrum was that the reformed second chamber should not even attempt to compete with the House of Commons in terms of electoral legitimacy. Its members should draw their authority from a range of different sources:

- the breadth of experience and range of expertise they possess
- their individual personal distinction
- the extent to which they are broadly representative of the society they seek to serve
- their ability to exercise an unfettered judgment, free from partisan political control
- perhaps above all, the quality of the arguments they can bring to bear

Before describing the implications of this conclusion for the Royal Commission's recommendations on the functions and composition of the reformed House of Lords, I will just say a few words about the second chamber's role as a formal voice for the different nations and regions of the United Kingdom.

Executive and some legislative powers have recently been devolved to administrations based on elected bodies in Scotland, Wales, and (falteringly) Northern Ireland. Some have argued that the UK is becoming a quasi-federal state and that reform of the House of Lords should be taken as an opportunity to respond to this development and counteract the centrifugal tendencies of the government's program of devolution. We did look at this possibility. In a modest way our proposals may indeed help to bind the UK together. But we recommended *against* giving seats in the second chamber to members of the devolved administrations or of the devolved assemblies. That would have confused and complicated the lines of responsibility and accountability established by the devolution settlements. It would have been unfair to England, where 85 per cent of the population lives, which does not have devolved government. It could not have contributed to intergovernmental liaison. As in Australia and Canada, intergovernmental liaison is most effectively and appropriately carried on *outside* parliamentary institutions.

Nevertheless, we concluded that the reformed House of Lords should contain a proportion of "regional members" to be a voice for Scotland, Wales, Northern Ireland, and the nine English administrative regions. As the second chamber of the United Kingdom Parliament, the reformed House of Lords should have members from throughout the United Kingdom.

Functions of the Reformed House of Lords

Having reflected on the roles of the reformed House of Lords, we turned our attention to the functions it should carry out and the powers it should exercise.

On powers, we recommended that the existing balance be entrenched. The reformed House should retain the ability to delay the enactment of legislation until the following session. But any Commons bill supported by the House of Commons in two successive sessions should be enacted. This is consistent with our view of the respective roles of the two houses of Parliament. The ultimate decision should rest with the House of Commons, but the House of Lords should have every opportunity to express and publicize its concerns and force the government and the House of Commons to look afresh at the issues before making the final judgment.

As regards the functions of the reformed House of Lords, we recommended that they be extended in some respects, through the establishment of more expert committees. These committees would report on the constitutional implications of proposed legislation, and on human rights issues. Other committees would review the impact of devolution and the implications of further decentralisation within England, and look carefully at secondary legislation and at draft treaties. In all cases the impact of these committees would rely on the quality of their input. By assembling relevant expertise and experience, we envisage that they would produce authoritative reports which would influence debate in both houses of Parliament, and more widely. Overall we believe that our recommendations would improve the ability of Parliament as a whole to hold the government more accountable.[4]

Characteristics

Given the decisions we had reached about the job which needed to be done, we asked ourselves what sort of people should be members of the reformed House of Lords. We concluded that they should, above all, be authoritative, confident, and broadly representative. We also recommended that they should have:

- breadth of expertise and a broad range of experience
- particular knowledge and skills relevant to constitutional matters and human rights
- an ability to bring philosophical, moral, or spiritual perspectives to bear
- personal distinction

- freedom from party domination
- a nonpolemical style
- the ability to take a long-term view[5]

Composition

Finally we asked ourselves how best to identify people with those characteristics. We reviewed the pros and cons of the various options and decided that we could not recommend either a wholly, or largely, directly-elected second chamber; or indirect election, whether from the devolved institutions or from among United Kingdom members of the European Parliament.

We were attracted by the concept of giving seats in the House of Lords to people drawn from a wide range of different professional or vocational groups and from organizations active in other sectors of society. However, we identified some objections of principle and several insuperable practical difficulties. We concluded that an independent appointment system would most reliably deliver a chamber with the characteristics we wanted to see. However, we noted that this would leave no voice at all for the electorate and might not result in the selection of people with whom the nations and regions would necessarily identify. As someone put it at our public hearing in Newcastle, a person selected by a London-based commission for the North East would stand no chance of being accepted in the area as a representative *of* the North East.

Our overall conclusion, therefore, was that an independent Appointments Commission should be supplemented by arrangements to secure a significant minority of "regional members," chosen to reflect the balance of political opinion within each region.[6]

We further recommended that the number of independents or "cross benchers" should be maintained at around 20 per cent of the total and that the political balance of the remaining members should be set by reference to the votes cast in the most recent general election. Since the Second World War, such an arrangement would always have produced a chamber in which the government was the largest party but in which no single party had a majority. This seemed to us to be a vital requirement for the reformed House of Lords. It would be dangerous to allow a situation in which the government of the day could control both houses of Parliament. Equally, if the House of Lords could fall under the control of an opposition party, it would be a recipe for legislative gridlock.[7]

As to the "regional members," a substantial majority on the Royal Commission favoured a model in which eighty-seven regional members would be directly elected, by thirds, for fifteen-year terms, at the same time as the existing elections to the European Parliament and using a similar electoral system.[8]

Appointed members would also serve for fifteen-year terms. Both appointed and elected members could be re-appointed for further terms. But elected members would not be eligible to stand for re-election and no member of the reformed House of Lords would be eligible to be elected to the House of Commons within ten years of ceasing to be a member of the House of Lords. The purpose of the relatively long terms and these other recommendations was to ensure the genuine independence of members of the reformed House. They would not have to worry about keeping in with their party or even with their electorate, to secure renomination or re-election. They would have no incentive to operate in a partisan way because there would be very limited openings for political preferment.[9]

The Appointments Commission, which would be responsible for selecting the bulk of the new members of the second chamber, would be entirely independent. There would be an end to the current system of prime ministerial and party patronage. The commission would be responsible for maintaining the appropriate political balance, but its main task would be to ensure that the reformed chamber was broadly representative of modern British society. We wanted to see gender balance, fair representation for minority ethnic groups, and a broad spread of expertise and experience.[10]

A key recommendation in our report was that the remaining links between the peerage and membership of the second chamber be severed. It should be possible to create life peers without imposing on them a duty to attend Parliament and to appoint members of the second chamber without requiring them to accept a peerage. As a transitional measure, however, those of the existing life peers who wished to do so would remain members of the reformed chamber until they died (or chose to step down).[11]

CONCLUSION

Our recommendations went with the grain of the traditional British evolutionary approach to constitutional development. They built on the strengths of the existing House of Lords but incorporated a number of radical departures from what has gone before. If implemented, our recommendations will bring about a series of fundamental changes to the House of Lords. These include:

- first, the final departure of the hereditary peers from the House of Lords

- second, the complete breaking of the link between possession of any peerage and membership of the House of Lords
- third, an end to prime ministerial control of the size, balance, and individual membership of the second chamber
- fourth, an end to party patronage in respect of the second chamber

The new second chamber would be authoritative, confident, and broadly representative of the society it is designed to serve. It would be more democratic than the old House of Lords because the regional members would be directly elected on a proportional basis and because the political balance of the House as a whole would reflect the votes cast in general elections. It would be more representative than the old House of Lords because it would contain people from all parts of the United Kingdom and every walk of life, broadly equal numbers of men and women, and representatives of all the country's main ethnic and religious communities.

Our report may not appeal to political theorists. But as someone with a reputation as a successful practitioner of the "black art" of politics, I believe that it stands a good chance of being implemented.[12] That is primarily because the hallmark of our report is political realism. My colleagues and I decided at the outset that we were not interested in producing a report that would only gather dust in a pigeonhole. Our aim was to produce a report which was intellectually coherent but which also took account of the personal and institutional factors likely to influence the political parties and the existing individual members of both houses of Parliament who would need to support any proposed changes.

The reformed House of Lords, as we envisaged it, would add value to the system of parliamentary democracy in the United Kingdom and improve the accountability of the executive. But it would do so in ways which would not undermine the pre-eminence of the House of Commons or seriously reduce the ability of the government of the day to implement its policies. For the United Kingdom at least, we believe we have solved the conundrum of second chamber reform.

NOTES

1 The 1949 Act provided that a bill passed by the House of Commons in two successive sessions (with at least twelve months having elapsed between Commons Second Reading in the first session and Commons Third Reading of an effectively identical bill in the second) could become law at the end of that second session without the positive consent of the House of Lords.

2 Between 1970 and 1999, average daily attendance more than trebled; the number of sitting days increased and the total number of sitting hours almost doubled; and the amount of time spent considering public bills rose substantially. The range of professional knowledge or occupational expertise among members of the House of Lords widened considerably. The nature of the House of Lords' input to scrutiny and debate also changed, with the introduction of specialist committees and new approaches to the scrutiny of delegated legislation and deregulation initiatives. On these developments, see United Kingdom, Royal Commission on the Reform of the House of Lords, *A House for the Future* (Her Majesty's Stationery Office, January 2000), 18–22.
3 *A House for the Future*, 31.
4 Ibid., 54–7, 65, 74, 88, 91.
5 Ibid., 96–103.
6 Ibid., 104–13.
7 Ibid., 114.
8 Ibid., 121–7.
9 Ibid., 117–21.
10 Ibid., 130–43.
11 Ibid., 144–9.
12 The British government published a White Paper on 7 November 2001, *The House of Lords – Completing the Reform* (Cm 5291), reflecting its intention to legislate for the second stage of House of Lords reform on broadly the lines recommended by the Wakeham Commission.

Responsiveness

In the introduction to this volume, some of the strengths of Westminster-type parliamentary government were discussed: accountability to citizens' representatives who compose the legislature; stability based on longstanding constitutional principles and conventions, notably responsible government; and the capacity to evolve in response to changing circumstances. For some, the varied channels of representation, with Parliament arguably the central forum, and the links that underpin accountability mean that the Westminster model encourages responsiveness in governance. For others, this argument is based more on theory than reality. Various critics increasingly question the actual responsiveness and influence of parliamentary institutions; advocate or at least see potential in direct democracy measures; and underline the importance of public policies and programs in responding to the needs and expectations of the population, particularly in highly diverse societies. Understandably, there are links to some of the questions of representation addressed in the three chapters grouped under that theme. Even if many critics believe that legislative institutions are too weak relative to the executive, they see the composition of those institutions as integral to their capacity to give voice to a range of views and interests, and thus to contribute to responsiveness in governance.

As the chapters in this section demonstrate, there is a lively debate about the degree to which the majoritarian principle that underlies the functioning of parliamentary institutions derived from the British system truly allows for responsiveness in governance. Indeed, Arend

Lijphart, in *Patterns of Democracy*, uses the terms "Westminster model" and "majoritarian model" interchangeably. Among its characteristics are a concentration of executive power in one-party cabinets and cabinet dominance of a legislature that is unicameral (as in New Zealand) or in which the weakness of the second chamber means that the Parliament's ongoing functioning approaches unicameralism. In addition, except for fairly infrequent instances of minority government, one-party government is the rule at Westminster and in Ottawa and Canberra. While some contend that responsiveness results from various interests and demands finding expression within the government party, for others this is a hollow claim because of the dominance of the executive (and, in large measure, the prime minister). This dynamic is not immutable, however. Some legislatures based on the Westminster model, for example the Scottish Parliament, have adapted their committee and other processes to allow for richer links with groups and citizens. In other cases, dissenting votes on non-confidence measures are not necessarily seen as "disloyal" acts. Here, as with so many aspects of the Westminister model, openness and political will on the part of the government party are key.

The rigidities of parliamentary institutions and demands for greater citizen participation help explain the heightened interest and somewhat greater use of democracy measures, notably referendums, in some of the countries reviewed in this collection. While few wish to use referendums as extensively as the Swiss or even Americans (at the state and local levels), they have become fairly well established as a mechanism to approve or reject changes to the constitution (as is required in Australia and occurred in Canada in 1992) or to major political institutions (for example, the two referendums that led New Zealand to adopt a proportional electoral system in 1996). In this context, the charge that referendums are incompatible with parliamentary government is now rarely heard. Views are more divided on other direct democracy measures such as citizens' initiatives and recall. In the rare cases where governments have decided to introduce such measures, they have usually set the thresholds (for example, the number of signatures required on a petition) at a fairly high level (as with British Columbia's initiative and recall legislation adopted in the 1990s). Despite certain currents of change, governments and other leading political actors often continue to view direct democracy measures as being in competition with, rather than complementary to, longstanding electoral and parliamentary processes.

Just as the political culture of the countries examined in this volume has been changing in response to demands for greater citizen participation, so too has it become more sensitive to the distinctiveness and rights of various societal groups. The position of indigenous peoples has been a significant, if sometimes contentious element of recent political debates in Canada, New Zealand, and Australia. As demonstrated in the first two chapters in this section, reparation of past injustices and ways of securing future progress have been sought not only through constitutional instruments but also through treaties, agreements, and statutes. Some measures, such as self-government agreements in Canada, seek to foster better socio-economic conditions and set the framework for governance of Aboriginal communities. In a sense, such measures seek to create space for aboriginal peoples to shape their lives in response to their differing histories, values, and goals. Both New Zealand and Canada have also taken steps to include representatives of their indigenous peoples within the political institutions of the larger society. New Zealand's long experience with designated seats for Mäori is noteworthy in this regard.

In the first chapter in this section, Paul Chartrand illustrates that, following a long period of Imperial and Canadian history during which Aboriginal peoples suffered from exclusion and domination, some progress is being made to respond to their varying situations and claims, and to involve them more fully in governance processes. Protections added to the Constitution in 1982, a small number of self-government agreements (such as the one with the Nisga'a, which Chartrand describes) and changes to various laws have begun a process of recognition and affirmation of Aboriginal group rights. The result, according to Chartrand, is that a new doctrine of constitutional law in emerging. While some decisions have put governments on the spot and have divided public opinion, leading Aboriginal spokespersons argue that if political institutions cannot respond effectively to their claims or cannot do so in a timely way they have no choice but to turn to the courts. Some continue to see potential in enhancing Aboriginal participation in legislative institutions. In the 1990s, the Royal Commission on Electoral Reform recommended there be designated Aboriginal seats in the House of Commons, and the Royal Commission on Aboriginal Peoples proposed an advisory Aboriginal Parliament. However, both ideas received little support from Aboriginal political organizations. For Chartrand, the challenge of recognizing and responding to Aboriginal peoples' distinctiveness within a multinational country can only be met by a sharing of governing authority within a "condominium of Canada."

In his contribution to this collection, Mason Durie examines ways in which New Zealand has provided for Mäori membership in

Parliament, the protection of Mäori interests in statute, and Mäori participation in the state sector. Designated seats in the House of Representatives date from 1867. While other parties, notably Labour, elect Mäori members, Durie's view is that without the designated seats Mäori influence within the political system would be diffuse and unfocused. Despite the Treaty of Waitangi, signed with the British in 1840, significant measures to protect Mäori interests within statutes and in the public sector date only from the 1970s. According to Durie, this recent phase is characterized by more dynamic participation, with the explicit recognition of Mäori customary and treaty rights and an expectation that a Mäori dimension can be reflected in practical terms alongside the conventional instruments of state, including through partnerships with Mäori governing bodies.

To conclude this section on the theme of "responsiveness," Jennifer Smith provides an analysis of recent debate about proposals to reform Canada's parliamentary institutions. In her view, criticisms of Canada's enduring system of representative and responsible government reflect dissatisfaction with aggressive and competitive behaviour on the part of parliamentarians and the partisanship of disciplined parties. The latter means that parliamentarians have "little in the legislative line" to do – in other words, limited capacity to foster responsiveness in governance by shaping the country's laws. Smith examines the basis for and potential impact of a range of reform proposals: direct democracy, and elected Senate, a restricted confidence convention and more free votes in the House of Commons, fixed elections, and electoral system reform. Her assessment is that taken together these measures would likely produce a radical change in the existing system: individual MPs would make huge gains in their standing in the legislative process, and at the same time, governments would need to develop the skills to assemble winning coalitions. While not rejecting the need for change, Smith concludes that the "combination of diversity and independent-mindedness" might enhance the political leverage of powerful minority interests at the expense of the majority. She suggests that the committee process offers avenues for MPs to contribute to the legislative process, and adds that there is little, except "the obstinacy of party leaders," to prevent MPs from pursuing ways of improving their role in the system.

Canada and the Aboriginal Peoples: From Dominion to Condominium

PAUL L.A.H. CHARTRAND

It is an unfortunate fact that the place of the indigenous peoples within Canada is not well understood. They have, for much of our history, been "put in their place" and relegated to the margins of society.[1] They have had virtually no role or influence in the governance of Canada or, indeed, in its main public institutions. History reveals a series of policies and practices of dispossession, exclusion, and domination by newcomers who set up a model of government patterned after the British system.[2]

Yet British imperial law and practice revealed a certain recognition of the existence and rights of the indigenous inhabitants,[3] and recent changes in the constitution and Canadian law have begun a process of recognition and affirmation of the group rights of the Aboriginal peoples,[4] the ones who were here "ab-origine," or from the beginning.

These rights are being articulated both in modern treaties based upon agreement between political representatives of the Aboriginal peoples concerned and of the Canadian government, and in an evolving judicial doctrine of Aboriginal rights.

A fundamental and outstanding question in this process of defining the place of the Aboriginal peoples in Canada is the nature and scope of their rights to govern themselves within the general legal and constitutional framework of Canada. Aboriginal people in Canada today have some limited self-government authority based mostly upon statutory regimes. These include "Indian band" authority over Indian reserves pursuant to the Indian Act; the local authority over lands set aside in modern Indian and Inuit land-claims agreements and governed by new statutory authorities that replaced the Indian Act governing system; and authority over Métis lands under the Alberta Métis Settlements legislation. The recent Nisga'a Treaty in British Columbia heralds the recognition of "self-government" as an Aboriginal right protected in a negotiated and constitutionally protected agreement.

The aim of this chapter is to survey some of the major issues involved in the evolution of Aboriginal self-government, the context in which these issues are being debated and developed, and some of the principles that can animate this most important national dialogue. This review suggests the idea of a change from dominion over the Aboriginal peoples to the concept of a condominium,[5] or an arrangement for the sharing of governance within Canada.

It is important to illuminate Aboriginal peoples' path to democratic participation in Canada as the peoples emerge from the shadows of historical marginalization. It is important to show those who are accustomed to putting people in their place that their own preferred concepts of democracy and constitutional principles require the accommodation within Canadian institutions of all of Canada's historic nations, even the smallest ones.[6]

A companion issue to the question of Aboriginal self-government is the participation of Aboriginal people as Canadian citizens within Canadian political institutions. Some observations will be made here on the very limited participation of Aboriginal individuals as elected political representatives, and on models of public government that attempt to accommodate Aboriginal populations that are the dominant majority in a particular geographic region.

THE DOMINION OF CANADA OVER ABORIGINAL PEOPLES

When Canada was created from four North American British colonies in 1867, the Aboriginal peoples whose homelands provided the territory and resources for the new country were not represented in the political discussions within the colonies and with British representatives.[7] They were, instead, treated as "subject races" to which principles of legitimate government did not apply, and therefore it did not matter that they were governed by laws over which they had no say.[8]

Traditionally, Canadian Aboriginal policy and practice reflected both emerging Canadian interests and, occasionally, pressures exerted by Aboriginal peoples, and were largely developed in an ad hoc fashion.[9] Historical policies treated Aboriginal people as a "problem" to be dealt with as political expediency might dictate and, where necessary, accorded them a place in the Canadian economy equivalent to "peasants."[10] On the national scene, the idea was to develop a new Canada modelled on a pale imitation of Britain, with no "Red Indians" in sight. The major national political preoccupation was not with the dispossession of the relatively weak indigenous nations, but with the struggle between the descendants of the French and English colonial settlers. The question was about which of these sides would define the vision of the new dominion.[11]

Within the last generation, however, the constitution of Canada has recognized and affirmed the status of Aboriginal peoples as "peoples," and international law and practice have increasingly given support to the concept of self-determination in its application to indigenous peoples living within the political boundaries of modern nation-states. This requires a shift in the principles that can legitimately determine the place of Aboriginal peoples in Canada. They must be viewed not as racial minorities subject to laws of general application, but as distinct social and political communities on traditional homelands, with the inherent rights that are vested in peoples or historic nations. This view, upon which future Aboriginal-Canadian relations must be built, is recognized not only by constitutional law but by evolving norms of international law and practice, and by human rights.[12]

The legitimacy of Canada's power over Aboriginal peoples is a core issue in current democratic politics that challenge Canada's national institutions, political processes, and representation. The old vision of Canada as a North American political and cultural extension of Europe that suffered the presence of an "Indian problem" is challenged by contemporary and emerging concepts of international and domestic moral, political, and legal norms.[13] A more just vision might be one of a multinational North American country, one where the historic Aboriginal nations have a place, and one which reflects not only the British influence but also the Aboriginal foundations of Canada.[14]

The outlines of this perhaps romantic vision may be discerned in recent developments towards Aboriginal self-government built upon a foundation of Aboriginal and treaty rights. These will now be examined before considering Aboriginal participation as individual Canadian citizens in the Canadian political system.

THE DECADE OF CONSTITUTIONAL REFORM: 1982 TO 1992

In 1982 an amendment to the constitution of Canada included the recognition and affirmation of the "existing Aboriginal and treaty rights of the Aboriginal peoples of Canada."[15] The constitution also required that the prime minister convene national conferences of first ministers and Aboriginal political representatives to identify these rights. The required conferences were held, but the mistrust evident in the need to give constitutional status to a series of meetings between Canadian and Aboriginal representatives was shown to be warranted by later events. By 1987 the conferences had produced no substantive agreement on the identification of Aboriginal and treaty rights, yet within months the same Canadian first ministers[16] had agreed on a package of constitutional reforms to respond to Quebec's demands that arose from its opposition to the 1982 amendments.[17]

Mistrust turned to cynicism and open defiance by Aboriginal people, highlighted by the "hot summer" of 1990 when Quebec police and federal army troops battled Mohawks in the Montreal area, bringing shame and embarrassment to Canada at home and abroad. A standing committee of the House of Commons that examined these events made recommendations to the government, including the establishment of a non-governmental body to deal with land disputes and a Royal Commission to inquire into and report upon relations between First Nations and other Canadians.[18] The Royal Commission was established in 1991, but no independent tribunal has yet been set up as recommended by both the committee and the Royal Commission.

In 1992 another round of constitutional reform talks, which included both Quebec and Aboriginal issues, produced a tentative agreement on reforms – the Charlottetown Accord – that was rejected 54.4 to 44.6 per cent in a national referendum on 26 October 1992. With the rejection of the accord, it seemed clear that a package of amendments that could be supported in all parts of Canada was not possible.[19] On the positive side, however, the provisions of the Charlottetown Accord on Aboriginal self-government represent the high-water mark of national discussions on this issue and a benchmark for future negotiations.[20] The Draft Legal Text of 9 October 1992 provided for the amendment of the Aboriginal and treaty rights section of the Constitution Act, 1982 to include this passage:

> The exercise of the right referred to in subsection (1) ["the inherent right of self-government within Canada"] includes the authority of duly constituted legislative bodies of the Aboriginal peoples, each within its own jurisdiction, a) to safeguard and develop their languages, cultures, economies, identities, institutions and traditions, and b) to develop, maintain, and strengthen their relationship with their lands, waters and environment, so as to determine and control their development as peoples according to their own values and priorities and to ensure the integrity of their societies.

With the demise of the Charlottetown Accord, the era of direct constitutional reform ended. Aboriginal peoples increasingly turned to the courts to secure their rights, while Quebec's politicians focused their attention on a political agenda for leaving Canada.

Citizen Rights and Aboriginal Rights

The Constitution Act, 1982 includes provisions that provide a forum for the two classic views about the place of Aboriginal people in Canada. The Canadian Charter of Rights and Freedoms proclaims the rights of individuals and liberal values. Its provisions apply to all Aboriginal individuals, as Canadian citizens and residents. On the other hand, the Aboriginal rights section, section 35, which stands alone outside the Charter, proclaims the rights of "peoples" and exposes the challenge that group rights and "special status" present to concepts of liberal individualism.[21] Section 35 rights are not vested in Aboriginal individuals but in the groups that comprise "peoples" with recognized Aboriginal and treaty rights. Only Aboriginal individuals who are members of these rights-bearing communities are entitled to exercise Aboriginal rights by virtue of their group membership.[22]

As Canadian citizens, Aboriginal individuals have Canadian citizenship rights. As members of Aboriginal groups with vested "aboriginal rights" affirmed and protected by the constitution, Aboriginal people, unlike other citizens, are entitled to enjoy the benefits of Aboriginal rights. This situation has attracted the label "Citizens plus."[23] The relationship between individual rights and group rights, particularly in the context of the emerging doctrine of Aboriginal rights, is complex and beyond the scope of this chapter.[24]

The language of the Charter contributes to the notion of the equality of all citizens and thereby feeds the confusion between citizenship rights and Aboriginal rights. The "racial equality" provision in section 15 seems to be behind some of the confusion in the public dialogue about the nature of Aboriginal and treaty rights.[25]

After declaring that all individuals are equal before and under the law, section 15 – the equality provision of the Charter – contains an "affirmative action" provision that permits laws and programs designed to "ameliorate" the conditions of disadvantaged individuals or groups "including those that are disadvantaged because of race, national or ethnic origin, colour, religion," etc. Section 15 permits governments to exercise their benevolent discretion in favour of disadvantaged groups but offers nothing to the dialogue on the rights of Aboriginal peoples.

Under section 15, governments are free to ameliorate the conditions of "disadvantaged" individuals who may be Aboriginal on account of their race, national or ethnic origin, or colour, but the membership of such groups of disadvantaged individuals must not be conflated with the membership of the "peoples" whose collective rights are protected in section 35. Many people in Canada may claim a personal identity as Aboriginal persons on account of their ancestry. Biological descent from an Aboriginal person, however, can never in principle be sufficient by itself to entitle an individual to claim rights as a member of an Aboriginal community with Aboriginal rights. Both objective factors, such as belonging to a family within a community, and subjective factors, such as self-identification, are essential elements of a definition of the membership of the Aboriginal peoples of Canada. Status as members of a historic political and social community must not be foisted upon individuals by birth and must yield to freedom of association with respect to both acquisition or renunciation of status.

As yet neither government policy nor judicial doctrine has properly dealt with the question of identifying the "Aboriginal peoples" whose ancestral rights are protected in the constitution. The explanation for Aboriginal rights is based in history and in the norms behind the right of self-determination, but the close association between "blood" and "belonging" in the concept of "ethnic nationalism" makes it very difficult terrain.[26]

The 1982 constitutional amendments contained promises to Aboriginal peoples. The promise that their basic rights would be defined by political agreement in a process of national statecraft failed, giving way to the competing interests of the more powerful.

The 1982 amendments also contained a challenge: they introduced into the Canadian constitution a new relationship between the judiciary and Parliament, which replaced the familiar concept of parliamentary sovereignty. Henceforth the courts could not only define the scope of parliamentary authority by defining the scope of rights that limit that authority; they could also develop concepts of positive obligations for both Parliament and the executive branch to protect those rights and make them effective. These limitations upon parliamentary sovereignty have been developed mostly with reference to individual Charter rights, but their logic is being extended to the realm of group rights and parliamentary obligations and is giving rise to a new doctrine of constitutional law that goes well beyond the terms of the amendments that gave it birth.[27]

THE ROLE OF THE COURTS IN DEVELOPING A DOCTRINE OF ABORIGINAL POLITICAL RIGHTS

As national statecraft has failed to define the nature of the basic Aboriginal and treaty rights of the Aboriginal peoples that were protected by the 1982 constitutional amendments, the courts have assumed a particularly significant role in this regard. It is important to emphasize that the courts charged with the development of a common law doctrine of Aboriginal rights and the law of Indian treaties are the courts of Canada, not the courts of the Aboriginal peoples. These courts owe their existence and legitimacy to Canada, and they have no effective means of enforcing their decisions against a recalcitrant government. In effect, the courts' ability to temper the unconscionable exercise of power by the state is thus limited. The courts then necessarily take on the role of rationalizing, *ex post facto*, the exercise of state power, even as they moderate its effects.

The Canadian doctrine of Aboriginal rights[28] is not at an advanced stage of development. Its origins are in the decisions of British colonial courts, and early cases that began to build the theoretical framework of Aboriginal rights were decided without the benefit of the views and arguments of the Aboriginal peoples themselves.[29] The new constitutional status accorded these rights through the historic 1982 changes have led to the development of new theoretical ground.

It is proposed that three broad categories of rights belong within the theoretical framework of Aboriginal rights being developed by the courts.[30] Early judicial attention in Canada focused on the land rights of Aboriginal peoples, and the concept of Aboriginal title or land-related uses based upon occupation and use led the development of a doctrine of Aboriginal rights.[31] A second category comprises cultural practices or customs that arise out of the social organization and distinctive cultures of Aboriginal peoples. The narrow scope of this category is revealed in the common law test that describes Aboriginal rights as "those customs, practices or traditions which were integral to a distinctive Aboriginal society prior to its contact with European society."[32]

The third category is that of political rights, or those rights that involve the authority of the group to make decisions that bind the actions of its members. The existence and function of this category may be discerned from principles evident in a theory of group rights,[33] in arguments advanced by legal and other scholars,[34] in the report of the Royal Commission on Aboriginal Peoples,[35] in principles of international law,[36] and in some lower court decisions,[37] notably the

Campbell case in the Supreme Court of British Columbia which upheld the validity of the historic Nisga'a treaty.

The common law doctrine of Aboriginal rights has yet to define the nature and membership of the communities in which Aboriginal rights are vested. This is true for all categories of rights proposed here. Although the Aboriginal peoples of Canada include the Indian, Métis, and Inuit peoples, the case law has been established almost exclusively around "First Nation" or "Indian" facts, and the courts seem to have assumed that the appropriate or legitimate group was a party to the legal action. The First Nations are recognized as "Indians" by virtue of federal legislation,[38] and it is not likely that a court would decide that "Indian" groups that have long been established by federal legislation are outside the constitutional category of Aboriginal peoples.

It is indisputable, however, that there are Aboriginal communities and peoples with rights protected by the constitution who are not recognized by current federal legislation. It is only a matter of time before the courts have to find the law which defines these groups. Although the current state of the law permits only tentative observations, it is assumed that judicial definitions will bear a functional relation to the Aboriginal rights that are the subject of litigation. For example, the Supreme Court has already decided that small, local Aboriginal communities have "site-specific" hunting and fishing rights, and the courts may find that these communities have certain rights to regulate the exercise of those rights by their members. However, there are good reasons, including practical efficiency and economies of scale, as well as democratic principles, to suggest that general governing authority over a community should be vested in larger communities, as the Royal Commission on Aboriginal Peoples proposed.

How might the evolving Aboriginal rights jurisprudence be developed to promote Aboriginal self-government negotiations? The Supreme Court has explained in recent cases[39] that the texts of Canada's written documents are not "exhaustive" and that "the Constitution also embraces unwritten, as well as written rules."[40] These underlying constitutional principles "animate the whole of our Constitution" and include federalism, democracy, constitutionalism and the rule of law, and respect for minorities.[41]

The Supreme Court has also said that Aboriginal and treaty rights themselves reflect an important underlying constitutional value. In discussing these authorities, a leading commentator has expressed the view that "Aboriginal peoples, unlike other minorities with constitutional rights, have an inherent and inalienable right to self-government which gives them a share of sovereign authority in Canada."[42] The rights of governance of Aboriginal peoples are pre-existing rights that do not depend on the constitution for their existence, while the powers of Canadian governments owe their existence entirely to the constitution.

The courts are also developing a theory of positive obligations that arise from the underlying constitutional principles. In the Quebec Secession Reference, the Supreme Court stated that "these principles may give rise to very abstract and general obligations, or they may be more specific and precise in nature. The principles are not merely descriptive, but are also invested with a powerful normative force, and are binding upon both courts and governments."[43]

In the context of a referendum that favoured Quebec secession, the Supreme Court stated that the principles of the constitution would place an obligation on Canada and the provinces to enter into negotiations. The same principles suggest that a democratic expression of the will of an Aboriginal "people"[44] to enter into negotiations on self-governing arrangements would give rise to an obligation to negotiate an appropriate agreement.[45]

A recent work by some leading scholars has proposed that the unwritten principles of the constitution lead to two distinct initiatives:

> In a reconciliation for the millennium, the organization of the Crown, government, courts, and economy require two reforms under section 35. First, Aboriginal peoples must exercise their inherent right to govern their peoples in their lands reserved to them and interpret their laws. Second, these Aboriginal peoples should be represented within the federal Parliament and provincial assemblies based on their constitutional rights, not on their race. Both of these reforms are consistent with the wording of section 35 and the constitutional conventions that seek to create a post-colonial Canada.[46]

TREATIES AS AGREEMENTS FOR SELF-GOVERNMENT

Treaties were entered into from the beginning of European settlement in the eastern parts of colonial North America that now form part of Canada. The process continued until 1923 as Canada expanded its territorial acquisitions and jurisdiction across the Prairies and the Northwest to the Pacific. More than sixty of these major treaties were signed, although there are no treaties for several large areas of Canada, particularly in some northern regions and most of British Columbia. In these areas, the lands are still legally encumbered by Aboriginal title.

In 1975, in response to the 1973 *Calder* case – a landmark judicial decision affirming Aboriginal title – and to political disputes over a massive hydro-electric power development on Cree territory in northern Quebec, the treaty process resumed with the signing of the James

Bay and Northern Quebec Agreement. More than a dozen such land-claims agreements or "modern" treaties have since been signed.

It seems clear that treaties are the best method for establishing self-government arrangements. Indian treaties are the most powerful symbol of First Nations' distinct status and identity, and may be viewed as historic repositories of intersocietal agreements upon which Canada was built. Modern treaty agreements can establish a degree of certainty concerning the rights to be exercised by the group that benefits everyone. It is an issue of particular interest to corporations engaged in the extraction of natural resources on Indian lands.

It also seems clear that treaty negotiations are the preferred legal and constitutional route to self-government agreements. The Supreme Court of Canada has specifically stated that section 35(1) of the Constitution Act, 1982 provides a solid constitutional base for negotiations and that the Crown is under an obligation to enter into and conduct negotiations on implementing Aboriginal and treaty rights in good faith.[47] Since 1995, the federal government has adopted a policy of negotiating self-government arrangements within modern land-claims agreements based on the recognition of an inherent Aboriginal right to self-government.[48]

However, ominous political developments work against the acceptance of these principles. The highly publicized Nisga'a treaty,[49] which came into effect on 11 May 2000 and includes recognition of some limited political and legislative authority in the Nisga'a nation, came under unprecedented attack from both the provincial and federal opposition parties during the process of legislative approval.

At the same time, a Supreme Court decision affirming rights to fish under the terms of a historic treaty on the Atlantic coast generated chaos, violence, and apprehension of tensions reminiscent of the "hot summer" of 1990. The *Marshall* case, delivered on 17 September 1999, involved a series of historic treaties with the Mic Mac people in what is now Nova Scotia and New Brunswick. The Court decided that a 1760 treaty was protected under section 35 of the Constitution Act, 1982 and that it allowed the beneficiaries to fish and sell their catch to obtain necessaries. The treaty rights were subject to federal regulation in accordance with justificatory standards established in previously decided case law. At trial the Crown failed to justify the existing regulations and the appellant was acquitted.[50]

Individual fishermen dashed to exercise those rights, with predictable chaotic results. The federal government did not seem prepared to react. The non-Aboriginal fishermen protested their disagreement, and some violence broke out. Canadians looking on must have sensed that no one was in charge; when there is a vacuum of public regulation, there is little security for those who would organize their affairs to stay on the right side of the law. This shows how critically important it is that immediate action be taken to resolve the questions of who the relevant rights-bearing communities are and what the lawful source of regulatory authority over the exercise of Aboriginal group rights is. The courts have yet to address the issue adequately, and the government seems content to sit back and manage crises.

The Nisga'a Treaty

We now turn to consider the first modern treaty that combined a settlement of the land question with self-government arrangements, the treaty with the Nisga'a people of the Nass Valley on British Columbia's middle coastal region.[51] Negotiations between the federal government and the Nisga'a had started in 1976 following the landmark 1973 *Calder* case. The province of British Columbia joined the talks only in 1990, and a tripartite agreement-in-principle was reached in 1996. This led to the ratification of the treaty by the Nisga'a in a referendum in November 1998 and to legislative ratification by British Columbia on 26 April 1998 and by Parliament on 13 April 2000. The Nisga'a treaty is seen as a model for the treaties to be negotiated with other First Nations in the province, where much of the territory remains subject to Aboriginal title.

The treaty is a complex and voluminous agreement that purports to set out all the treaty rights of the Nisga'a Nation. It has four basic components. First, the Aboriginal title of the Nisga'a is replaced by a grant to the Nisga'a Nation of a fee simple estate of just under 2,000 square kilometres of land within the much larger traditional territory. Second, the treaty defines the existing hunting, fishing, and trapping rights in the Nisga'a lands and permits participation in wildlife and fisheries management over a much larger area known as the Nass Wildlife Area. The Nisga'a thus have defined legislative power over the lands granted to them and certain specified hunting, fishing, and trapping rights over a larger area. The third basic component of the treaty is the payment of money over a period of years, which can be seen as compensation either for what the Nisga'a have given up or possibly for the negative impact of the arrival of Europeans upon the Nisga'a.[52] The fourth component comprises the "self-government" provisions, with elements of legislative jurisdiction being specified in chapter 11 of the treaty.

The Nisga'a government comprises two levels. The first is the Nisga'a Lisims government, which is responsible for intergovernmental relations between the Nisga'a Nation and Canada or British Columbia, and for matters that affect all Nisga'a citizens, such as language and culture. Second, there are four village governments responsible for local matters. There are also non-legislative "Urban Locals" in three urban locations where non-resident Nisga'a citizens can participate in Nisga'a government by electing representatives to the Nisga'a Lisims government. The governments are representative, elected at least every five years, and subject to a constitution that is itself subject to the constitution of Canada, including the Charter of Rights and Freedoms. There are detailed "citizenship" provisions on enrolment and eligibility, with the latter extending to individuals descended from a Nisga'a tribe on the maternal side, adopted children, and those married to Nisga'a citizens and duly adopted by a tribe.

There is authority to set up both a police service and a court, but this is subject to provincial approval and both must fit within the provincial system. The legislative power of the Nisga'a government extends to areas that concern Nisga'a identity, education, preservation of culture, the use of land and resources, and the means by which the Nisga'a will make decisions in these areas. In this category, Nisga'a laws prevail over conflicting federal and provincial legislation. In a second category of legislative authority, when a Nisga'a law conflicts with a provincial or federal law, the federal or provincial law will prevail.

The Nisga'a Treaty attracted attention for a number of firsts:

- It combined negotiations on self-governing authority of the Nisga'a people with negotiations on the land rights of the Nisga'a and incorporated rights of self-government into a section 35 treaty. For previous modern treaties, including those with the Yukon First Nations in 1995, there had been parallel negotiations, but the legislative authority of the First Nations had a statutory, not a treaty, basis.
- It included provisions for the creation of a Nisga'a court system, although it would have to fit within the provincial court system.
- It attempted an exhaustive listing of land and resource rights and eschewed the language of "extinguishment," long an irritant in Aboriginal-government relations.[53]
- It recognized the Nisga'a authority to create legislative bodies and provided for commercial fishing rights.

These provisions tend to reflect the judicial development of the law of Aboriginal rights and evolving federal policy. Other provisions that attracted wide attention, such as the citizenship and enrolment code – which include provisions for the participation of non-residents in

Nisga'a government – had already been introduced in earlier agreements such as the Yukon First Nations agreements.[54]

In a legal challenge to the self-government provisions launched by British Columbia's leader of the opposition at that time, the Supreme Court of British Columbia upheld the constitutional validity of these provisions. It explained that section 35 of the Consititution Act, 1982 guarantees, among other things, a limited form of self-government recognized by common law, which was defined and given content in the Nisga'a Treaty.[55]

What also seems clear, in addition to the merits of treaty-making as expounded in law and policy, is that gains that may be made in the development of judicial principles and federal policy must be balanced against the political opposition to Aboriginal rights that seems to be growing in Canada.[56] In the face of uncertainty and political opposition on major national policy issues, governments have often turned to commissions for advice. We now consider the approach of the Royal Commission on Aboriginal Peoples to the questions of Aboriginal self-government and of Aboriginal relations and policy in Canada generally.

THE ROYAL COMMISSION ON ABORIGINAL PEOPLES

Through its legacy of research and argument, the final report of the Royal Commission on Aboriginal Peoples aimed to contribute to the national dialogue on the place of Aboriginal peoples in Canada. It also aimed to create a historic shift in the way Canadians view Aboriginal peoples, just as previous Royal Commissions had changed views on other important issues.[57] In various quarters, the view of Aboriginal peoples as a "problem" still persists, often expressed through the desire to "buy peace at the best price"; this must be overcome if Aboriginal relations are to be put on a firm foundation.[58]

The Royal Commission also saw the need to legitimize the claims being made by Aboriginal representatives during discussions on national constitutional reform. Consequently, it argued that the common law of Canada recognizes an inherent right of Aboriginal self-government that is protected by the constitution and is vested in Aboriginal "nations."[59] In this regard the commission was sensitive to the need to debunk the myth of "race-based" special status and explained that Aboriginal peoples comprise historic nations that are dynamic social and political communities, not racial minorities.[60]

The Royal Commission's massive final report, issued in 1996, proposed a vision of a national process in which some sixty to eighty "nations" of Aboriginal peoples would enter into newly negotiated treaties with the Crown. It also proposed the establishment of an Aboriginal Lands and Treaties Tribunal to play a supporting role in treaty processes. In addition, it proposed the establishment of an Aboriginal Parliament, the main function of which would be to advise the House of Commons and the Senate on legislation and constitutional matters relating to Aboriginal peoples. The report also urged the federal government to adopt a long-term strategy on the construction or reconstruction of Aboriginal nations, while assisting communities to overcome the economic and social problems that continue to plague them. A twenty-year plan was proposed: it included the restructuring of federal government institutions and the establishment of a national political framework to guide negotiations on self-government and land rights.

By the time the Royal Commission issued its final report, the government that had appointed it was no longer in power. The federal policy response of January 1998 contained few of the fundamental structural and policy changes that had been urged by the Royal Commission.[61] The most significant financial investment was a $350-million "healing fund" to deal with the legacy of abuse at Indian residential schools.[62] However, nothing changed in the structures of the federal government. They continue to react to crises as they arise, and there is little apparent coordination among federal departments.[63]

THE "URBAN DILEMMA"

The "urban dilemma" as perceived in relation to the goal of Aboriginal self-government is rooted in the observation that a majority of Aboriginal people live in urban areas.[64] It is obviously more difficult to govern Aboriginal people in urban areas, where they are shoulder to shoulder with others, than on lands under the exclusive authority of an Aboriginal government.[65]

Aboriginal people in Canada today have some recognized legal authority to local self-government over Indian reserves under the Indian Act; to lands set aside in modern Indian and Inuit land-claims agreements governed by new statutory authorities that replaced the Indian Act; and to Métis lands under the Alberta Métis Settlements legislation.[66] Elsewhere, Aboriginal people are generally subject to the laws that apply to all Canadians, and they receive public services under general legislative and administrative authorities.

The legitimate concern that Aboriginal self-government is a weak response to the circumstances of most Aboriginal people today does not have to do with the right of self-government as such but with the need for feasible implementation strategies. Some believe that the dispossessed who have moved to the urban areas do not have a sufficient degree of social and political solidarity to build or rebuild Aboriginal nations or "peoples." They prefer to characterize the members of fractured Aboriginal communities as "racial minorities" who either need assistance from benevolent affirmative action programs or should be allowed to acculturate and assimilate into the general population.

The Royal Commission argued for a three-pronged approach in response to the "urban dilemma."[67] First, affirmative action programs should be delivered to persons of Aboriginal ancestry residing in urban areas. Second, where members of the urban Aboriginal community wished to do so, "self-government" arrangements for service delivery could be negotiated with governments. These arrangements would not, of course, be based upon any recognition of group rights, which belong only to historic "nations," but upon agreements with an Aboriginal "community of interest." Third, those historic nations that would negotiate self-government treaties to operate from their homeland bases could in theory provide services to their non-resident members in urban areas.

In order to implement the third approach, Aboriginal self-governing nations could build community institutions in urban areas. Until such treaties are negotiated, however, the advantages of cities may be gained by aggregating the resources of existing First Nation and Inuit governments. With this model, schools, training centres, and medical and economic institutions that would be beyond the capacity of individual "Indian bands" or Inuit communities could be built. Aboriginal people should not be denied the advantages of living in urban areas; it is better to create welcoming institutions than to lament the fact that today many reserves are far from urban centres and located in economically depressed areas. If the city's advantages cannot move to the reserve, in theory the reserve can move to the city's advantages.[68]

No matter what approach is eventually adopted, the challenges to the establishment of a comprehensive "nation" approach to Aboriginal self-government are daunting, not only because of the legal, policy, and public opinion factors that have been considered briefly in this paper, but also because of some factors inherent in Aboriginal communities themselves, and their historic and current circumstances. Canada is a vast country, with many culturally, socially, economically, and politically diverse Aboriginal communities spread from coast to coast. There is little or no history of cooperative political relations between them that can build whatever political leverage may be gained from working together in the pursuit of common interests. In trying to gain political support for their regional or national projects, the national and provincial political organizations[69] must compete with the interests of the representatives' own home communities. For communities other than "Indian bands," there is no recent or current tradition of group decision-making that binds members in public or community matters.

From a historical perspective, it seems that Aboriginal representatives are now at the point of emerging from the shadows of marginalization. The first order of business is to proclaim the survival of the group – a vision that sees a new day where the community can again marshall its resources for the common benefit. This shows the importance of recognizing the Aboriginal peoples' right of self-government.

It is the second order of business, that of reconstructing these nations, that concerned the Royal Commission and led it to propose a long-term plan of reconciliation and reconstruction. A national vision of a multinational Canada cannot be realized without the effective capacity and participation of the representatives of the historic Aboriginal nations. The commission's proposal for a national meeting of first ministers and Aboriginal leaders to agree on a national negotiating framework has received no official response from the federal government, despite its support from Aboriginal leaders.

The challenges posed by the "urban dilemma" work their way into the second order of business, but are not reason enough to abandon it or weaken a national commitment to it. In fact, the large urban population may offer Aboriginal governments the advantage of an increased pool of potential members who can stimulate economic and social growth. A feasible strategy to implement self-government should include plans for developing closer and more functional links between the urban and the rural, remote, and reserve-based populations. Such a proposal is in fact suggested, if not made necessary, by the judicial activism that has begun to rearrange the legal and policy distinctions upon which the "rural or remote Indian reserve" model and the "urban Aboriginal" model have been constructed.[70] Furthermore, the provisions in modern agreements, such as the Yukon First Nations agreements and the Nisga'a treaty, that enable non-resident members in urban areas to participate in the governance of the land-based Aboriginal community demonstrate the acceptance of the idea and provide models for future development.

CANADIAN MODELS OF ABORIGINAL ACCOMMODATION IN PUBLIC FORMS OF GOVERNMENT

The new territory of Nunavut[71] has been widely touted as a Canadian form of Aboriginal self-government. The territory is governed by a public form of government representing all its residents. The boundaries of the new territory, however, have been drawn around a population of Inuit people, who comprise about 85 per cent of its population. The Inuit people thus have, by virtue of their numerical majority, a de facto power to govern. They have no power to govern as Inuit or as representatives of the Inuit people.

The Nunavut model is a type of political and institutional accommodation of the presence of a predominant ethnic majority in a certain territory. The ostensible "self-government" goal is to permit the ethnic majority to exercise its numerical dominance at the ballot box and in the local legislative body, with the result that its preferred cultural and political values are reflected in those aspects of public life over which the local government has jurisdiction. An examination of other such public government responses to protect and promote ethnic self-government[72] may promote understanding of this Canadian political adaptation.

The creation of the province of Manitoba in 1870 was a response to the demands of the local population, whose members were mostly an indigenous people of the West, the Métis.[73] However, the Manitoba Métis model did not work. By the end of the decade, the province had been inundated by immigrants from Ontario, and the Métis had lost all political power in the public government of Manitoba.[74] Today the Métis are in court battling Canada and the province to which they gave birth over unresolved land rights.[75]

The history and mythology of the creation of Manitoba has had a profound and enduring significance in Canada,[76] but not as great as that of the creation of the province of Quebec. The province of Quebec was created out of the united province of Canada that had been created by the 1840 Act of Union. In 1867, the province with a French-speaking majority acquired legislative authority over education, culture, and most private law.[77]

Quebec's separatist movement has implications for the national project of defining the place of Aboriginal peoples within Canada, especially in the context of Aboriginal self-government. The political influence and power of Quebec is a significant factor in shaping the Canadian political context in which Aboriginal peoples can assert their group rights.

Response to the Quebec political movement shows that claims calling for "ethnic self-government" have difficulty gaining popular support in Canada. Throughout Canada's history, Quebec seems to have been the main battleground of the fight for French-Canadian nationalism,[78] although there are significant and widespread French minority populations across Canada. Recently, the traditional idea of French-Canadian nationalism has largely evaporated in the claims of a new Québécois civic[79] nationalism. Quebec's politicians have not been blind to the advantages of legal control over a territory for advancing ethnic claims and have invented the idea of a new Québécois people defined not by history, culture, and place but by Quebec's provincial boundaries, which include not only the historic English minority and all immigrants but also the Aboriginal peoples. The Québécois claims have included the rights of "peoples" at international law[80] and introduced an added layer of complexity in the public dialogue about the identity and constitutional rights of the "Aboriginal peoples."[81]

There are also important differences between the claims of Aboriginal peoples and those of contemporary Quebec sovereignist politicians. Aboriginal peoples want to join Canada and negotiate a just and appropriate place within it; they do not want to separate from Canada.[82]

It is apparent that the Nunavut model cannot be applied in many places in Canada to accommodate claims to Aboriginal self-government. Looking at the only enduring success in the Canadian experiment with public government to accommodate ethnic group claims, it would seem rather farfetched at the moment to speculate that Nunavut may in time spawn an Inuit nationalist movement akin to that of Quebec's nationalist movement which would challenge Canada's claim to Arctic sovereignty.

ABORIGINAL PARTICIPATION IN CANADA'S PUBLIC INSTITUTIONS

The history of Aboriginal participation in the Parliament of Canada begins with the story of Louis Riel, the Métis leader who was ejected from Parliament in 1873[83] and hanged for treason in 1885 for inspiring the last military stand against the Canadian annexation of the West. Riel continues to evoke strong passions. Notwithstanding enduring enmity, mainly among Ontario Orangemen, he continues to be widely viewed in Quebec as a hero in the struggle for French-speaking hegemony; some in the West view him as a historic figure battling Western alienation and domination from the East; and of course the Métis revere him as the symbol of their historic struggle for justice in Canada.

Aboriginal individuals have not participated much in Canadian public government, other than in the recent territorial public governments where Inuit people comprise the majority. An examination of the parliamentary records shows that only ten members of the Senate and sixteen members of the House of Commons have identified themselves or been identified as Aboriginals since 1867.[84]

In Manitoba, the current government party counts four Aboriginal members, including the Speaker[85] and two cabinet ministers.[86] This is an exceptional situation which may in time help us understand the prospects for advancing Aboriginal issues through the participation of Aboriginals in Canadian government institutions.

Recommendations such as that for Aboriginal federal seats made by the Royal Commission on Electoral Reform and Party Financing,[87] and that of the Royal Commission on Aboriginal Peoples for an Advisory Aboriginal Parliament on the Scandinavian model,[88] have received little support from Aboriginal political organizations and are not being implemented.

CONCLUSION

The dominion of Canada over the Aboriginal peoples is having to give way to new policies compelled by modern principles that require a sharing of governing authority and capacity within a condominium of Canada. These principles are derived from domestic constitutional amendments and judicial activism, and from evolving norms in the international law of human rights.

The views of the old era that saw Aboriginal peoples as a "problem to be solved at the best price" must give way to national institutions that seek reconciliation and reconstruction of the historic nations upon which Canada was built. We are all in the same boat metaphorically speaking, and no one should be heard to say "Oh, the leak is in their end of the boat."[89]

A national forum must produce a national framework of principles to guide the negotiation of treaties with representatives of individual nations. Democratic and constitutional principles recognize the right of each distinct "people" to determine for itself the nature and scope of its "public interest" in accordance with respect for human rights. At another level, although globalization tempts us to look away from regional and ethnic pressures, they are imperatives that must not be ignored.[90]

There are significant challenges to the implementation of a vision of Canada as a North American multinational country, some of which have been briefly considered here, but it is in everyone's interest that we strive for accommodation. Our common interests oblige us to accommodate our differences.

NOTES

1 In its 1989 report, the Canadian Human Rights Commission commented that "if there is any single issue on which Canada cannot hold its head high in the international community, any single area in which we can be accused of falling down on our obligations, it is in the area of aboriginal

relations," Canadian Human Rights Commission, *Annual Report 1989* (Ottawa: Minister of Supply and Services, 1990), 15. See also Ronald Wardhaugh, *Language and Nationhood: The Canadian Experience* (Vancouver: New Star Books, 1983), chap. 10. The Aboriginal population of Canada numbers less than a million people, or about 3 per cent of the total population.

2 The best historical account is probably J.E. Chamberlin, *The Harrowing of Eden: White Attitudes Toward Native Americans* (New York: The Seabury Press, 1975). The preamble to the *Constitution Act, 1867* provides that the Constitution of Canada is to be "similar in Principle to that of the United Kingdom."

3 See generally Brian Slattery, *The Land Rights of Aboriginal Canadian Peoples, as Affected by the Crown's Acquisition of Their Territories* (Saskatoon: College of Law, University of Saskatchewan, 1979).

4 The term "indigenous peoples" is generally used in the international context, but in Canada the constitutional provision that protects the rights of the indigenous peoples uses the term "Aboriginal peoples." The latter term will be used here; it includes the Indian, Métis, and Inuit peoples who are expressly mentioned in section 35 of the Constitution Act, 1982.

5 The term "condominium" refers more commonly to "the joint control of a State's affairs by other States" (*Concise Oxford Dictionary*, 8th ed. [Oxford: Clarendon Press, 1990], 238), but its core meaning of "a joint control" *(Gage Canadian Dictionary* [Toronto: Gage Publishing Ltd., 1983], 244) is adopted here for the purpose of illustrating a central idea of this chapter.

6 Editorial and other commentaries that attack the idea of Aboriginal self-government as undemocratic and unprincipled are very frequently published in Canadian newspapers and seem to be on the increase in recent years. For example, Henry Srebrnik, an associate professor of political studies at the University of Prince Edward Island, has written "Can special rights and entitlements for Aboriginal peoples be reconciled with liberal democratic values that entail equal individual rights, including the right to govern, for all citizens of a state?" ("The Fiji Coup: A cautionary tale," *National Post*, 30 May 2000). This article, like others of its ilk, contains errors of fact, including the assertions that "many native reserves [sic] ... are already de facto aboriginal statelets" and that "the Assembly of First Nations (AFN) functions as a legislative body, invested with legitimacy by natives and non-natives alike." In fact, Indian "bands" on Indian reserves have only a few powers of local government, which are enumerated in the federal Indian Act, while the AFN is a government-funded political representative group comprised of the chiefs of all the Indian bands created by federal law. The AFN has no powers to legislate and does not make decisions that are binding upon bands.

7 Roger Gibbins, "Constitutional Politics," in *Canadian Politics,* 3rd ed., ed. James Bickerton and Alain-G. Gagnon (Peterborough: Ontario Broadview Press, 1999), 263.

8 This point is discussed in Paul L.A.H. Chartrand, "Aboriginal Self-Government: The Two Sides of Legitimacy," in *How Ottawa Spends: A More Democratic Canada ... ?* ed. Susan D. Phillips (Ottawa: Carleton University Press, 1993), 231–56.

9 J.R. Miller, ed., *Sweet Promises: A Reader on Indian-White Relations in Canada* (Toronto: University of Toronto Press, 1991).

10 See Chamberlin, *The Harrowing of Eden*; and Sarah Carter, "Two Acres and a Plough: Peasant, Farming for the Indians of the Northwest, 1889–1897," in Miller, *Sweet Promises*, 353. The underlying objective of keeping Aboriginal people in a peasant economic status is evident not only in the historical provisions of the Indian Act that prohibited free trade between Indian reserves and the rest of the world, as is discussed in Carter's article, but also in judicially developed policy. Examples include the Mitchell Tax Case (*Mitchell v. Peguis Indian Band* [1990] 2 SCR 85), which ruled that no commercial advantage is to be gained by Indians from an Indian Act tax exemption applicable on reserves, and the recent Marshall treaty case that limits Mic Mac commerce to results in a "modest livelihood" (*R. v. Marshall* [1999] 4 CNLR 161 (SCC)).

11 This struggle between the ethnic nationalism of the French Canadian population and the competing notion of a new single Canadian identity based largely upon an English cultural and political tradition is an important part of the history of Canada. There is a voluminous literature on this topic; see, for example, Thomas S. Axworthy and Pierre E. Trudeau, eds, *Towards a Just Society: The Trudeau Years* (Toronto: Penguin Books, 1992).

12 Paul Joffe, "Assessing the Delgamuukw Principles: National Implications and Potential Effects in Quebec," *McGill Law Journal* 45 (2000): 155–208; James Crawford, ed., *The Rights of Peoples* (Oxford: The Clarendon Press, 1988).

13 Crawford, *The Rights of Peoples.*

14 Paul L.A.H. Chartrand, "Aboriginal Self-Government: Towards a Vision of Canada as a North American Multinational Country," in *Issues in the North,* vol. 2, ed. Jill Oakes and Rick Riewe (Winnipeg: Canadian Circumpolar Institute and Department of Native Studies, University of Manitoba, 1997), 81–6.

15 Section 35 of the Constitution Act, 1982. See also note 4.

16 "First Ministers" means the prime minister of Canada, the premier of each province, and the leader of each territory.

17 See, for example, David C. Hawkes and Marina Devine, "Meech Lake and Elijah Harper: Native-State Relations in the 1990s," in *How Ottawa Spends 1991–1992: The Politics of Fragmentation,* ed. Frances

Abele (Ottawa: Carleton University Press, 1991), 33; Alain-G. Gagnon, "Quebec's Constitutional Odyssey," in Bickerton and Gagnon, *Canadian Politics*, 279.

18 18 Canada, House of Commons, *The Summer of 1990: Fifth Report of the Standing Committee on Aboriginal Affairs* (May 1991).

19 See Peter Hogg, *Constitutional Law of Canada,* student ed. (Toronto: Carswell, 1998), 65–9.

20 Shin Imai, *Aboriginal Law Handbook* (Toronto: Carswell, 1993), 67–70. Hogg believes that the agreement by all first ministers that the Aboriginal peoples have an inherent right of self-government "should probably be regarded as an informal recognition that the right exists now, albeit in inchoate form, despite the failure to ratify the express declaration to that effect in the Accord" (*Constitutional Law of Canada*, 596).

21 Will Kymlicka argues that traditional liberal philosophy allows for Aboriginal self-government: *Multicultural Citizenship: A Liberal Theory of Minority Rights* (Oxford: Clarendon Press, 1995). See also the articles in Joseph E. Magnet, *Constitutional Law of Canada*, 7th ed., vol. 2 (Edmonton: Juriliber, 1998), and specifically "The Charter of Rights and Aboriginal Peoples." The most persistent critic of Aboriginal rights, who uses liberal ideas as a launching pad for his attacks, is Gordon Gibson. For an example of his misconceived views, some of which are rebutted in this chapter, see "A Separate Political Class," *National Post*, 27 July 2000, in which he criticizes the *Campbell* decision.

22 *R v. Sparrow* [1990] 1 SCR 1075.

23 Alan Cairns, *Citizens Plus: Aboriginal Peoples and the Canadian State* (Vancouver: University of British Columbia Press, 2000).

24 Group rights are necessary because they protect Aboriginal peoples from the erosion of their communities' integrity by the exercise of state power in the promotion of the general public interest. This requires little coercive authority of the Aboriginal group vis-à-vis its own members, and in theory does not pit group rights against individual rights. The rights of the Aboriginal group protect the interests of the Aboriginal group against the competing interests of the general public interest.

25 See Chartrand, "Aboriginal Self-Government."

26 See Michael Ignatieff, *Blood and Belonging: Journeys into the New Nationalism* (Toronto: Penguin Books, 1994); and R.L. Barsh and J.Y. Henderson, *The Road: Indian Tribes and Political Liberty* (Berkeley: University of California Press, 1980).

27 See Joffe, "Assessing the Delgamuukw Principles" and Brian Slattery, "Making Sense of Aboriginal and Treaty Rights," *Canadian Bar Review* 79 (2000): 196–224.

28 The rights are Canadian in the sense that they are Canadian legal and constitutional constructs and do not necessarily reflect the concepts of Aboriginal societies about "rights" concepts. The evolving doctrine

is discussed in Hogg, *Constitutional Law* and in James Y. Henderson, Marjorie L. Benson and Isobel M. Findlay, *Aboriginal Tenure in the Constitution of Canada* (Toronto: Carswell, 2000), 316 ff. See also Paul L.A.H. Chartrand, "On the Aboriginal Rights Dialogue," in *Ideas in Action: Essays on Politics and Law in Honour of Peter Russell*, ed. Joseph F. Fletcher (Toronto: University of Toronto Press, 1999), 75.

29 See Henderson, Benson, and Findlay, *Aboriginal Tenure*, 313, where the St. Catherine's Milling Case is discussed.

30 Slattery, "Making Sense of Aboriginal and Treaty Rights."

31 This is also true of New Zealand and African countries. American jurisprudence, on the other hand, developed a doctrine of Indian political rights in the first half of the nineteenth century; see Felix S. Cohen, *Handbook of Federal Indian Law* (Washington, D.C.: United States Government Printing Office, 1942). Only recently have Australian courts begun to articulate a domestic theory of Aboriginal rights, and their analysis is significantly different from that of Canadian courts. On the Australian law, see Richard H. Bartlett, *Native Title in Australia* (Sydney: Butterworth's, 2000).

32 See *R v. Van der Peet* [1991] 4 CNLR 177 (SCC).

33 It has already been established that Aboriginal rights are communal in nature. For those rights to have any substance, there must be an effective institution of community governance to safeguard and administer them. The individual enjoyment of the community rights must be subject to the regulatory authority of the community. The community rights are in essence a legal aspect of community relations, and individuals cannot have authority to regulate the relations between community members.

34 Kent McNeil, "Aboriginal Rights in Canada: From Title to Land to Territorial Sovereignty," *Tulsa Journal of Comparative and International Law* 5 (1998): 253–98; Hogg, *Constitutional Law*, 576; Kymlicka, *Multicultural Citizenship;* and Peter Hogg and Mary Ellen Turpel, "Implementing Aboriginal Self-Government: Constitutional and Jurisdictional Issues," *Canadian Bar Review* 74 (1995): 187–224; and the sources cited in Joffe, "Assessing the Delgamuukw Principles."

35 Canada, *Report of the Royal Commission on Aboriginal Peoples,* vol. 2 (Ottawa: Canada Communication Group, 1996), 184 ff.

36 Joffe, "Assessing the Delgamuukw Principles"; Barbara Hocking, ed. *International Law and Aboriginal Human Rights* (Sydney: Law Book Co., 1988); Alison Quentin-Baxter, "The International and Constitutional Law Contexts," in *Recognizing the Rights of Indigenous Peoples* (Wellington, New Zealand: Institute of Policy Studies, 1998), 22.

37 *Campbell v. A.G. B.C.* [2000] 4 CNLR 1; *Eastmain Band v. Gilpin* [1987] 3 CNLR 54, at 67. CSP (Q).

38 *Indian Act*, RSC 1985, c.I-5.

39 The leading case is *Reference Re Secession of Quebec* [1998] 2 SCR 217, where the other authorities are discussed.

40 *Secession Reference,* citing the *Reference re Remuneration of Judges* [1997] 3 SCR 3.

41 Ibid, para. 32. See also *Reference Re Amendment of the Constitution of Canada* [1981] 1 SCR 753, at 874 where it is said that the constitution of Canada includes "the global system of rules and principles which govern the exercise of constitutional authority in the whole and every part of the Canadian state."

42 P.H. Russell, "The Supreme Court Ruling, A Lesson in Democracy," *Cité Libre*, English ed., 26, no. 4 (1998): 30. See also the discussion in Joffe, "Assessing the Delgamuukw Principles"; and Andrew Orkin and Joanna Birkenbaum, "The Aboriginal Argument: the Requirement of Aboriginal Consent," and Paul Joffe, "Quebec Secession and the Aboriginal Peoples: Important Signals from the Supreme Court," both in *The Quebec Decision* (Toronto: James Lorimer and Co., 1999), 83 and 137, respectively; Henderson, Benson and Findlay, *Aboriginal Tenure,* chap. 29.

43 *Secession Reference,* note 34, supra, para 54.

44 On the meaning of a "people," Joffe in "Assessing the Delgamuukw Principles" writes that "while there is no legal definition of what constitutes a 'people,' the practice of the United Nations is to retain a very broad meaning of the term for questions pertaining to self-determination. Both objective elements (e.g., common language, history, culture, race or ethnicity, way of life and territory) and subjective elements (the will of a particular group to identify and assert its existence as a people) have been identified." See also M.J. Bryant, "Aboriginal Self-Determination: The Status of Canadian Aboriginal Peoples at International Law," *Saskatchewan Law Review* 56 (1992): 267–96.

45 The unwritten principles relied upon are discussed in Joffe, "Assessing the Delgamuukw Principles" and in Henderson, Benson and Findlay, *Aboriginal Tenure.*

46 Henderson, Benson and Findlay, *Aboriginal Tenure,* 448–9.

47 See the authorities and discussion of the law in Jack Woodward, *Native Law,* loose leaf ed. (Toronto: Carswell, n.d.), section 3.5 "Protective and Fiduciary obligations of Federal Crown."

48 *Federal Policy Guide. Aboriginal Self-Government: The Government of Canada's Approach to Implementation of the Inherent Right and the Negotiation of Aboriginal Self-Government* (Ottawa: Minister of Public Works and Government Services Canada, 1995).

49 The text of the Nisga'a Treaty and related information are available at <http://www.aaf.gov.bc.ca/aaf/treaty/nisgaa/>.

50 See *R. v. Marshall*, [1999] 4 CNLR 161–212 and the Court's written response to an application for a re-hearing and a stay by the West Nova Fishermen's Coalition delivered on 17 November 1999, 301–23.

51 The Nisga'a Treaty is discussed in Christopher McKee, *Treaty Talks in British Columbia: Negotiating a Mutually Beneficial Future,* 2d ed. (Vancouver: University of British Columbia Press, 2000); Douglas Sanders, "'We Intend to live here forever': A Primer on the Nisga'a Treaty," *University of British Columbia Law Review* 33 (2000): 103–28; and Paul Rynard, "'*Welcome In, But Check Your Rights at the Door*': The James Bay and Nisga'a Agreements in Canada," *Canadian Journal of Political Science* 33 (2000): 211–43.

52 This is the way the money payments are explained by the judge in *Campbell v. A.G. B.C.* [2000] 4 CNLR 1, at 10, per Williamson, J.

53 The Treaty nevertheless specifies that the rights it sets out comprise a "full and final settlement in respect of the Aboriginal rights" of the Nisga'a Nation (chap. 2, art. 22), and that any Aboriginal rights that might survive the agreement are "released" to Canada (art. 26). This appears to have the same effect as an extinguishment provision. For a review of the doctrine of extinguishment and the Royal Commission's recommendations for abandoning it in the context of treaty negotiations, see Royal Commission on Aboriginal Peoples, *Treaty Making in the Spirit of Coexistence: An Alternative to Extinguishment* (Ottawa: Minister of Supply and Services Canada, 1996).

54 *Yukon First Nations Self-Government Act.* SC 1994, c. 35, as amended. Information about the Yukon Agreements is available at <www.ainc-inac.gc.ca>. I acknowledge the helpful discussion on various aspects of the modern treaties with Professor Brad Morse of the University of Ottawa.

55 *Campbell v. A.G. B.C.* [2000] 4 CNLR 1.

56 Aboriginal representatives have expressed concern that increased immigration will lead to a lessened appreciation of the historical rights of Aboriginal peoples and have recommended that educational curricula include appropriate information.

57 Canadian Human Rights Commission, *Annual Report 1989;* see page 15, where the commission called for "a thorough-going enquiry into those problems, modelled on the Royal Commission on Bilingualism and Biculturalism of twenty-five years ago."

58 The view that Aboriginal people present problems to be bought off at the best price is a common idea in newspaper commentaries. An example is Vaughn Palmer, "Native Treaty Turmoil," *National Post,* 3 June 2000.

59 *Report of the Royal Commission on Aboriginal Peoples*, vol. 2, 177.

60 Ibid., 176.

61 *Gathering Strength: Canada's Aboriginal Action Plan* (Ottawa: Government of Canada, 7 January 1998).

62 Ibid. On the history of abuse at Indian residential schools, see John S. Milloy, *A National Crime: The Canadian Government and the Residential School System: 1879 to 1986* (Winnipeg: University of Manitoba Press, 1999); and *Report of the Royal Commission on Aboriginal Peoples*, vol. 1, 333.

63 The federal government has set up some interdepartmental committees of officials to coordinate policy in some limited areas, but the lack of policy coordination is a significant problem in the operations of Canadian governments. In the United States, each federal department is required by executive order to have an Indian "desk" or policy capacity. In Australia, the Aboriginal and Torres Strait Islanders Commission was created to help provide better and more coordinated services to Aboriginal people.

64 Table 2.1, "Comparison of Demographic Characteristics," in *Report of the Royal Commission on Aboriginal Peoples*, vol. 4, 10. See also the excellent critique of the Royal Commission's approach by Alan Cairns, *Citizens Plus*; Cairns's reference to the slight urban majority is at page 154.

65 The criticism has its parallel in arguments that responded to the call for self-determination by indigenous peoples in the international arena. There, the observation that it was easier, and incidentally more politically and economically expedient, to recognize self-determination for colonized peoples overseas led to the absurd "blue water" thesis which sought to limit the application of self-determination to overseas colonies and exclude it in respect to the so-called metropolitan territories of United Nations member states. For a discussion of the "blue water" theory in international law, see Russel L. Barsh, "Indigenous Peoples and the Right to Self-Determination in International Law," in *International Law and Aboriginal Human Rights*, ed. Barbara Hocking (Sydney: Law Book Co., 1988), 68–83, from which the information in this note is taken.

66 See note 4. See also *Consolidated Native Law Statutes, Regulations and Treaties 2000–2001* (Toronto: Carswell, 2000); the *Indian Act* is at page 1 and several of the land claims agreements legislative enactments are found between pages 219–561. Information about the Alberta Métis Settlements, and their history and governance is available in Catherine E. Bell, *Contemporary Justice: The Settlement Way* (Saskatoon: Native Law Centre, University of Saskatchewan, 1999).

67 *Report of the Royal Commission on Aboriginal Peoples*, vol. 4, 519–621.

68 This could be done either by creating an Indian reserve or by purchasing lands on the market. Some of the Indian Act's current limitations on the

creation of reserves would have to be overcome to create "nation-based" or jointly held reserves.

69 The Assembly of First Nations is composed of the chiefs of the more than 600 "Indian bands" defined and recognized by federal law. The Congress of Aboriginal Peoples represents "Indians" who are not federally registered and other Aboriginals not represented by the other national organizations. The Inuit Tapirisat of Canada represents Inuit people, and the Métis National Council represents the Métis people of Western Canada.

70 In *Corbière v. Canada (Minister of Indian and Northern Affairs)* [1999] 3 CNLR 19, the Supreme Court of Canada relied on section 15 of the Charter to strike down a provision of the Indian Act that restricted voting rights to resident band members, thereby excluding non-resident band members. The political rights at issue are created by federal legislation; they are not inherent Aboriginal rights of the Indian band, which is itself a creature of federal statute. In contrast, the Nisga'a Nation is recognized in the Nisga'a Treaty as an Aboriginal nation with an inherent right to govern itself.

71 The territory was created by the Nunavut Act, chapter N-28.6 (1993, c. 28). An agreement on the Inuit land rights in the territory was approved by Parliament in the Nunavut Land Claims Agreement Act, chapter N-28.7 (1993, c. 29) General information about Nunavut is available at <http://www.inac.gc.ca/nunavut/>.

72 For a discussion of ethnic nationalism, see Ignatieff, *Blood and Belonging*. For a discussion of the rights of minorities in respect to preservation of their culture, see Kymlicka, *Multicultural Citizenship*.

73 W.L. Morton, ed. *Manitoba: The Birth of a Province* (Winnipeg: The Manitoba Record Society Publications, 1965); Paul L.A.H. Chartrand, *Manitoba's Métis Settlement Scheme of 1870* (Saskatoon: University of Saskatchewan Native Law Centre, 1991). The most readable history of the Métis is still Joseph K. Howard's *The Strange Empire of Louis Riel* (Toronto: Swan Publishing Co., 1965).

74 Gerald Friesen, "Homeland to Hinterland: Political Transition in Manitoba, 1870 to 1979," *Canadian Historical Association Historical Papers*, (Ottawa: 1979), 33–47.

75 *Dumont v. A.G. Canada* [1998] 3 CNLR 39 (Man. CA) The case has been to the Supreme Court of Canada and sent down for trial. For a legal analysis of the issues, see Chartrand, "Manitoba's Métis."

76 Louis Riel, the Métis leader who has been recognized as the "Father of Manitoba" by the provincial legislature, is still a powerful figure in English-French relations because of the association of the Métis with the Catholic Church and the French language, and in Métis-Canada relations.

In recent years, a number of federal politicians have proposed private members' bills to exonerate Riel from the charge of treason for which he was convicted and hanged in Regina in 1885. This approach has been supported by some, and opposed by some, both among the public and among the Métis people.

77 See Hogg, *Constitutional Law of Canada,* 33–7, for a brief history of the creation of the Dominion of Canada.

78 There is a voluminous literature on the Quebec issue. Some of the different views may be found in Magnet, *Constitutional Law of Canada,* vol. 1 (Edmonton: Juriliber, 1998).

79 For a discussion of the differences between "ethnic" and "civic" nationalism, see Ignatieff, *Blood and Belonging,* 5–9. On ethnic identity and conflict, see Lola Romanucci-Ross and George DeVos, eds, *Ethnic Identity: Creation, Conflict, and Accommodation* (London: Altamira Press, 1995).

80 See Royal Commission on Aboriginal Peoples, *Canada's Fiduciary Obligations to Aboriginal Peoples in the Context of Accession to Sovereignty by Quebec,* vol. 1 (Ottawa: Minister of Supply and Services, 1995).

81 See Joffe, "Assessing the Delgamuukw Principles," 202, where it is explained that certain Quebec politicians have taken the position that the collective will of Quebecers prevails over the rule of law.

82 This point is different from the claim that Canada's assumption of jurisdiction over Aboriginal peoples is illegitimate. It is directed to the intention of Aboriginal peoples in the exercise of their right of self-determination. It is future-oriented and not concerned with the separate issues of legitimization of the past or rejection of the present.

83 Maggie Siggins, *Riel: A Life of Revolution* (Toronto: Harper-Collins Publishers Ltd, 1994), 227 ff.

84 Prior to the 2000 election, the House of Commons record listed one Inuk, three Métis, and one Indian. In previous Parliaments, there had been three Inuit, four Métis, and three Indian MPs. In mid-2000 there were two Inuit, two Métis, and one Indian senator. Previously, there had been no Inuit or Métis senators and four Indian senators (information from the Library of Parliament, Information and Documentation Branch). See the discussion of the limited participation in Canadian politics by Aboriginal people in *Report of the Royal Commission on Aboriginal Peoples,* vol. 2, 375–7.

85 George Hickes, a distinguished Inuk member of the New Democratic Party that currently governs the province.

86 Eric Robinson is minister of Aboriginal Affairs, and Oscar Lathlin, a member of the Treasury Board, is minister for Conservation.

87 See *The Path to Electoral Equality*, published by the Committee for Aboriginal Electoral Reform, which contains the committee's recommendations to the commission (n.d.; n.p.).

88 *Report of the Royal Commission on Aboriginal Peoples*, vol. 2, 377–9.

89 This comment is attributed to Miles Richardson, a Haida and Chief Commissioner of the B.C. Treaty Commission, in Millar, "Sweet Promises," 465.

90 See Kaplan, *The Ends of the Earth*.

Mäori in Governance: Parliament, Statutory Recognition, and the State Sector

MASON DURIE

Unlike during the early colonial period, when paternalistic Crown protection did not permit direct participation in directing the affairs of the new state, the Mäori of New Zealand are now explicitly involved in several spheres of governance. The increased levels of Mäori participation have mirrored not only dynamic change within the nation but also transformations elsewhere as indigenous peoples the world over have sought new relationships with states and more decisive roles in decision-making.

As part of that process there has been a re-evaluation of the rationale for fair representation, greater awareness of the privileges conferred by treaties, a corresponding acknowledgement of the rights of under-represented groups, and increasing concern about disparities between groups who live side by side but have endured quite different levels of well-being. Sometimes those distinctions have been blurred so that indigenous relationships with the state have been variously interpreted on demographic, historic, socio-economic, or democratic grounds. Often they are all relevant, although any special indigenous claim to participation in governance cannot be entirely explained as a function of minority status or disparities in living standards.

In the New Zealand context, Mäori involvement in governance is not new: four Mäori seats were established in the House of Representatives in 1867; two Mäori members were appointed to the Legislative Council in 1872; and Mäori participation in government departments at senior levels occurred as early as 1900 when Dr Maui Pomare was appointed "Medical Officer to the Mäoris." Over the past two decades, however, Mäori participation in governance has entered a new phase, not only as to the numbers involved and the positions held, but also in the opportunities to assert a more decisive influence on policy and on the institutions of state themselves. In the new era, Mäori participation depends less on adapting and conforming to institutional conventions than on challenging accepted norms and standards to better reflect New Zealand's cultural and social mix. Moreover, there is an acceptance, however tentative, that Mäori should decide Mäori policy and that New Zealand's governing bodies should play a positive role in encouraging Mäori leadership.

While progress in that direction has been significant, or perhaps because it has been significant, the relatively high levels of Mäori involvement in governance have exposed new sets of tensions that raise uncertainties about the underlying rationale and pose challenges for future consideration. First, the increased Mäori presence has inevitably led to greater potential for conflict between the objectives of the state and Mäori aspirations. Second, views are divided as to whether the Mäori position is best served by integration within the institutions of state or by the establishment of a Mäori focus somewhat removed from the state. Third, is the exercise fundamentally about equal opportunities to ensure proportional representation, is it about achieving the best outcomes for Mäori, or is it about the exercise of a constitutional right?

These issues can be illustrated by considering Mäori membership in Parliament, the protection of Mäori interests in statute, and Mäori participation in the state sector. Four phases of representation can be identified. First, there was an initial absence of any representation of Mäori. Second, when Mäori representation was accepted in Parliament, the law, and within the state, it took place in an otherwise conventional system of governance that made few concessions to Mäori cultural values and fewer still to aspirations for autonomy, and the governance was strongly influenced by an overriding assumption that assimilation would be the not- too-distant outcome. A third phase saw more dynamic participation, with the explicit recognition of Mäori customary and treaty rights and an expectation that a Mäori dimension would take its place alongside the conventional instruments of state. The fourth phase has yet to happen. If it does, it will see a move away from an emphasis on participation within a single system to a fuller exploration of the theme of partnership.

CONTEXT

In order to better understand Mäori participation in governance, it is important to explore three contexts that give some shape to the New

Zealand situation: the Treaty of Waitangi, Mäori demographic trends, and positive Mäori development. All three are relevant to issues of representation, although it is not always clear whether one provides more rationale for change than the others.

The Treaty of Waitangi

After nearly 100 years of legal and political dismissal, the Treaty of Waitangi is now accorded greater respect as a source of constitutional rights for Mäori. Signed in 1840 by Britain and most tribes, the treaty provided for British governance, certain guarantees to the tribes relating to properties and (at least in the Mäori version) to continuing tribal authority, and the conferment of citizenship rights on individual Mäori people. In the early years, the treaty and its lofty goals were taken seriously by the Crown so that, when Governor Fitzroy took it upon himself to alter the terms of the treaty, in *R.* v. *Symonds* the court made it clear that the treaty was more than a convenient instrument of annexation: it was binding on the Crown.[1] However, in 1877 a claim by the Ngäti Toa tribe to land previously gifted to the Church of England led the Supreme Court to quite a different view (*Wi Parata v. Bishop of Wellington*). The treaty, said the judges, was "a simple nullity."[2] Although contested by the Privy Council in 1902, the decision offered some comfort to the government and largely dissipated any sense of a treaty fetter, especially in the acquisition of land.

By 1975, however, governments were less inclined to dismiss indigenous claims to traditional rights or to argue, as the court had in the *Wi Parata* case, that cession of sovereignty spelled an end to aboriginal title. New Zealand followed the international trend, not simply to comply with global pressures but because Mäori agitation was forceful. A respected Mäori leader, Whina Cooper (later Dame Whina), led a march of some 5,000 from the far north to Parliament where a Memorial of Rights was presented to the prime minister petitioning the government to cease unjust alienation of Mäori land.[3] In that same year the rehabilitation of the treaty commenced with the passage of the Treaty of Waitangi Act and the establishment of a tribunal to investigate grievances against the Crown where there had been a breach of Treaty principles. Since then some 780 claims have been lodged and wider acknowledgement of the treaty has led to its recognition in legislation, policy, and resource management. In 1986 there was also recognition of the treaty's relevance to social and economic domains.[4]

A commitment to the treaty by the fourth Labour government in 1984 gave it greatly increased prominence across the range of government activities and ushered in a Mäori constitutional revolution.[5]

Mäori were asking for, as a Treaty of Waitangi right, a greater say in the affairs of the nation, more control over their own resources, and a greater share of the nation's resources. Moreover, the Waitangi Tribunal and the courts were developing treaty jurisprudence that positioned Mäori rights within a treaty framework and, at least in two cases, used the treaty as an aid for the interpretation of the law.[6] A change of government did not reduce the momentum, although the focus shifted towards the settlement of historic grievances and introduced an element of uncertainty about the treaty and social policy.[7] But by then the treaty discourse had become germane to the courts and legislators, and there was no real inclination to return to the rhetoric of a simple nullity, even though public attitudes were generally less than sympathetic.[8] Former prime minister Sir Geoffrey Palmer concluded that "for all its humble beginnings and its inconsistencies, the Treaty of Waitangi is now firmly embedded in the legal and constitutional firmament and is unlikely to be dislodged."[9] The politics of Mäori participation had shifted from a debate on Mäori inclusion within a conventional colonial system to participating as Mäori and the recognition of a Mäori dimension as an integral part of the New Zealand norm.

Mäori Demographic Trends

Quite apart from any status conferred by the Treaty of Waitangi, the position of Mäori in New Zealand is increasingly determined by demographic realities. Even though changes to the definition of Mäori have made it difficult to make comparisons over time, there is strong evidence of a substantial and sustained increase in the Mäori population since 1900.

For the past two censuses, it has been possible to determine the number of people descended from a Mäori as well as the number who choose to identify themselves as Mäori. Both are valid measures, although identity is regarded as the more meaningful measure. In 1991, for example, some 511,278 claimed Mäori descent while only 434,847 identified themselves as Mäori. In the 1996 census the differential was again present. A total of 579,714 people indicated they were descended from a Mäori, though only 85 percent, 523,374, actually identified themselves as Mäori[10] (see Table 1 below). The difference between the two figures is significant. If self-identification is the only basis for determining ethnicity, then 56,340 people descended from a Mäori are not regarded as Mäori even though their health (and other) problems are more like those of the Mäori than the Päkehä (non-Maöri).

Mäori population growth was the most striking feature of the 1991–96 inter-census period; it increased by more than 20 per cent while the

Table 1: Mäori descent and ethnic populations

Census Year	*Mäori Descent Population*		*Mäori Ethnic Population*	
	Numbers	*Total NZ Population (%)*	*Numbers*	*Total NZ Population (%)*
1991	511,278	15	434,841	13
1996	579,714	16	523,374	15
2051			993,000	22

Source: Statistics New Zealand

national increase was 7 per cent. The trend will continue. Although accounting for some 15 per cent in 1996, by 2051 the Mäori ethnic population will almost double in size to close to one million, or 22 per cent of New Zealand's population. Even more dramatic, by 2051, 33 per cent of all children in the country will be Mäori, and Mäori of age to work (fifteen to sixty-four years) will increase by 85 per cent.[11]

But for now Mäori are a youthful population, with the number of people under fifteen years of age accounting for some 37 per cent of the total Mäori population, and the median age being 21.6 years. While for New Zealand as a whole the proportion of people fifteen to nineteen years old is declining, the 46,584 Mäori youths represent 20 per cent of the Mäori population, and Mäori constitute 14 per cent of the total number of people in that age group.[12] By 2006 Mäori will make up a quarter of New Zealand's school-age population. Although the younger age groups will continue to grow, the population will begin to age quite rapidly, with the proportion of men and women over sixty-five increasing from 3 per cent in 1996 to 13 per cent in 2051.

Like many New Zealanders, Mäori are mobile. Following the Second World War, urbanization resulted in major migrations from country areas to towns and cities. By 1976 more than 80 per cent of Mäori were living in urban settings, a quarter in the greater Auckland area. While there has been a slow increase in the Mäori population in the South Island, more than half are still living in Auckland, Waikato, or Bay of Plenty Regional Council areas. In some regions Mäori make up a significant proportion of the population – 45 per cent in the Gisborne region and 32 per cent in Northland. Emigration overseas has also become a significant trend, with some 30,000 Mäori now being recorded as residents in Australia. More recently still, there has been a shift in internal migratory patterns away from urban areas, where unemployment is high, back to tribal areas such as Northland, from where grandparents had moved some thirty or forty years earlier.[13]

Demographic patterns clearly indicate that the Mäori population is both dynamic and diverse. Younger, urban Mäori, now three or more generations removed from their own traditional lands, their *turangawaewae*, face quite different challenges from their cohorts who have remained close to tribal lands and resources. Migration to other regions, or overseas to find work, has added to the complexity of associations and affiliations that must inevitably characterize a highly mobile population. In that process, the meaning of "being Mäori" has also changed, and there is currently discussion about the place of tribes alongside urban collectives. Central to the debate is whether Mäori resources are best developed and distributed through tribal systems or through regional systems configured around urban institutions closer to where Mäori actually live.

Positive Mäori Development

In 1984, and for reasons beyond the scope of this paper, the process of dismantling the welfare state began, and was initiated, ironically, by the same political party that had established it. The new free market approach required radical restructuring of the economy, a reduction in state expenditure, deregulation, and wherever possible the introduction of competition. Driven by economic expediencies that included the removal of state subsidies for the agricultural and forestry sectors, "temporary" stress on all New Zealanders was seen as inevitable. Mäori, however, carried more than their fair share of the burden. Overnight, Mäori unemployment skyrocketed to more than 20 per cent. It remains unacceptably high at 18 per cent and is higher still for school leavers.[14]

But just as the welfare state had a downside for Mäori, the free market environment had unexpected benefits. The Mäori 1984 Economic Summit meeting, the *Hui Taumata*, prescribed a decade of positive Mäori development premised on the themes of tribal development, economic self-reliance, social equity, and cultural affirmation. The new call was for "Mäori solutions to Mäori problems." Both the lack of confidence in the capacity of the state to offer positive solutions and a desire to capitalize on existing Mäori structures and values combined to inject a sense of independence and renewed commitment to alternate approaches. Significantly, a sound economic base was seen as a crucial step towards achieving any real social or even cultural survival.

As part of the restructuring of the Mäori world a range of organizations evolved. Many were based on tribes, though they were not necessarily traditional; nor did they always have full tribal support. Since the onset of urbanization, tribal structures had diminished in importance, except for cultural matters, and there was a lack of experience in tribal economic and social development. There were the inevitable disagreements between tribes about boundaries, prior claims, and previous agreements, but competition within tribes also developed. Debate about which particular group had the authority to advance tribal interests, and to vie for government funds, often led to more than one body claiming the mandate. For government agencies it was confusing, though to some extent the problem had been created by hastily imposed government policies that had emphasized structures at the expense of relationships.

Two implications of these and other developments should be emphasized. First, it has become increasingly clear that Mäori reject the notion of assimilation and, with it, the concept of universality. Instead, the expectation now is that all Mäori young people should be able to grow up as Mäori. If that choice is not available, or if economic circumstances forbid access to Mäori structures and indeed the culture itself, then disadvantage has occurred.

The second point arising from a decade of positive Mäori development is the desire of Mäori people to develop their own economic and social systems in ways that are consistent with Mäori aspirations and priorities. While the state as a provider had certain attractions, seldom was it inclined to recognize Mäori preferences. In contrast, large numbers of Mäori health, education, and social service providers are now creating effective links with Mäori networks and are enabling families *(whänau)*, communities, and tribes to steer their own canoes. The trend is also consistent with article 21 of the Draft Declaration of the Rights of Indigenous Peoples: "Indigenous peoples have the right to maintain and develop their political, economic and social systems, to be secure in the enjoyment of their own means of subsistence and development, and to engage freely in all their traditional and other economic activities. Indigenous peoples who have been deprived of their means of subsistence and development are entitled to just and fair compensation."[15]

MÄORI IN PARLIAMENT

Although four seats were set aside for Mäori under the Mäori Representation Act 1867, the motives for their establishment were complex. On a per capita basis some fourteen or fifteen seats might have been expected, though it is unlikely that proportionality was a significant consideration. Donald McLean, who sponsored the bill, saw it as a peace measure, probably a temporary expedience until assimilation had become a reality.[16] In any event the Mäori seats were tolerated, though not welcomed, and as early Mäori politicians James Carroll and Maui Pomare were to discover, it would be some decades before a holder of a Mäori seat could gain full ministerial rank.[17] At the same time, although their electorates were geographically large and difficult to manage, the fact that Mäori were in Parliament as representatives of their own people was in itself highly significant. Some achieved high standing. Maui Pomare, for example, was minister of health in 1922, and Apirana Ngata was native minister from 1928 to 1934 and deputy prime minister as well.

In 1935 all four Mäori seats were held by the Independent Ratana movement. With a promise of political power sharing, the Ratana members joined the Labour government to serve under Michael Joseph Savage. It was a coalition of convenience, guaranteeing strong Labour support for Mäori causes in return for increasing the Labour majority.[18] Mäori had held the balance of power.[19] But the alliance had serious consequences. Because the seats were assured for Labour, many Mäori voters opted out of the Mäori roll and onto the general roll so that they could exert political muscle in marginal seats. Further, the strong Labour emphasis on state provision and social security created a sense that the Mäori seats were about social inequalities and tacit support for the welfare state. The National Party, whether in opposition or in government, had less time for the philosophy of welfarism and for the four seats, and from time to time advocated their abolition. The National view was that because there were two or three National Mäori members of Parliament representing general seats, the need for separate Mäori seats was outmoded. Mäori participation rather than Mäori representation appeared to be its main concern. In the event, because of expected Mäori opposition, no attempt to disestablish the seats actually occurred.[20]

Mäori confidence in the parliamentary system gained a new lease of life after the introduction of Mixed-Member Proportional Representation (MMP). As first presented, MMP would have led to the abolition of the four Mäori seats. The Royal Commission on the Electoral System had concluded that a Mäori party would provide adequate safeguards for Mäori and the four seats would therefore be redundant.[21] When the Electoral Reform Bill was drafted it therefore made no provision for the four Mäori seats. Widespread Mäori indignation followed, the abolition of the seats being seen as an erosion of an established constitutional convention.[22] The result was the reinstatement of dedicated Mäori seats, without very much debate, but with a new formula for deciding the number of seats. Whereas previously the number of seats had been fixed at four, regardless of the total Mäori population or the number of voters, under the Electoral Reform

Act 1993, the number of seats would be a function of the number of people enrolled on the Mäori roll.

Now there was some incentive to focus on the Mäori roll. It had been estimated that there were more Mäori enrolled on the general roll than the Mäori roll and that a substantial number, perhaps 50,000, were on neither roll. After a campaign to increase awareness of the new provisions and to provide information on MMP, there was a significant increase in the number of voters enrolled on the Mäori roll so that five seats were contested in the first MMP election in 1996 and six in 1999. By then, about equal numbers or Mäori voters were on the Mäori and the general rolls.

After the 1996 election, the potential of the five Mäori members to carry the balance of power was felt. Although not billed as a Mäori party, New Zealand First captured all five Mäori seats. The party's subsequent position of strength as a coalition partner was due entirely to the Mäori bloc. In addition, a further nine Mäori had entered Parliament as list members and one Mäori represented a general electorate. With 15 members in a 120-member House, and 4 Mäori appointed to the cabinet, Mäori political might had dawned. There had been some prior discussion about a Mäori caucus within Parliament so that on issues important to Mäori a unified approach might be taken. In the event, party allegiances prevented any serious agreements. But even by the end of the three-year term, party allegiances had also been eroded; New Zealand First all but collapsed as four of the five Mäori members left its ranks in search of a new home. A hastily put together party, Mauri Pacific, failed to make a showing and all five Mäori members lost their seats. Their time in Parliament, however, had not been fruitless. As a result largely of Mäori insistence, access to the Privy Council had been retained, the fiscal cap on Treaty of Waitangi settlements had been lifted, the Ngai Tahu Settlement was approved, and the government accepted responsibility for the reduction of socio-economic disparities between Mäori and non-Mäori.

The 1996 experience had convinced Labour that success in the next MMP election would depend on voters in the Mäori electorates, and political overtures were successfully made to Mäori. In 1999 all six Mäori electorate representatives were elected to Parliament within the bosom of Labour. This time a Labour-Alliance coalition formed the government and again there were four Mäori cabinet ministers. There were also further demonstrations of Mäori political influence. When the government was auctioning third generation radio frequency spectrums, the Mäori members were adamant that one-quarter of the spectrum should be offered to Mäori, initially on the basis that the Waitangi Tribunal had recognized the spectrum as a developmental property right to which Mäori were entitled.[23] The previous National government had simply dismissed the claim, but under pressure the current Labour government awarded a spectrum share to Mäori, not because it was a property right but because it was one way in which the disparities between Mäori and non-Mäori could be reduced. The Mäori members of Parliament had brokered the deal.

Despite concerns that the MMP system would not guarantee increased accountability to Mäori,[24] the limited MMP experience suggests that Mäori are now better served than under the first-past-the-post system. However, three important points need to be highlighted. The first is that, without the designated Mäori seats, Mäori influence within the system would be diffuse and unfocused. The significance of the seats does not stem from any increase in the number of Mäori members in Parliament but from the capacity for dedicated representation of Mäori. A Mäori member of Parliament is not the same as a Mäori member who represents a Mäori electorate. The second point is that a single Mäori party capable of capturing the six or more seats(depending on the number of voters on the Mäori roll) could lead to a Mäori coalition partner that did indeed hold the balance of power. Mäori opinion is divided on that matter. Party loyalties run deep, and there is some worry about entering the House as a minority player rather than with a major party. The third point, however, is that the Mäori vote has assumed a new strategic importance to all political parties, partly because of the demographic realities, but also because, as both Labour and, before it, New Zealand First discovered, the six Mäori seats can make the necessary difference to forming a government.

Although there is a view that Mäori in Parliament will always be condemned to the fate that marginalizes all minorities, there is also a recognition that under MMP having six Mäori seats and the prospect of another three or four greatly improves the chances for effective Mäori representation. The presence of fifteen or so Mäori members in the current House of Representatives has the potential to make a substantial difference. Nor is influence in shaping the law confined to a simple show of hands among parliamentarians. In the new MMP environment, participation in select committees and agreements between parties, and greater sensitivity to electorate demands may have an even more important effect. In this sense, Mäori are better placed than ever to have their aspirations translated into legislation.

MÄORI AND THE STATUTES

Ultimately, the point of having Mäori representation in Parliament is to ensure that domestic law recognizes Mäori interests. However, for most of New Zealand's legislative history, statutes have not only failed to acknowledge Mäori interests but have actively discouraged any notion of a Mäori dimension in the wider affairs of New Zealand. Three main mechanisms were used to limit Mäori recognition within the law. The first substituted Mäori understandings for British concepts and processes. The 1862 and 1865 Native Land Acts, for example, replaced traditional forms of land tenure with British systems, thereby accelerating the alienation of tribal estates. In the second approach, Mäori interests were acknowledged but marginalized to avoid conflict with the law's wider provisions. Under the Oyster Fisheries Act 1866, Mäori rights to oyster beds were recognized but it was wrongly assumed that those rights were at subsistence levels only. Mäori were forbidden to sell oysters from their own reserves until 1874, by which time it was anticipated they would have "acquired other tastes."[25] The third way of negating Mäori interests through statute was simply by prohibiting aspects of custom. Traditional healers and political leaders were outlawed in the Tohunga Suppression Act 1907,[26] while the use of Mäori language in court had been blocked through the Pleadings in English Act 1362. The latter had become part of New Zealand law by virtue of the English Laws Act 1858 when the settler government adopted all the laws of England that had been in force in 1840.[27]

However, while laws in the past were used to restrict Mäori interests, since 1975, when the Waitangi Tribunal was established under the Treaty of Waitangi Act, there has been an increasing recognition of Mäori rights in statute. The position of Mäori within statute is sometimes linked to the Treaty of Waitangi which appears to suggest a special relationship between Mäori and the Crown (e.g., Resource Management Act 1991). At other times Mäori are viewed as a disadvantaged minority (e.g., Health and Disability Services Act 1993), a culturally different client group (e.g., Children, Young Persons and their Families Act 1989), an indigenous people with a distinctive culture (e.g., Mäori Language Act 1987), or a group with a distinctive constitutional right (e.g., Electoral Reform Act 1993).

Five main approaches to strengthen the Mäori position have been used. They are shown in Table 2.

Although the Treaty of Waitangi is mentioned in several statutes, there is no uniform wording of clauses referring to the treaty. A clause limiting all aspects of the act was used in section 9 of the State Owned Enterprises Act: "Nothing in this Act shall permit the Crown to act in a manner that is inconsistent with the principles of the Treaty of Waitangi." But the more usual pattern, and one that is less likely to invite litigation, is a clause limiting the administration of an act. Section 8 of the Resource Management Act, for example, requires that

Table 2: Recognition of Mäori interests in statute

Basis for recognition of a Mäori interest	*Effect of statutory provisions*	*Examples of statutes*
The Treaty of Waitangi	The Treaty is enforceable where it is incorporated into legislation.	• State Owned Enterprises Act 1986 • Conservation Act 1986 • Resource Management Act 1991
Protection of customary assets	Mäori language and Mäori land are afforded protection.	• Mäori Language Act 1987 • *Ture Whenua* Mäori Act 1993
Fairness and social well being	There is a requirement to consider Mäori social networks, Mäori cultural processes, and Mäori custom.	• Children Young Persons and their Families Act 1989 • Health and Disability Services Act 1993 • Law Commission Act 1985
Mäori constitutional position	Mäori representation in Parliament is guaranteed.	• Electoral Reform Act 1993
Settlement of Treaty of Waitangi claims	A process for investigating claims against the Crown is established; the terms of settlement cannot be varied except by repealing the law.	• Treaty of Waitangi Act 1975 • Treaty of Waitangi (Fisheries Claim) Settlement Act 1992 • Treaty of Waitangi (*Tainui Waikato*) Settlement Act 1995

those who administer any part of the act must "take into account" the principles of the treaty.

Although the incorporation of the Treaty of Waitangi into legislation is largely limited to resource areas (land, fish, minerals, and the environment), in an early draft of the Code of Health and Disability Services Consumers Rights, compliance with the principles of the treaty had been initially included. Subsequently the minister of health, Jenny Shipley, explained the removal of the clause: "I was concerned that the Crown's Treaty duties in respect of health and disability services have yet to be determined by the courts or the Waitangi Tribunal. Accordingly the reference to recognition of Mäori as tangata whenua [indigenous people of New Zealand] under the Treaty of Waitangi could create legal uncertainty as to its meaning in practice. In my view, it is desirable that the Code avoid such uncertainty."[28] However, in 2000 the Labour-Alliance government introduced a treaty clause into the first draft of the *Public Health and Disability Bill.* The proposed wording was not dissimilar to section 8 of the Resource Management Act 1991 in that it required those with responsibility for the implementation of the act to take into account the principles of the Treaty of Waitangi. But there was substantial opposition on the grounds that Mäori might be able to make a claim on health services for preferential treatment. That would have been an unlikely consequence given other aspects of the bill, but the wording was nonetheless changed. When returned to the House, the new treaty clause simply noted that the treaty was being recognized in the way District Health Boards were structured.

A more usual pattern for social policy legislation is to recognize a Mäori interest, although the basis for recognition does not appear to follow a consistent pattern. For example, an objective of the Health and Disability Services Act is that Mäori health be at least as good as the health of non-Mäori, implying a focus on disparities. On the other hand, the Children, Young Persons and their Families Act acknowledges customary values and the balance between individual and group rights. The draft bill was felt by many Mäori to overemphasize the paramount interests of the child, ignoring *whänau* (family) rights. As a result it was redrafted to reflect "a family centered focus," "*whänau* decision making," and "family oriented practice," a philosophical shift that some commentators thought could compromise the safety of the child.[29] Nonetheless, the act goes some way towards maintaining equilibrium between an exclusive focus on the child and a consideration of the child's needs in association with *whänau*. It "represents a major change in policy towards Mäori family forms and *tikanga*."[30]

A requirement in the Law Commission Act 1985 to "take into account *te ao Mäori* (the Mäori dimension) and to give consideration to the multicultural character of New Zealand society seems to encourage the recognition of Mäori custom in law. Commission reports such as the 1989 Mäori Fisheries Report[31] have attempted to reflect that dimension, and the president of that commission urged the legal profession to use Mäori norms when deciding Mäori issues. "Counsel have not performed their task where they have failed to identify some relevant Mäori custom, not excluded by the cession or a statute, which therefore subsists as a matter of New Zealand law."[32]

Two acts deserve special mention because they secure Mäori customary assets, albeit at a late stage when the assets are seriously eroded. The Mäori Language Act 1987 declares Mäori language to be an official language of New Zealand, establishes a Mäori Language

Commission, and enables the use of Mäori in courts. *Te Ture Whenua* Mäori Act 1993 (Mäori Land Act) aims to keep Mäori land in Mäori hands by balancing individual land rights with group land rights. Traditional forms of tenure are upheld, and *hapu* (tribal groups) are encouraged to avoid further alienation of their holdings by giving first preference for purchase or succession to "preferred classes of alienees" drawn from a close kinship circle. Although Mäori land interests have dwindled from nearly 30 million hectares to 1.5 million hectares, the intention of the act is to protect whatever remains of tribal estates for future generations.[33]

Recognition of a special Mäori constitutional position is most likely based on the Treaty of Waitangi, but as already noted the Mäori Representation Act 1867 was not explicitly linked to the Treaty, and the Electoral Reform Act 1993 simply carried forward the provision for Mäori seats, again without reference to the Treaty though with a new mechanism for determining the number of seats. Of greater potential constitutional significance was the 1985 White Paper on a Bill of Rights. It recommended the entrenchment of the Treaty of Waitangi as part of the fundamental law of New Zealand, a step that caused difficulties for many communities, including some Mäori communities. In the event the Bill of Rights was passed as ordinary law and without any special acknowledgement of the Treaty or Mäori interests.[34]

Legislation to facilitate Treaty of Waitangi settlements provided initially for the establishment of a tribunal to inquire into claims against the Crown for breaches of the principles of the Treaty of Waitangi Act 1975. The Tribunal has registered some 780 claims and has not only earned a reputation for high quality reports but also been credited with initiating a bicultural jurisprudence and rehabilitating the treaty back into a legislative and constitutional framework. Subsequently, legislation has been passed to enforce settlements between Mäori and the Crown where a Treaty of Waitangi grievance has been shown to have adversely affected claimants. Although not encoded in the law, the government has opted for a settlement process that relies heavily on direct negotiation between claimants and the Crown. Generally, settlements are made full and final by the removal of further recourse to the courts or the Waitangi Tribunal. They are also constrained by a capped settlement budget, the exclusion of the conservation estate and natural resources from settlement packages, and the delivery of a Crown apology.[35]

While there has been a significant turnaround in the use of legislation to endorse rather than negate a Mäori identity, there is room for greater coherence and some clarification about the place of the Treaty of

Waitangi across the raft of legislation, especially in social policy areas. There is also a need for further clarification of traditional concepts and the use of Mäori words in statute so that judicial interpretation can provide its own level of consistency and maintain integrity with Mäori understandings of custom and lore.

MÄORI PARTICIPATION IN THE STATE SECTOR

The state's responsibility to actively protect Mäori interests has been recognized as a Treaty of Waitangi obligation existing alongside the state's duty to all citizens. It is reinforced by the State Sector Act 1988, which requires public sector management to recognize the aims and aspirations of Mäori people, and the employment requirements and need for greater involvement of Mäori people in the public service. However, the parallel obligations are not always readily reconciled, and there is some concern that an inherent conflict exists between the principle of equal rights and the principles arising from the Treaty of Waitangi that allocate different entitlements for Mäori.[36] While this conflict is a source of ongoing debate in New Zealand, a Treaty obligation on the state has been part of government policy since at least 1984. The way in which that obligation is met, however, is often confusing because of the uncertain justification for recognising Mäori interests: at times a Treaty-based rationale is used, at others a recognition of socio-economic disparities, and often a blurred combination of both.

Whether on the basis of the Treaty of Waitangi or for reasons of equity, four approaches to recognizing Mäori interests have been adopted by the state over the past two decades: biculturalism, active Mäori recruitment into the state sector, mainstreaming, and delivering effective outcomes.

Even though the bicultural parameters have not been carefully defined, the New Zealand public service has promoted a model of biculturalism. However, biculturalism has a range of meanings that can be represented across a continuum: at one extreme a type of cultural exchange, at the other an independent or semi-independent Mäori organization.[37] Initially, the bicultural objective was simply to introduce Mäori values and cultural norms, so that Mäori staff and clients could feel greater affinity with the department's processes. In 1991–92, for example, an objective of the State Services Commission was to improve awareness of *tikanga Mäori* (Mäori custom and lore) within the commission.[38] Later, because the cultural focus did not seem to make much difference, Mäori groups (largely state employees) argued for making the department's core business more relevant to

Mäori. In their view biculturalism should have been more about delivering positive results than celebrating culture. Central to this new goal was increasing the Mäori labour force and establishing units within departments where a critical mass of Mäori staff could provide leadership in policies and programs for Mäori.[39]

Although recruitment to the public service has been a government strategy for twenty years or more, in fact the size of the workforce has not increased in any spectacular way. The real numbers of Mäori public servants have actually decreased significantly since 1988, largely because of the overall downsizing of the state; but the proportion has remained relatively stable, around 8 per cent and close to the level of Mäori participation in the labour force.[40] However, it is still well below the level of Mäori representation in the population of age to work. When the distribution of Mäori state employees is considered, there is a more obvious dearth of Mäori at senior management levels. By 1996 only 3.6 per cent of public service managers were Mäori compared with representation in the public service as a whole of 8.2 per cent; and only one chief executive was Mäori. At the same time Mäori are over-represented in the lower salary brackets.[41]

Prior to 1984, Mäori leadership in the public service was firmly wedded to the Department of Mäori Affairs, and relatively few Mäori were employed elsewhere in the public service. Devolution and mainstreaming changed that. The current Ministry of Mäori Development is a small ministry; many of the former Mäori Affairs' functions have either been devolved beyond the state sector or transferred to other government departments. Although the mainstreaming process appears to have created fragmentation rather than solidarity, and there is some scepticism about the capacity of the so-called mainstream to deliver in an effective manner,[42] there is nonetheless an expectation that all departments will be responsive to Mäori.

The government's strategic objectives and goals for Mäori are largely set out in Strategic Result Area 8. It requires evidence of "significant progress towards negotiating and implementing fair and affordable settlements to well founded grievances arising under the principles of the Treaty of Waitangi; and, consistent with the Crown as a Treaty partner, development of policies and processes that lead towards closing the economic and social gaps between Mäori and non-Mäori."[43] Despite the fact that the result area has been labelled ineffective because there are no firm targets or mandatory milestones, it sends a clear signal to departments that the state has a collective responsibility for improving outcomes for Mäori. To facilitate the process, the controller and auditor general has recommended the adoption of an audit model so that departmental progress towards meeting Strategic Result

Area 8 can be assessed. Processes relating to strategy, policy advice and service delivery, human resources, structure, and working environment are contained in the model, and guidelines for implementation and measurement are offered.[44]

In applying the model to strategic planning, for example, the auditor general expects that public sector organizations will take account of the Treaty of Waitangi, involve Mäori appropriately, and produce performance measures to assess progress towards strategic goals, objectives and outputs, and changes in outcomes for Mäori. Moreover there is a related expectation of Mäori input into service design, delivery of services, and monitoring and evaluation. Regarding the structure of a public sector organization, it is recommended that the agency have administrative and management arrangements that enable the monitoring of organizational performance with respect to Mäori and sufficient control of quality to ensure effective outputs for Mäori. A variety of structures have been adopted, although most major Crown agencies have established Mäori units or advisory positions.[45]

State responsiveness to Mäori depends not only on the level of Mäori participation in the public service but also on the capacity of the state to contribute to Mäori advancement through other mechanisms. These two variables, workforce participation and the implementation of effective policies and programs, are linked. However, they are essentially different concerns and one does not necessarily follow the other. Increasing the level of direct Mäori involvement in the state is important and can be justified on several grounds, but unless the effort leads to demonstrable benefits for Mäori, the exercise is essentially one of creating equal employment opportunities rather than one of specifically advancing Mäori people. The goal is not insignificant but it is a different goal from achieving the best outcomes for Mäori.

The present Labour-Alliance government underlined the state's obligations to Mäori when it extended the monitoring role of the Ministry of Mäori Development to include an active auditing function. All other departments can now be called on to demonstrate how they have addressed Mäori aspirations and contributed to a reduction in disparities between Mäori and non-Mäori. If progress cannot be shown, then departmental budgets and resources will move to more responsive agencies, either within or outside the state.

CONCLUSION

Mäori participation in Parliament, statutes, and the state have undergone substantial change in less than two decades, although much of the change builds on agreements and protocols negotiated much earlier in New Zealand's history. The 1840 Treaty of Waitangi, for example, remains central to the current arrangements, and even though the rationale for advancing Mäori interests sometimes lacks sharp definition, there is nonetheless an established convention that the Crown will recognize the interests of Mäori – not only because they are a minority ethnic group or a disadvantaged population, but also because they are partners to the Treaty of Waitangi.

There is considerable division in New Zealand about the extent to which Mäori interests might be promoted. While there is some agreement, by no means universal, that the injustices of the past must be righted, there is less agreement about the provision of special ongoing or new arrangements for Mäori, other than to address socio-economic disparities. For example, the opposition to the reservation of a parcel of the radio frequency spectrum for Mäöri suggests that the right to development is not held as highly as the right to compensation for historical grievances. Yet the Treaty of Waitangi was never about fossilizing Mäori endeavours within an 1840 timeframe; it was essentially about a shared approach to development and to New Zealand's future.

Mäori participation in governance is essentially premised on the right to development and a perceived entitlement to an active role in decision-making. There has been progress as some laws now recognize Mäori perspectives, the electoral system allows for significant Mäori participation, and the state sector seeks to deliver outcomes that are consistent with Mäori aspirations. Inevitably there are criticisms that it is all too slow, too late, and excessively constrained by the Crown's reluctance to cast off the final vestiges of a colonial past. As well, from opposite viewpoints, there are claims that the recognition of a special right by Mäori to participate in governance clashes with the principles of democracy and the equality of all citizens, and that the Treaty of Waitangi should no longer be reflected in New Zealand's mechanisms for governance.

At the heart of the matter is whether indigenosity confers rights and creates special obligations on states. In the New Zealand context, the Treaty of Waitangi strengthens the position of Mäori as an indigenous people, but the fundamental issues are nonetheless about the way in which arrangements for governance should address indigenous rights and the purpose of those arrangements. Reducing socio-economic disparities, remedying past injustices, recognizing cultural diversity, guaranteeing human rights, and developing equal employment opportunities all provide some justification for encouraging active Mäori participation, but they do not entirely capture the essence of the indigenous arguments for autonomy and a distinctive place within the state. It is unlikely that the issue will be resolved without a more focused debate on the future of New Zealand's constitutional arrangements. At a constitutional conference held in Wellington in 2000, the position of Mäori and the ongoing relevance of the Treaty of Waitangi proved to be a major focus for debate, without any clear resolution.[46]

Meanwhile, Mäori participation has led to significant changes within New Zealand's systems of governance. First, the language has changed. To a greater or lesser extent, mono-cultural attitudes and assumptions have been replaced by a set of cultural values and protocols that more appropriately reflect New Zealand as a nation in the South Pacific with its own unique heritage. While the Westminster system is still clearly the basis for governance, a New Zealand style that is able to incorporate the Mäori dimension within a unitary framework has emerged. Second, there has been a dynamic shift in the balance of power. Mäori now hold a level of influence that depends not only on representation in Parliament but also on the dawning of a bicultural jurisprudence and some appropriation of the instruments of state. Third, increasingly the measures of good governance are being construed in terms that go some way towards recognizing Mäori aspirations and Mäori advancement. Although achieving the best outcomes for all New Zealanders is a fundamental governance goal, there is also recognition of an obligation to actively promote Mäori culture, language, and well-being. In meeting that objective, the need for more than a single set of measures has become apparent.

Ultimately, the effectiveness of wise governance must be reflected in outcomes that make sense to Mäori as Mäori, but also as citizens of New Zealand. In that respect increased Mäori participation has not been accompanied by any dramatic improvement of Mäori standards of living, at least not compared to those of other New Zealanders. But there have been gains in the promotion of language and culture, and in the quest for a greater say in decision-making. Moreover, it appears fairly certain that assimilation of Mäori into the wider population has at last been discounted as the ultimate goal, and, in keeping with the Treaty of Waitangi, the Crown's obligation to actively protect Mäori interests has been acknowledged.

While increased reflection of Mäori interests in governance and statutes has occurred over the past two decades, it would be simplistic to imply that there is a formula to guide the process or that there is a fixed end point towards which the country is moving. Instead, the developments are subject to a wider context based not only on structural arrangements but also on the dynamic nature of the Crown's relationship with Mäori.[47] It is likely that the focus for the relationship will shift, from a preoccupation with levels of representation to the development of mechanisms for creating effective partnerships. In the future, Mäori participation in governance may be less about inclusion within a unitary system of control and authority, and more about the establishment of Mäori governing bodies to control Mäori resources and provide a fulcrum for interacting with the Crown. Integral to that shift will be the formation of a national Mäori body that has the capacity and the mandate to act as a governing body and to interact with the nation's other governance structures. This does not mean the splintering of a single nation state. Rather, in line with the emergence of Scottish and Welsh Parliaments in the UK, and a Saami Parliament in Norway, it would lead to systems of governance that have different jurisdictions but close ongoing relationships.

NOTES

1 Frederika Hackshaw, "Nineteenth Century Notions of Aboriginal Title," in *Waitangi: Mäori and Pakeha Perspective of the Treaty of Waitangi,* ed. I.H. Kawharu (Auckland: Oxford University Press, 1989), 102–8.

2 Paul McHugh, *The Mäori Magna Carta: New Zealand Law and the Treaty of Waitangi* (Oxford: Oxford University Press, 1991), 113–17.

3 Michael King, *Whina: A Biography of Whina Cooper* (Auckland: Penguin Books, 1983), 215–19.

4 The Terms of Reference for the Royal Commission on Social Policy described the principles of the Treaty as one of the "foundations of our society and economy."

5 Geoffrey Palmer, *New Zealand's Constitution in Crisis: Reforming our Political System* (Dunedin: John McIndoe, 1992), 71–102.

6 *Huakina Development Trust* v. *Waikato Valley Authority* [1987] 2 NZLR 188 (High Court) *Attorney-General* v. *New Zealand Mäori Council* [1991] 2 NZLR 129 (Court of Appeal).

7 Mason Durie, *Te Mana, Te Käwanatanga: The Politics of Mäori Self-Determination* (Auckland: Oxford University Press, 1998), 203–4.

8 W.H. Oliver, "The Fragility of Päkehä Support," in K.S. Coates and P.G. McHugh, *Living Relationships Kökiri Ngätahi* (Wellington: Victoria University Press, 1998), 222–31.

9 Mai Chen and Geoffrey Palmer, *Public Law in New Zealand* (Auckland: Oxford University Press, 1993), 435.

10 Statistics New Zealand, *New Zealand Now Mäori* (Wellington: Department of Statistics, 1998), 13–15.

11 Ibid., 17–18.

12 Judith Davey, *Tracking Social Change in New Zealand From Birth to Death iv* (Institute of Policy Studies, Victoria University, Wellington 1998), 73–4.

13 Statistics New Zealand, *Population Issues for New Zealand: New Zealand National Report on Population* (Wellington: Department of Statistics, 1994).

14 Te Puni Kokiri, *Progress Towards Closing Social and Economic Gaps Between Mäori and Non-Mäori* (Wellington: Ministry of Mäori Development 1998), 14–16.

15 United Nations, *Draft Declaration of the Rights of Indigenous Peoples as Agreed upon by the Members of the Working Group at its Eleventh Session* (United Nations Document 1993) E/CN.4/Sub.2/1994/2/Add. 1.

16 Danny Keenan, "A Permanent Expedience?" *He Pukenga Körero: A Journal of Mäori Studies* 2, no. 1 (1996): 58–61.

17 G.V. Butterworth, *Mäori Affairs* (Wellington: GP Books, 1990), 53–5.

18 J. Henderson, *Ratana: The Man, the Church, the Political Movement* (Wellington: The Polynesian Society, 1963), 90–1.

19 Dominic O'Sullivan, "The 1996 General Election and the Labour Vote in the Mäori Electorates," *He Pukenga Korero: A Journal of Mäori Studies* 5, no. 1 (1999): 40–56.

20 M.P.K. Sorrenson, "A History of Mäori Representation in Parliament," in *Towards a Better Democracy: Report of the Royal Commission on the Electoral System* (Wellington, 1986), B-58.

21 Royal Commission on the Electoral System, *Towards a Better Democracy: Report of the Royal Commission on the Electoral System* (Wellington, 1986), 108.

22 Justice Committee, *The Treaty of Waitangi and Constitutional Implications of the Electoral Reform Bill* (Wellington: Mäori Congress, 1993).

23 Waitangi Tribunal, *Radio Spectrum Management and Development Report, Wai 776* (Wellington, 1996).

24 Ann Sullivan, "Mäori Politics and Government Policies," in *New Zealand Politics in Transition*, ed. Raymond Miller (Auckland: Oxford University Press, 1997), 368–9.

25 Waitangi Tribunal, *Muriwhenua Fishing Report* (Wellington: Waitangi Tribunal Department of Justice, 1988), 81–8.

26 P. Webster, *Rua and the Mäori Millennium* (Wellington: Victoria University Press, 1979), 221–4.

27 Durie, *Te Mana, Te Käwanatanga: The Politics of Mäori Self-Determination*, 60.

28 Hon. Jenny Shipley, *An Introduction to the Code of Health and Disability Services Consumers' Rights* (Wellington: Parliament of New Zealand, 1996).

29 Pauline Tapp, David Geddis, and Nicola Taylor, "Protecting the Family," in *Family Law Policy in New Zealand*, ed. M. Henaghan, B. Atkin (Auckland: Oxford University Press, 1992), 178–180.

30 Donna Durie-Hall and Joan Metge, "Kua Tutü te Puehu, Kia Mau: Mäori Aspirations and Family Law," in *Family Law Policy in New Zealand*, ed. M. Henaghan, B. Atkin (Auckland: Oxford University Press, 1992), 79.
31 New Zealand Law Commission, *Report on the Treaty of Waitangi and Mäori Fisheries* (Wellington, 1989).
32 Justice Baragwanath, *The Treaty of Waitangi and the Constitution*, NZLS Seminar series (Wellington: New Zealand Law Society, 1997).
33 Te Puni Kokiri *Newsletter Special,* Ministry of Mäori Development (Wellington, March 1993).
34 Palmer, *New Zealand's Constitution in Crisis,* 51–70.
35 New Zealand, *Crown Proposals for the Settlement of Treaty of Waitangi Claims: Detailed Proposals* (Wellington: Office of Treaty Settlements, 1994).
36 Jonathon Boston et al., *Public Management: the New Zealand Model* (Auckland: Oxford University Press, 1996), 10–11.
37 M.H. Durie, "Mäori and the State: Professional and Ethical Implications for a Bicultural Public Service," *Conference Proceedings of the Public Service Senior Management Conference* (Wellington: State Services Commission, 1993), 23–35.
38 New Zealand, State Services Commission, *Corporate Plan 1991/92* (Wellington, 1993), 21.
39 H. Parata and M.H. Durie, *Mäori Health Review: A Report for the Department of Health On How It Can Meet the Government's Health Objectives* (Wellington: Department of Health, 1993).
40 New Zealand, State Services Commission, *Mäori in the Public Service: A Statistical Profile* (Wellington, 1997), 10–11.
41 Te Hao Roa, *Central Government Strategy, Systems and Capability for Outcomes for Mäori* (Wellington: Forum of Senior Mäori Public Servants, 1997).
42 Boston et al., *Public Management: The New Zealand Model*, 156–8.
43 New Zealand, Department of Prime Minister and Cabinet, *Strategic Result Areas for the Public Sector 1997–2000* (Wellington, 1997).
44 New Zealand, Controller and Auditor General, *Report of the Controller and Auditor General – Third Report for 1998, Four: Delivering Effective Outputs for Mäori*, (Wellington: Parliament of New Zealand, 1998).
45 Report of the Controller and Auditor General – Third Report for 1998.
46 "Building the Constitution," (a conference sponsored by the Institute of Policy Studies, in Victoria at the University of Wellington in April 2000).
47 Ken S. Coates and P.G. McHugh, *Living Relationships Kokiri Ngätahi: The Treaty of Waitangi in the New Millennium*, (Wellington: Victoria University Press, 1998), 170–9.

Debating the Reform of Canada's Parliament

JENNIFER SMITH

At the dawn of the millennium, Canada's system of parliamentary government is the target of sustained and serious criticism, perhaps the most sustained and serious in its long life. This is because the criticism reaches the foundations of the system.

Criticism of such a fundamental kind was bound to happen at some time or other. After all, the system has never undergone a serious overhaul. It reflects the same principles of representative and responsible government now that it did in 1867.[1] These principles and the institutional mechanisms that give effect to them may be summarized as follows:

- The principle of representation by population, or "rep by pop." This refers to the election of the members of the legislature by the people, currently accomplished under the single-member plurality system of election, sometimes referred to as the first-past-the-post system.
- The accountability of the political executive – the government of the day – to the elected legislature. This is secured by (1) mandating that money bills originate in the House of Commons, (2) conferring on the executive a monopoly of the authority to sponsor money bills there, and (3) requiring that the executive so empowered maintain the confidence of a majority of the membership of that body.
- A constitutional opposition. The idea that it is a patriotic duty of the parliamentary opponents of the government to criticize its policies and performance is symbolized by the words of the phrase "Her Majesty's Loyal Opposition." Opposition to the government is not a disloyal act.

No one opposes the principles of representation by population, or the accountability of the government to the elected legislature, or the constitutionality of the opposition. However, the effects of the principles and the mechanisms used to support them are no longer widely admired. The most noticeable effect is the conduct of the elected representatives, which is adversarial. It must be stressed immediately that adversarial behaviour is not a necessary condition of the operation of the system of representative and responsible government, and there is evidence of this point in Canadian political history.[2] However, the combination of the system *and* disciplined political parties nourishes it. Certainly the House of Commons is organized in an adversarial fashion, with the government being pitted against the opposition. The government does not share power with the opposition. Instead the two sides are ranged against one another, the government proposing measures and defending them, the opposition attacking the measures and occasionally offering alternative ideas. Many find the aggressive and competitive behaviour of parliamentarians that flows from this arrangement to be puzzling at best and obnoxious at worst.

Another effect that some find questionable is the partisanship of disciplined parliamentary parties. Again, the simple requirement that the government maintain the confidence of a majority of the elected legislature does not require that there be disciplined parties. But certainly it makes them highly valuable. It is much easier for political leaders to meet the confidence requirement of responsible government with loyal followers as opposed to unreliable independents. Finally, it has been noticed that the system gives many parliamentarians little to do in the legislative line – or at least not what they want to do. They can criticize legislation constructively and supportively or they can seek to demolish it. But they cannot originate public bills that involve the raising or spending of money, and so they have a limited role as public-policy makers. The category of the members who are thus legislatively underemployed includes all opposition members, and possibly members of the governing party who are not ministers – collectively referred to here as private members. This is a substantial number. In an age dominated by the thinking of the business world, it is hardly surprising to find that the lack of meaningful work gives rise to a certain restiveness.

It is essential to stress that the organizational pattern of government versus opposition that gives rise to these ills is compelled by the combination of responsible government and disciplined political parties, as described above. Therefore those who oppose, say, the adversarial character of the House of Commons confront two practices that lie at the heart of the system. This lends the campaign for reform of the system an intriguing if dangerous edge.

The purpose of this chapter is to consider the case for the reform of the parliamentary system. To this end, both the major criticisms that are levelled against the system and the proposals of reform attendant upon them are reviewed. Next the potential effects of the proposals are considered. Understandably this last is an exercise in abstraction. So is the effort to recommend some lines of reform, with which the essay concludes. They are abstract exercises because it is impossible to test the ideas beforehand, as it were. Fortunately there is the experience of parliamentary systems in other countries where, as reported in this volume, interesting changes have been underway for some time. The insights of the authors are helpful in the consideration of reform proposals in Canada. Still, it is wise to refrain from advancing proposals of reform with an air of certainty. The risk of overlooked and unwelcome ramifications is too grave. It is enough to suggest some ideas of reform that might be studied in greater depth by students and practitioners of parliamentary government, which I do in the conclusion.

First, however, it is useful to recall the major efforts that have been made thus far to improve the existing system from the standpoint of the government as well as the standpoint of the private member, a task to which I turn now.

THE RECORD OF REFORM

In *The Parliament of Canada*, published in 1987, author C.E.S. Franks began with this sentence: "Ours is an age of reform."[3] He pointed out that between 1960 and the mid-1980s, when he was writing, Parliament was subject to a series of reforms. Moreover, the activity has continued until today. There has been no lack of well-intentioned effort. Those who are unhappy with the parliamentary system, then, cannot complain about that. Instead, their complaint must be that it has accomplished very little.

In general, reform has meant reform of procedure in the House of Commons. At the risk of oversimplification, it can be said that two objectives are pursued. One is to streamline the handling of the business of the House. The other is to engage private members in useful and productive activities. The two objectives are not necessarily compatible. The government is inclined to define efficiency in terms of getting its business done speedily. For their part, private members who want to make a contribution to the process are bound to be less concerned than the government about the length of time that such a contribution might take. The objectives of each might well be pursued simultaneously, since major procedural overhauls are often the product of all-party agreements that contain something for the government and something for the opposition. This occurred in 1968, when the moribund committee system was revitalized to engage members in the press of legislative business with which the House had hitherto struggled in an increasingly inefficient manner in Committee of the Whole. This was a change that portended advantages for both sides. However, as Louis Massicotte states, the government made the efficiency gains at the expense of the opposition, which lost opportunities to stall government business, and at the expense of private members generally, who made little headway in meaningful legislative work in the committees.[4]

In the 1980s, there were two rounds of procedural reform, the first of which again uneasily yoked together the government's interest in prosecuting its legislative program smoothly with the interest of private members in legislative work. In 1982 an all-party committee chaired by Thomas Lefebvre found ways to streamline proceedings and enhance the role of the committees. Among the most noteworthy were the abolition of evening sittings of the House and the establishment of a legislative calendar with fixed dates for the periods when the House is in session.[5] By contrast the next round, in 1985–86, was devoted to the objective of enhancing the role of the private member, whether on the government or the opposition side. The McGrath reforms, named after the chair of the special committee that produced them, James McGrath, boosted that role in a number of ways. For example, the adoption of the secret ballot in the election of the speaker of the House effectively transferred the choice from the prime minister to the members; the establishment of special legislative committees to scrutinize public bills left standing committees with more time to initiate inquiries into public issues and publish detailed reports thereon; and a new routine established to deal with private members' bills offered members some assurance that their handiwork might see the light of day in the form of a vote.[6]

One recommendation of the McGrath Committee was for party leaders to adopt a more relaxed attitude to the idea of members voting according to their own lights rather than the party's. As Louis Massicotte points out, without such a shift in attitude, members could not make full use of the new opportunities made available to them. But there was no such shift.[7] As a result, although the committee system continued to strengthen, the adversarial character of the House remained unchanged, as did the governing party's control of legislative business. Further, in the next series of changes, secured in 1991 by the government against the wishes of the opposition, the government made gains.

For example, the number of days assigned to debates on the throne speech and the budget were trimmed, a change that could only favour the government side.[8]

In the most recent round of changes adopted in 1994, the committee system was tackled in another attempt to strengthen its hand.[9] The legislative committees were scrapped, and the standing committees resumed the task of scrutinizing government bills, which added considerably to their workload – and importance – since they maintained their authority to hold inquiries and issue reports. Moreover, an intriguing innovation was made to the traditional legislative process according to which a bill is referred to committee following second reading, the stage at which the House votes to adopt the principle of the bill. Now it is possible to send the bill to committee after first reading, which enables the committee to assess the principles of the bill and to propose any alterations thought to be necessary at that point – in other words, before the House has set the bill's course, as it were. As might be expected, the procedure is rarely initiated by the government. By contrast, the change under which the Finance committee was authorized to hold pre-budget hearings has taken hold, and is regarded to be permanent – and important. Undoubtedly this is because the committee initiates the hearings. Once again, then, an effort had been made to enhance the role of the private member in his or her law-making capacity.

It is evident from this brief account that members of Parliament have worked hard to adapt the system of responsible government to current thinking about the desirability of engaging all members in the legislative process in a meaningful way – not simply government ministers. They are not content with the idea that a Parliament is essentially a debating chamber. They think that it ought to be a legislating chamber, as well. If it remains essentially a debating chamber, then that is testimony to the rock-hard impact of the simple principles and mechanisms of responsible government outlined at the start. Those principles and mechanisms overwhelm reforms made at the margin. The question now is whether they would remain impervious to the more radical proposals for change in circulation in the last few years.

CURRENT CRITICISMS AND PROPOSED CHANGES

The parliamentarians who have worked on the changes noted above are committed to the improvement of the existing system. They are cognizant of the trade-offs involved between the governing party's desire for efficient law-making and the ordinary member's desire to engage meaningfully in the process. However, others take a noticeably harsher tone. There is talk about majority government being an "elected dictatorship" and the prime minister being an "elected dictator," jarring phrases that are meant to describe the concentration of power in the office of the prime minister.[10] Alternatively, there are fears about "minority tyranny," by which is meant the undue influence of special interests. Preston Manning, who helped to found the western-based Reform party in 1987 and became its first and only leader, stressed that the new party was part of the "current worldwide movement to democratize undemocratic institutions and processes, and to break the tyranny of modern 'Family Compacts' of bureaucrats, politicians, and special interests that exercise the tyranny of a minority over democratic majorities."[11] In Manning's considered view, there are in effect no institutional instruments in the existing system that collect the majority's view on any issue of public policy. The House of Commons, the obvious candidate, fails because the members are disciplined partisan voters.

The Reform Party's crusade against the existing system has not been without effect. Indeed, the charge that the system is undemocratic has become commonplace, a point demonstrated in the recent general election, which saw much derisory comment about the prime minister's power to call it at his own convenience and pleasure.[12] Shortly after the election, which the prime minister and his party won, one of the country's national newspapers ran a lead editorial entitled "How the PM can fix Canada's democracy," which is said to be ailing and in need of a cure.[13] Of course the Reform Party was hardly a lone critic, nor is the successor Canadian Alliance, which carries the banner forward – although today the Alliance is the political party most closely associated with the issue. Academics have warned about the "democratic deficit" for years,[14] and in 1999 one of the country's leading political scientists published an exhaustive analysis of the concentration of power in the organization of the government.[15]

Equally commonplace are the changes that are thought to be required to fix the allegedly undemocratic parliamentary system, some of which have long been advanced by the Reform Party, and now the Alliance;[16] some by individual MPs;[17] and some by analysts.[18] The leading proposals are listed below. The first few are part of an overall package that is advanced by the Alliance and defended on the basis of the same arguments made by its Reform predecessors, and I refer to those arguments. On the other hand, the proposal to strengthen the committees belongs to the longer tradition of efforts to reform parliamentary practice adverted to above in the section on the record of reform.

Similarly, the idea of a change in the electoral system from the existing single-member plurality (SMP) system to a system of proportional representation (PR) has been a subject of intermittent interest for years.

Beginning with the Alliance's package, there are the extra-parliamentary vehicles of change or the techniques of direct democracy: specifically, the referendum, the citizens' legislative initiative, and the recall (a mechanism for recalling elected representatives). They are proposed as complements to parliamentary democracy.[19] Long a staple of the Reform Party's policy arsenal, these ideas received their first serious public airing in the recent general election, when the Alliance was grilled on the number of sponsors required to launch a citizens' initiative. The Reform Party had set the figure at 3 per cent of the electorate but Alliance leader Stockwell Day hedged on the issue. As matters transpired, he had good reason to do so. Newfoundland comedian Rick Mercer sponsored an initiative to change the name of Stockwell Day to "Doris" Day and met the 3 per cent threshhold with ease over the Internet. The figure of 3 per cent is now widely held to be too low.

Next is Parliament, beginning with the existing Senate, the members of which are distributed among the provinces on the basis of an ancient regional formula and appointed by the prime minister for a term that lasts until the age of 75. The proposal of a "Triple E" Senate – equal, elected, and effective – was Reform's calling card in the early days, and possibly its greatest public relations success outside of the province of Quebec, where the proposal was and continues to be looked upon with considerable skepticism. In the West and in the Atlantic provinces it is well received. Then there is the House of Commons, the subject of equally far-reaching proposals.

The Reform Party was always critical of the disciplined party voting that is characteristic of the Commons. The argument is that the practice transforms members into trained seals who invariably support the party leadership rather than give expression to the views of their constituents, which might well vary from the party's views. The challenge is to find ways to undermine the need for disciplined voting, and thus the practice itself. Accordingly, Reform latched onto the confidence vote and the timing of elections as vehicles for change.

On the confidence vote, the idea is to restrict the definition of the House's want of confidence in the government to motions expressly worded to that effect, or formal want-of-confidence motions. The government's defeat on such motions would require it to resign. For the rest of the votes – meaning almost all of them – government defeats would not require the government to resign.[20] Liberated from this major reason for partisan solidarity, from time to time the government's own members might be open to persuasion to vote differently than their leaders recommend – or so the thinking goes. The phrase, "free votes," really means independent-minded voting. On the timing of elections, the idea is to eliminate prime ministerial discretion and to replace it with fixed election dates, the government's defeat on a formal want-of-confidence motion being the only reason to go early. The fixed election date again reduces the need for unfailing party solidarity, and at the same time removes from the prime minister a disciplinary lever over the back-bench troops in the form of the ever-unpredictable election threat.[21]

Certainly these proposals pack a punch and so it is worth pausing here to interpret them in the light of a larger rationale, and one more specific than the current cliché about the need for more democracy. The only rationale on offer was elaborated by Manning. As indicated above, his central concern from the start has been the fate of the majority's voice within the existing system. He believes it to be suppressed. Some of the proposed changes, like the use of referendums, are among the more obvious measures to give effect to this voice. Less obvious, but designed with the same purpose in mind, are the proposals to weaken the confidence convention and establish fixed elections. According to Manning, the immediate effect of these proposals is to produce a more independent member, that is, more independent of the party. But why would this favour majority rule? The answer lies in the theory of representation.

Manning argues that disciplined party voting favours the domination of the political process by minority interests. He writes: "In the House of Commons, the practice of making every vote a partisan confidence vote frequently prevents members from faithfully and accurately representing the wishes of the people who elect them. Its decisions are often completely contrary to majority opinion across the country."[22] The restriction of the need for partisan voting, then, would open the windows of the legislature to the blast of popular majorities. Does this mean that members become delegates of their constituents? Not entirely. Manning has a "unified field" theory of representation in which the three kinds of representation – mandate, delegate, and trustee – are knit together. It is a difficult trick. Essentially, he tries to finesse mandate representation (adhering to the party's advertised platform) and delegate representation (voting the way the constituents specify) by arguing that the Reform Party generates its platform out of the people's will as expressed by the party's membership and its parliamentary caucus. The trustee concept of representation enters in the form of the respect paid to the elected member's judgment about various issues.

In applying as a standard of evaluation the likely impact of the more radical of the proposed changes on the system of responsible government, it needs to be kept in mind that Manning's own standard of evaluation is quite different. His standard is the extent to which the changes would give effect to the will of the majority. This is a populist standard, of course. As such it is a fitting one for a man who regards himself and the party that he founded to be part of the tradition of Western populism,[23] a subject to which he has given careful thought. But it is not without its own problems, largely because the will of the majority might turn out to be a transient thing, easily subject to manipulation by political leaders. Manning's only real antidote to this is the idea of "the common sense of the common people," which amounts to the hope that most people share the same good sense about the issues of the day.[24]

As noted above, there are at least two other avenues of reform that are often explored, neither of which was a focus for the Reform Party, or is a focus now for the Alliance. One is the switch to an electoral system of proportional representation. Sometimes this is advanced in relation to a reformed Senate,[25] and sometimes in relation to the House.[26] The issue of the electoral system is too complex to pursue here. However, it is a live one, and worth mentioning in connection with parliamentary reform, since a change in the existing system could be expected to have a significant impact on parliamentary politics, a point discussed in the next section. Finally, there is the matter of the standing committees of the House. Recently, and on the basis of extensive consultation with MPs, themselves, Peter Dobell has identified some changes that, taken together, would strengthen the committees and improve the quality of the contribution that they make to the legislative process. They include more stable committee membership; extra remuneration for committee chairs; the use of opposition members as chairs; and the use of committee hearings at an earlier stage than is usual now in the consideration of bills.[27]

EVALUATING THE PROPOSED CHANGES

Turning first to Parliament, there is the trio of changes proposed for the House of Commons. To repeat, they are the restriction of the confidence convention to formal want-of-confidence votes in the government; fixed election dates that run on a four-year cycle, unless an early election is triggered by a formal want-of-confidence vote; and a theory of representation that encourages members to vote independently of party. The first two are concrete rule changes that are meant to bolster the third, which might be described as an alteration in attitude. Would they undermine the system of responsible government? Quite possibly not.

Under these rule changes, there is nothing to prevent the parliamentary parties from maintaining the traditional, disciplined solidarity. And there is everything that there always was to encourage them to maintain it, namely, the rewards of office. These remain undiminished. To the victor – a majority governing party – go the rewards. On the rationale that they have nothing to lose, the opposition parties might choose to enter into the spirit of the changes and let their members act like independents. But this would weaken their profile with the electorate, weaken their capacity to inflict damaging criticism on the government, and thereby assist the governing party – a charitable course of action but not a savvy one.

On the other hand, were the opposition *and* the governing party members who are not ministers keen to pursue an independent voting path, it is still the case that the system of responsible government stands. It must be stressed that responsible government strongly encourages disciplined parties but it does not require them. It merely requires that a government maintain the support of a majority of the legislature for its legislative program. A more independent-minded legislature would tax its diplomatic and negotiating skills, but that is no bad thing.

Of course it has long been held that governments facing independent-minded legislators are bound to fall, possibly in succession, the result being a series of weak governments. Viewed in that context, the changes advanced by the Reform Party and now by the Alliance might be thought to forestall such an unsavoury prospect. In contemplation is a government insulated from defeat by the restriction of the confidence rule to formal want-of-confidence votes and the expectation of a four-year term. This opens up the fascinating question of whether a government that continually lost votes – although not the critical votes as defined by reformers – could stay in office. How many defeats could the electorate stand to watch? How many could a government stomach? The simple and compelling rule that the government command the support of the legislature might well weigh heavily against a robust stand for independent voting, should that entail a string of defeats.

It is argued here that responsible government emerges unscathed from these rules. There remains the standard of the majority will of the electorate, which is the real standard for Manning. Essentially this comes down to the question of whether opposition members would gain any purchase on a genuine role in the shaping of legislation. Would the proposed rules encourage the government to consult them? The answer depends on the behaviour of the government's own backbench members. If the temptations of freedom, independence, and fame make them unreliable supporters, then the government might find itself paying more attention to opposition concerns. And this is especially so if an elected Senate is added to the mix. Indeed, the elected Senate is a far more significant event for the idea of representing majority opinion *and* for responsible government than the changes discussed thus far.

It is the elective feature of the Senate proposal that is bound to make it effective, not the feature of equal provincial representation, which is an unlikely prospect in any event and best set aside for the purposes of this analysis. Certainly in a democracy, an elected body is a legitimate legislative actor. Therefore an elected Senate becomes as legitimate a legislator as the elected House of Commons. If it is assumed that each body retains the veto over bills that it possesses now, then by definition a democratically-chosen Senate adds to the range of public opinion that is represented in the legislative process. To that extent it might be held to advance Manning's objective of realizing the preferences of the majority of the electorate in the process. Alternatively, however, it might be held to block that objective by multiplying the opportunities for the dreaded "special interests" to seek to stall a legislative measure or to influence its content as it proceeds through an increasingly complicated course.

As for responsible government, the question that immediately arises is whether an elected Senate is also a confidence chamber. Is the government expected to be responsible to both houses of Parliament? This is not an academic question by any means. The Australian example is instructive. There, an equal number of senators per state is elected under a system of PR. The senators have longer fixed terms than members of the House of Representatives and for the most part an independent election cycle. As Cheryl Saunders points out, over time these factors, among others, have helped to generate an upper house with something of an identity and will of its own. Certainly it is not a body that is routinely dominated by the government of the day. The Australian Senate was not designed to be a confidence chamber, and for the most part has not functioned as one. However, in a critical constitutional episode in 1975 it did by denying passage of the government's key financial bills. Accordingly, the governor general dismissed the government and called fresh elections, making the point that the Commonwealth Parliament had refused supply. In Saunders' view, the action was a departure from normal practice according to which it is the elected, lower house that signals a loss of confidence in the government by refusing supply.[28]

The Reform Party never did work through this problem, and the Alliance has yet to do so. It should. The picture that begins to emerge is of an institutional structure beautifully designed to block the will of the majority at a number of key junctures in the legislative process. The legislative process necessarily would slow down. Manning himself approvingly remarked upon this prospect in connection with his proposal to restrict the application of confidence votes to formal want-of-confidence motions, stating that it would "also promote fiscal restraint in government."[29] Eliminating the routine application of the confidence convention to money bills, he continued, would end the role of the House of Commons as a rubber stamp of the expenditure budget. It hardly needs to be said that throwing an elected Senate into the mix, particularly one that threatens to become a confidence chamber in its own right, would only exacerbate such a development. Then there is PR.

PR is the proverbial straw. The addition of PR to the aforementioned list of changes completely finishes any idea of squeezing the will of the majority through these institutional twists and turns, which is undoubtedly why the Reform Party never countenanced it. The whole idea of PR is to give effect to individual voter preferences. It is anti-majoritarian. The combination of diversity *and* independent-mindedness in the legislature is lethal from the standpoint of majoritarianism. It simply gives too much leverage to too many individuals across a wide partisan range to be otherwise. However, it is not lethal from the standpoint of responsible government. It simply makes the requirement of the support of the legislature difficult for any government to meet. It is rare in Canada for the winning party to gain a majority of the popular vote cast in a general election. That being so, the options are minority government, in which the government seeks support from opposition members from vote to vote; or coalition government, in which the government seeks a more reliable guarantee of support in the form of a coalition partner or partners. As Jonathan Boston writes about New Zealand, which in the mid-1990s adopted a form of PR known there as the mixed-member proportional system, the formation of a governing coalition can be a time-consuming process.[30]

Thus far it is clear that the real winner in this package of proposals is not so much the will of the majority as the elected representative, the legislator, the parliamentarian. This individual makes huge gains in terms of his or her standing in the legislative process. As the utility of unthinking partisanship declines, the price of a vote soars. Meanwhile, the need for governments to develop the skills to assemble winning coalitions rises sharply. But they would develop the skills. It is never helpful to overlook the role of the learning curve in the face of changes in the rules. However, there are still the extra-parliamentary techniques of direct democracy to consider – the referendum, the initiative, and the recall.

On the face of it, these techniques appear to be vehicles of majority opinion. Products of the populist movement in North America that arose at the end of the nineteenth century, they were designed to counter the perceived tendencies of political parties to ally with established interests at the expense of the interests of the ordinary citizen. They were and are still meant to enable popular majorities to circumvent legislative obstacles that stand in their way. From the standpoint of opponents of minority tyranny such as Manning, then, they are the very apotheosis of reform. However, the record of these techniques in, say, California, where they are used with notable regularity, shows they are often weapons in the hands of powerful minority interests. There are many reasons for this, among them the fact that today they are costly weapons, and cost rations use.[31] Whatever the reasons, the point is that in the mass age, the techniques of direct democracy are no longer the reliable vehicles of majority opinion that many suppose them to be. And being extra-parliamentary, they are hardly consistent with responsible government which is, after all, a system of government based on representation.

There remain the proposals designed to strengthen the standing committees of the House of Commons. Dobell characterizes them as modest and incremental, and points out that they could be implemented without the need for amendments to the rules of procedure. Indeed, he continues, they could be adopted on an experimental basis to see if in fact they do enable MPs to contribute to the legislative process without at the same time destabilizing the government's legislative agenda. Dobell's view is that they would not destabilize it and that they are consistent with the essentials of the parliamentary system, which means responsible government.[32] In this respect the key proposal is the use of the committees in an earlier stage of the legislative process. Dobell's suggestion, which clearly is framed to ensure that the principles of responsible government remain intact, is that the government send to the committees drafts of bills on which it has not signed off, thereby signalling a receptivity to amendments. He foresees that in such circumstances, committee members, particularly members from the governing party, might feel free to climb outside of the box of party discipline and tackle the bills in a more independent fashion. For its part, he continues, the government is not compromised by accepting advice from the committee because this stage of the proceedings is still an informal one. Only when the government formally tables bills in the House need it take full responsibility for them and defend them. Dobell seems on solid ground in his view that the responsible-government system can accommodate the "pre-study" stage of draft bills by standing committees. In the meantime, as he points out, the British House of Commons is testing this innovation, a development that will assist students of parliamentary reform to evaluate it.[33]

CONCLUSION

Two solid conclusions can be drawn from the review of these proposals, various of which are a staple in the diet of reformers. The first conclusion is that, taken together, the proposals for direct democracy, an elected Senate, a restricted confidence convention in the House and more free votes there, fixed elections – presumably for both houses – and a change in the electoral system in the direction of PR are likely to produce a radical change in the existing system. The second conclusion is that the direction of the change is unpredictable. It might very well be the exact opposite of the direction intended by the authors of the proposals. In other words, these reforms might enhance the political leverage of powerful minority interests at the expense of the majority, meanwhile leaving the foundations of responsible government entirely intact. Does the prospect of such a debacle – at least from the standpoint of many reformers – mean that nothing ought to be done? Not at all. It is merely a caution against an expectation of easy institutional change in pursuit of "more democracy." We would do well to join the eighteenth-century British parliamentarian Edmund Burke, who felt "an insuperable reluctance in giving [his] hand to destroy any established institution of government, upon a theory, however plausible it may be."[34]

The caution duly noted, there is no avoiding the fact that two themes are struck again and again in public discussions of the political system. They are the role of the parliamentarian and the role of the citizen in his capacity as voter. Parliamentarians, specifically those who are not members of the cabinet, think that they ought to contribute to the legislative process. For their part, citizens are beginning to think that their votes – every last one – ought to count towards the result of an election. These are analytically distinct problems. The role of parliamentarians needs to be dealt with in the context of the parliamentary process. The role of voters needs to be dealt with in the context of the electoral system.

As far as the parliamentarians are concerned, particularly members of the House of Commons, the better course for them is once more to pick up the mantle of parliamentary reform and pursue ways of improving their lot. And there is every sign that they intend to do so, judging from the public comments of some in the days following the 2000 general election.[35] Undoubtedly this will mean improving their lot in the committees, possibly along the lines that Dobell suggests. The committees are an obvious forum in which members need to make a contribution to the legislative process, if they are to make one at all. Changes like these are not flashy. But they get at the fundamental problem of the existing system for many parliamentarians, which is that it leaves them stranded, unable to contribute to the legislative process. Moreover they are practicable, and this is an important consideration.

Dobell contends that it is possible to enhance the role of the standing committees, and by extension the role of MPs, without getting involved in formal amendments to the rules of procedure. This is helpful, but the real obstacle to change, as Dobell acknowledges, lies elsewhere. He is realistic about the need for the party leaders, and especially the prime minister, to see the desirability of parliamentary reform in order for change to occur. To that end, his argument is that a more effective role for MPs can only strengthen Parliament, and the public's image of Parliament and parliamentarians, a prospect that is positive for the government as well. Thus, in reference to the idea of committee hearings at an early stage in the development of legislation, he suggests this might help to "increase public acceptance across the country of government legislation."[36] This is a thought for the government to ponder rather than dismiss, as all too often it is wont to do.[37]

The voter's role in determining the result of an election is another matter entirely and requires the consideration of an electoral system based on the principle of proportionality instead of the principle of plurality, on which the current system is based. Nevertheless, it must be kept in mind that such a significant change in the electoral system would have a considerable impact on the membership of the House of Commons, and therefore on the way that the House operates. As already noted, the shift to a proportional system is unlikely to produce easy one-party majorities. In all probability, the governing party would need to find support beyond the ranks of its own members. Such a circumstance would have a profound effect on the ordinary member, the value of whose leverage could be expected to rise appreciably. The combination of a change in the electoral system *and* a strengthened committee system would only intensify the effect.

In conclusion, it is worth recalling the two key objections to the existing system advanced by critics, namely, the idea of the prime minister as an elected dictator and the concern that minority interests are subverting the will of the majority. Of course the prime minister is not an elected dictator but instead a beneficiary of the system of responsible government when he leads a majority party in the legislature. As for the dreaded minority interests, they are hard to define and harder to measure. There is little use in chasing chimeras. Nevertheless, to the extent that objections such as these have any merit at all, they are addressed by the effort to enhance the role of the elected representative in the legislative process and the effort to enhance the role of the voter in the determination of election outcomes. Happily, there is little – save the obstinacy of party leaders – to prevent the elected representatives from pursuing ways of improving their role in the system. The electoral system, on the other hand, is a proposition for the longer term.

NOTES

1 For a discussion of the development of representative and responsible government in Canada, see F. Leslie Seidle and Louis Massicotte, eds, *Taking Stock of 150 Years of Responsible Government in Canada* (Ottawa: Canadian Study of Parliament Group, 1999).

2 The five variations of Premier Bracken in Manitoba supply some interesting variations of the adversarial theme. See Jennifer Smith, "Responsible Government and Democracy" in Seidle and Massicotte, *Taking Stock*, 19–49.

3 C.E.S. Franks, *The Parliament of Canada,* (Toronto: University of Toronto Press, 1987), 3.

4 Louis Massicotte, "Parliament in the 1990s" in James Bickerton and Alain-G. Gagnon, *Canadian Politics*, 3d ed. (Peterborough: Broadview Press, 1999), 168.

5 Canada, House of Commons, *Votes and Proceedings of the House of Commons*, 5 November 1982.

6 The McGrath Committee produced three reports: *Votes and Proceedings of the House of Commons*, 20 December 1984; *Votes and Proceedings of the House of Commons*, 26 March 1985; and the separately published *Report of the Special Committee on Reform of the House of Commons*, June 1985.

7 Massicotte, "Parliament in the 1990s," 172.

8 *Votes and Proceedings of the House of Commons*, 11 April 1991.

9 See *Votes and Proceedings of the House of Commons*, 7 February 1994.

10 See Gordon Gibson, "It's Time for a Backbenchers' Bill of Rights," *The Globe and Mail*, 28 November 2000.

11 Preston Manning, *The New Canada* (Toronto: Macmillan Canada, 1992), 321.

12 Alan Fotheringham, "It Was That Kind of Campaign," *The Globe and Mail*, 28 November 2000.

13 *The Globe and Mail*, 13 December 2000.

14 As an example, see Jane Jenson, "The Costs of Political Elitism" in *Canada's Century: Governance in a Maturing Society*, ed. C.E.S. Franks et al. (Montreal and Kingston: McGill-Queen's University Press, 1995), 217–37.

15 Donald Savoie, *Governing from the Centre: The Concentration of Power in Canadian Politics* (Toronto: University of Toronto Press, 1999).

16 Chuck Strahl, House Leader of the Alliance Party, *Building Trust: A Plan to Make Parliament More Responsive to Canadians*, <http://207.229/hotissues/viewby/ind…14&category=4&department=34&readarticle=1> (9 January 2001).

17 See the notes of a meeting of then sitting and former MPs on the plight of the ordinary member in the fall of 1998, *Occasional Papers on Parliamentary Government*, no. 7 (Ottawa: Parliamentary Centre, 1998).

18 Peter Dobell, "Reforming Parliamentary Practice: The Views of MPs," in *Policy Matters* 1, no. 9 (Montreal: Institute for Research on Public Policy, 2000).

19 Manning, *The New Canada*, 324–7.

20 Strahl, *Building Trust*, "Free Votes," 1.

21 Manning, *The New Canada*, 322–3.

22 *The New Canada*, 321.

23 Ibid., 7.

24 Ibid., 25.

25 Peter Aucoin, "Regionalism, Party and National Government" in *Party Government and Regional Representation in Canada*, Volume 36 of the studies of the Royal Commission on the Economic Union and Development Prospects for Canada, ed. Peter Aucoin (Toronto: University of Toronto Press, 1985), 137–60.

26 Kent Weaver, "Improving Representation in the Canadian House of Commons," *Canadian Journal of Political Science* 30, (1997): 473–512.

27 *Reforming Parliamentary Practice*, 33.

28 Cheryl Saunders, "The Australian Republic: Act 1," this volume.

29 Manning, *The New Canada*, 324.

30 Jonathan Boston, "Institutional Change in a Small Democracy: New Zealand's Experience of Electoral Reform," this volume.

31 See S. Bowler, T. Donovan and C. Tolbert, eds, *Citizens as legislators: Direct democracy in the United States* (Columbus: Ohio State University Press, 1998); B. Gamble, "Putting Civil Rights to a Popular Vote," *American Journal of Political Science* 41, no. 1 (1997): 245–69; E. Garrett, "Money, Agenda-Setting, and Direct Democracy," *Texas Law Review* 77, no. 3 (1999): 1845–90.

32 *Reforming Parliamentary Practice*, 34.

33 Ibid, 29.

34 Edmund Burke, excerpt from "Speech on Mr. Fox's East India Bill" in *The Philosophy of Edmund Burke*, ed. Louis I. Bredvold and Ralph G. Cross (Ann Arbor: The University of Michigan Press, 1977), 156.

35 Preston Manning, "We Must Fix Our Ailing Democracy," *The Globe and Mail*, 11 December 2000.

36 *Reforming Parliamentary Practice*, 33.

37 Liberal House Leader Don Boudria regards the Alliance proposals for parliamentary reform to be "half-baked." See Bruce Cheadle, "Rivals Dismiss Alliance Proposal to Reform House," *Kitchener-Waterloo Record*, 9 January 2001.

Multi-Level Governance

In the final section of this book, three authors address the functioning of parliamentary institutions within countries that also have federal systems of government, whether officially (Canada) or in practice (South Africa), or in which there has been significant power-sharing with sub-national governments (the United Kingdom). (Although Australia, also a federation, does not receive separate treatment here, important elements of its federal structure, such as the Senate, are discussed in Cheryl Saunders's chapter.) While the constitutional and institutional frameworks of the three countries examined here vary considerably, in all three cases parliamentary institutions exist at two levels and are part of a dynamic in which sub-national governments carry out significant responsibilities assigned to them but in a context marked by significant interdependence. An additional element is the reflection and protection of diversity. In countries such as those reviewed here, the interests of minorities can be expressed in parliamentary and other political institutions at two levels; multiple forums may strengthen the representation of such interests, but the overall dynamic is necessarily more complex.

One influential view of federalism, perhaps expressed most clearly in K.C. Wheare's *Federal Government*, focuses on federalism as a system in which authority is divided between two levels of government that are largely autonomous within the spheres of responsibility assigned to them. From this perspective, parliamentary institutions, whether at the national or provincial/state levels, are mostly concerned with representing citizens, passing laws, and carrying out other duties in relation to the areas of public policy for which they are responsible. While federations such as Canada and Australia may have been established largely on the basis of this concept, the practice of federalism in these countries (and others) has been adapted to reflect the marked *interdependence* in public policies and programs within modern states. Under what is referred to in the literature as "interstate federalism," intergovernmental processes that involve officials, ministers, and even first ministers provide channels that help governments manage that interdependence, including through the negotiation of major agreements. While the latter usually require legislative sanction, critics suggest that *interstate* federalism which excludes elected representatives except those who also happen to be ministers has contributed to the further marginalization of parliamentary institutions.

In contrast, *intrastate* federalism reflects a view of the functioning of contemporary federations that places a premium on representing the interests of the citizens or governments (or both) that comprise the constituent units within the institutions of the national government. The second chamber of the federal Parliament is often intended to play a key role in this regard; in theory, this would mean that a large part of the interplay between national and subnational interests, including on major public policies, should take place within parliamentary institutions. To the degree that linguistic and other minorities are concentrated in particular provinces or states (such as Quebec within Canada), intra-parliamentary processes can also help accommodate the societal diversity that Daniel Elazar and others see as one of the most salient characteristics of many federations. However, theory and practice are not often aligned: Canadian senators' claims to act on behalf of provincial or regional interests are hampered by their weak authority (derived from what many see as an outdated selection method); and Australian senators are considered to be stronger advocates of the positions of their political parties than those of their states. That said, principles of intrastate federalism underlie the composition and mandate of the South African National council of the Provinces. Even the Wakeham royal commission (see Lord Wakeham's chapter) was concerned with finding ways of representing the regions (or nations) of the United Kingdom in a reformed House of Lords.

In the opening chapter of this section, Stéphane Dion uses interdependence as his leitmotif: a determining factor of federalism today is the ability of governments to work together while respecting each other's spheres of autonomy. He provides a survey of the "land of intergovernmental relations in Canada" – a rich landscape that reflects the strength of the provinces (and their small number), the power of the executive in relation to the legislative branch (at both levels), Quebec's ongoing search for greater autonomy, and a second chamber that does not really compete with provincial governments as to regional representation. Dion then proposes a series of principles for productive intergovernmental relations. These reflect not only the enduring importance of intergovernmental processes in the development and adaptation of major public policies and programs (such as health care but also his view that federalism is an apprenticeship in negotiation and the art of conflict resolution.

In the late 1990s, as Robert Hazell notes in his chapter, the United Kingdom saw the birth of a whole set of new political institutions through the Blair government's devolution program. Hazell describes the backdrop to this initiative, which included pressure from nationalists in Scotland and Wales, as well as the main elements of the constitutional arrangements. He notes that leading political figures wanted the regions' legislative assemblies to be different from Westminster. Drawing on research on the first years of the Scottish Parliament. Hazell demonstrates that in a number of ways – such as through more powerful committees and efforts to draw in the views of a wide range of organizations and citizens – Scottish political leaders have sought to increase responsiveness within governance. In addition, owing more to Labour's candidate nomination policy than the proportional election system itself, women accounted for 38 per cent of members elected to the Scottish parliament in 1999 – much higher than the proportion elected to Westminster in 1997 or 2000. While public attention was perhaps more focused on the establishment of the legislative assemblies. Hazell sees greater and more public intergovernmental bargaining between Edinburgh, Cardiff, Belfast, and London as a highly significant outcome of devolution – one that may exacerbate tensions between different parts of the country. Differences could become greater if at some point in the future the governing party at Westminster and the leading party in one or more of the devolved assemblies are of different political stripes.

In the final chapter of this collection, Christina Murray provides an analysis of another newly established legislative institution, the South African second chamber, the National Council of Provinces (NCOP). Its composition and powers, inspired in good measure by those of the German Bundesrat, place the NCOP squarely within the intrastate federalism model: each province sends a ten-member delegation, the members of which are appointed by the provincial legislature, to the NCOP; the legislatures prepare mandates for their delegations; and legislation "affecting" the provinces must usually be passed by the NCOP. For Murray, the NCOP was intended to compensate for the limited powers accorded the provinces under the constitution and contributes to cooperative government. A major difficulty in implementation has been the limited capacity of provincial legislatures to deal with the sheer volume of national legislation that the NCOP generates. South Africa continues to face enormous challenges in securing democratic processes in a highly diverse country where decentralized forms of governance do not have deep roots. Its own adaptation of parliamentary government combined with multi-level governance will bear watching as it continues to evolve.

The Interdependence of Governments in Canada

STÉPHANE DION

Federalism may be defined as a system in which two orders of government possess constitutional powers. Each order of government is sovereign within its own legislative sphere, in the sense that the constitution recognizes it as the only one empowered to legislate in that sphere.

And yet there are some fields of governmental activity that do not lend themselves well to a watertight distinction of roles and responsibilities between orders of government. Therefore the constitutions of federations generally provide for a number of shared constitutional jurisdictions within which both orders of government are called upon to play a role and to work together.

In addition, the expansion of the role of governments in the lives of citizens throughout the twentieth century has increased the responsibilities of both federal governments and governments of constituent entities, and as a result, their areas of jurisdiction increasingly touch. They have had to learn to work more closely together and to manage these intense interactions.

The federalism of today is characterized as much by the interdependence of responsibilities as by the division of powers. The ability of governments to work together while respecting each other's spheres of autonomy is a determining factor in the functioning of modern federations.

However, for a host of reasons, this dynamic between autonomy and interdependence is experienced to a particularly high degree in Canada. You would be hard pressed to find another federation whose political life is marked as much by its intergovernmental relations.

I will first describe the factors which place intergovernmental relations at the centre of Canadian political life, and then propose seven principles which, I believe, ought to guide governments in federal systems so that their relations best serve the public interest.

THE LAND OF INTERGOVERNMENTAL RELATIONS

Canadian political life is largely punctuated by federal-provincial meetings. An example is the political event of the summer, which for a number of years now has been the annual meeting of provincial and territorial premiers generally held in August. Over a few days, the premiers devote the main part of their meeting to coordinating their strategies so as to exert effective pressure on their federal counterpart.

Meetings of the prime minister and premiers have led to agreements on important policies and programs, ranging from medicare and pensions in the 1960s to the National Child Benefit in the 1990s. In September 2000, a first ministers meeting led to accords on health renewal and early childhood development. All first ministers agreed on priorities to strengthen the health care system, which will include measuring, tracking, and reporting on performance to citizens. Given the extent of intergovernmental dialogue and compromise before and during the first ministers meeting, Premier Bouchard of Quebec was correct in describing the agreement as a dynamic partnership.[1]

This political event attracted a great deal of media coverage. But there are also a host of other, less publicized meetings that have a cumulative effect that shapes our country. Between 1 April 1999 and 31 March 2000, alone, sixty-one federal-provincial-territorial meetings were held, covering almost all fields of governmental activity: twenty-six among senior officials and thirty-five among ministers.[2] And that does not include the innumerable informal contacts.

These meetings, of both elected representatives and government officials, reflect the pervasiveness of intergovernmental issues in almost every sector. I believe there are five underlying factors that explain the great importance of intergovernmental relations in Canada and which give them a unique character among world federations.

The Strength of Our Provinces

In Canada both orders of government are strong enough in their respective spheres that they can act relatively autonomously. Compared to the constitutions of other federations, Canada's constitution creates few shared powers, and our provinces have broad legislative jurisdictions of their own. The provinces have jurisdiction over education and play the primary role in the design and management of health and social services. Over time, the provincial governments have also increased their tax revenues in comparison with those of the federal government. The latter does not make substantial use of its spending power, and attaches few conditions to it. Federal transfers to the provinces are much less conditional today than they were in the 1960s and 1970s.[3] This is very clear in the fields of health and social assistance, for example. So the federal government can initiate few policies without having to work with the provinces.

The Small Number of Our Provinces

There are relatively few provinces in Canada, a fact which facilitates intergovernmental contacts. There are only ten Canadian provinces, compared with sixteen German *Länder*, twenty-six Swiss cantons, and fifty American states. The relatively small number of Canadian provinces makes it easier not only to hold frequent interprovincial or federal-provincial meetings but also to build interprovincial cohesion. Moreover, the largest provinces, Ontario and Quebec, as well as British Columbia and Alberta, have political and administrative structures of appreciable size compared to those of the federal government.[4] They are major actors in the Canadian political system.

Our Type of Second Chamber

Compared with other Senates, Canada's, which is not elected, is in less of a position to compete with the provincial governments in terms of regional representation. For example, the competition in the United States between the two senators and the governor of a given state has no equivalent in our Canadian political system. Furthermore, because our senators are appointed by the federal executive branch, and not by the executive branches or the legislatures of the constituent entities, intergovernmental relations in Canada thus take place between executive branches that are clearly distinct and that are not institutionally linked through Parliament.

The Strength of the Executive Branch in Relation to the Legislative Branch

Among the twenty-four existing federations, only four combine a parliamentary system and a simple majority vote electoral system: Canada, India, Malaysia, and St. Kitts and Nevis. This combination tends to produce governments, at both the federal and provincial levels, that are formed by a single party that is usually able to pass the legislation it proposes. As a result, intergovernmental relations are conducted between strong governments. In comparison, federations that combine a presidential system, some with and some without a proportional representation system, tend to have intergovernmental relations that are more diffuse and that are strongly defined by the balance between the executive and the legislative branches and by party coalitions.[5]

The Existence of a Minority Group That Is a Majority In One of the Constituent Entities

In addition to their belonging to Canada, francophone Quebecers also identify strongly with their province, where they make up 81.5 per cent of the population. The Quebec government plays a key role in promoting provincial autonomy in Canada. Moreover, the presence in Quebec of a separatist party in power or in opposition over the last three decades has often imparted an existential nature to intergovernmental relations that is unknown in other federations.

These are the five factors that I feel fundamentally explain the exceptional importance of intergovernmental relations in Canada. No other federation combines all five. The United States, one of the longest standing federations, does not have any of these characteristics. Australia, for its part, has two: a small number of constituent entities (there are only six states) and the relative strength of the executive branch in relation to the legislative branch. But the Australian states have substantially fewer powers and autonomous means than do the Canadian provinces; the Australian Senate is elected; and Australia does not have a national minority that constitutes a majority within one of its states.

SOME PRINCIPLES TO OBSERVE FOR PRODUCTIVE INTERGOVERNMENTAL RELATIONS

Precisely because intergovernmental relations are of such importance, it is essential that they serve the general interest well. To this end, I proposed, at the international conference on federalism in Mont-Tremblant on 6 October 1999 seven fundamental principles which, if observed, should guide intergovernmental relations for the better. These seven principles should be viewed as a whole; respecting one of them must not be used as a pretext for ignoring the others.

First, the constitution must be respected. We must do away with the all-too-convenient excuse that a given governmental initiative responds to a need that is too urgent to be obstructed by issues of jurisdiction. Infringement of legislative jurisdiction creates confusion which damages the quality of public policy.

Second, cooperation is essential. More often that not, it is necessary to cooperate, because government jurisdictions touch on each other in almost all sectors of activity. Such cooperation has led to innovative government partnerships and co-management arrangements for better service delivery in areas such as training our workforce, collecting taxes, promoting tourism, and protecting the country's food and blood supplies. There are few policies or programs that the Canadian government can implement without the active cooperation of the provinces.

Third, the ability of governments to act must be preserved. We must not let our quest for cooperation lead us to create a federation where no government can move without the permission of the others. The capacity for initiative and innovation must be preserved within each autonomous sphere of activity. We must not fall into what the Europeans call a joint decision trap.

Fourth, the federation must be flexible. The quest for joint action must take into account the diversity of the country. It must reconcile the pursuit of common objectives and the citizens' desire for government services of comparable quality throughout the country with the constituent entities' capacity to innovate and establish a healthy emulation among themselves.

Fifth, the federation must be fair. Federations must encourage redistribution among their constituent entities, so that even the less wealthy among them are able to provide their citizens with services of acceptable quality. In Canada, this has been a constitutional principle, which we call equalization, since 1982. In Europe, some federations prefer to talk of a solidarity fund.[6] Perhaps we should use the same designation in Canada, because a national solidarity fund is what equalization gives Canadians.

Sixth, the exchange of information is essential. Unilateralism and surprises must be avoided. Governments must be notified in advance of any new initiatives that could have a significant impact on their activities. Exchanging information also allows governments to compare their performance, assess their respective initiatives, and establish among themselves a healthy emulation.

Seventh, and last, the public must be aware of the respective contributions of the different governments. Visibility does indeed count.

While visibility should not be the main motivation for government action, citizens have the right to know what their governments are doing. Visibility encourages transparency, enabling citizens to assess the performance of each government. And governments will agree more readily to work together if they are sure to receive credit for their initiatives.

These are the principles which I believe could guide intergovernmental relations within federations. In any event, I feel that they are certainly important in Canada. I am not saying that we Canadians fully succeed in respecting these principles. I am saying we must try our best to do so.

Certainly, this is not achieved without some difficulty. A degree of creative tension is inherent in the federal system. The perspective of the federal government is not the same as that of the constituent entities. The federal government, representing all the voters, is naturally concerned with the second principle: the need for cooperation, and for pooling resources and talents to achieve national objectives. The governments of constituent entities are mindful of the third and fourth principles: their sphere of autonomy and their capacity for initiative and innovation. For intergovernmental relations to yield positive results, each government must accept the merits of the others' views and everybody must respect the other principles: fairness, exchange of information, transparency, and respect for the constitution.

Conclusion

It seems clear to me that Canada is the land of intergovernmental relations. I have proposed five factors that can explain this phenomenon, and seven principles for action that should enable us to draw on the best of it.

The stakes are considerable, because federalism is more than just an effective method of governance. It is also an apprenticeship in negotiation, the art of conflict resolution, an inevitable dimension of life in society. In a federation, governments are well positioned to set an example for their citizens. They can prove that it is possible to work together for the good of the whole country, while respecting differences of parties, regions, languages, cultures, or ethnic mix. Federalism is proof that diversity in a country is not a problem, but rather a strength. Of course, intergovernmental relations within a federation are often highly complex. But as practitioners we must never forget that beyond that necessary complexity, which is our daily bread, federalism is first and foremost a profoundly human undertaking.

NOTES

1 Comments by Premier Bouchard in a press conference following the meeting (11 September 2000).

2 Information from Intergovernmental Affairs, Privy Council Office (Government of Canada).

3 Conditional shared-cost transfers accounted for approximately 75 per cent of all federal transfers to provincial governments in the early 1960s. By 1996, following the establishment of the Canadian Health and Social Transfer, conditional transfers had dropped to approximately 4 per cent of all federal transfers to the provinces. Ronald L. Watts, *Comparing Federal Systems*, 2nd. ed., (Kingston, Ontario: Institute of Intergovernmental Relations, 1999), 49.

4 As of March 1999, there were 186,314 public service employees in the government of Canada, 66,000 in the government of Ontario, 66,875 in the government of Quebec, 38,197 in the government of British Columbia, and 20,446 in the government of Alberta. Canada, Treasury Board Secretariat, *Employment Statistics for the Federal Public Service* (1999); Ontario, Civil Service Commission, *Annual Report* (1999); Québec, Secrétariat du conseil du trésor, *L'effectif de la fonction publique du Québec* (1999); British Columbia, Public Service Employee Relations Commission, *Annual Report* (1999); Alberta, Personnel Administrative Office, *Annual Report* (2000).

5 Watts, *Comparing Federal Systems*, 84–5.

6 Most federations, with the notable exception of the United States, have some formal equalization program, though the scope of such transfers varies greatly. For more information, see Watts, *Comparing Federal Systems*, 50–3.

The UK's Rolling Program of Devolution: Slippery Slope or Safeguard of the Union?

ROBERT HAZELL

It is rare for students of politics to witness the birth of a new political system and a whole set of new political institutions in their own country. Devolution in the United Kingdom has introduced such major changes that any commentary on them is bound to be highly selective. This chapter begins with a description of the essential features of devolution in the first three years since the election of the Labour government in May 1997. Next there is an analysis of the quasi-federal system that is emerging as a result, and some of the gaps remaining at the centre are identified. Finally, the last part of the chapter describes how the devolved assemblies are trying to break from the model of their creator, the Westminster Parliament.

DEVOLUTION SINCE 1997

Devolution has a long history, going back to Gladstone's attempts to grant Home Rule to Ireland in the 1880s and 1890s. With the partition of Ireland in 1920, devolution disappeared from the political agenda, but resurfaced in the late 1960s in Scotland and Wales, when the two nationalist parties, the Scottish National Party and Plaid Cymru, began winning by-elections and gave the Labour Party a severe electoral fright. The last Labour government (1974–79) legislated for devolution in the Scotland Act and Wales Act of 1978, but its proposals were defeated at referendums in 1979.

Thus it was that John Smith, Tony Blair's predecessor as leader of the Labour Party, described devolution as Labour's "unfinished business."

Labour's manifesto in 1997 committed the party to legislating for devolution in Scotland and Wales in its first year, which it did. In its first year in office the new Labour government unleashed five separate devolution initiatives, each with a different dynamic, whose cumulative effect will be to transform the nature of the UK as a multi-national state. But this speed came at a price. Each initiative has been planned with little or no regard to the other elements in the devolution package, and with no sense of the package as a coherent whole. As devolution is implemented in this piecemeal fashion, there will be a growing need to develop a coherent framework, if only after the event, for practical and political reasons. Coherence need not mean symmetry or federalism by another name; but it should imply the development of common solutions to common problems, and a common institutional framework to bind the devolution settlement together.

Scotland

Scotland will have the most devolved power. The Scotland Act 1998 provides for the Scottish Parliament to be able to legislate in all matters except the UK constitution; foreign policy; defence and national security; immigration and nationality; macro-economic, monetary, and fiscal policy; regulation of markets; employment; and social security. The Scottish Parliament will regard itself as being in the devolution vanguard, and will want to retain that position; and with a population of five million it will be the largest of the devolved units, except London, but with far greater powers and a much bigger budget.

The Scottish Parliament will give the Scottish National Party (SNP) a much stronger platform from which to broadcast its separatist message. With only six MPs elected to Westminster in 1997, their voices were difficult to hear among the louder noise. In Edinburgh it became the main opposition party, thanks to the proportional voting system,[1] which in 1999 gave the SNP thirty-five members (seven constituency and twenty-eight additional) in the 129-seat Parliament. With the usual alternation, they are likely in time to form a government in Scotland; but they are unlikely to increase their representation at Westminster. Opinion polls on voting intentions show a significant gap between support for the SNP at Scottish elections (running at an average of 34 per cent from May 1999 to July 2000) and support for the SNP at Westminster (running at an average of 27 per cent). Scottish politics may increasingly resemble Quebec politics, with the sovereignist party polling more strongly at the provincial than federal level. Scottish politics will also put pressure on the highly centralized Labour Party to relax its grip, in order to allow Scottish Labour to compete more effectively against the SNP in Scotland. Whether we will see the same degree of autonomy emerge as in Canada (e.g., between the provincial Liberal Party in Quebec and the federal Liberal Party) remains to be seen.

What if the SNP does form a government in Scotland: will that lead to the break-up of the UK? Veteran Labour backbencher Tam Dalyell has said that devolution is "a motorway without exit to an independent state."[2] But he is not necessarily right. There are a number of roadblocks the SNP would have to overcome. First, it would have to command a majority in the Scottish Parliament to hold a referendum. Because of the proportional voting system, that is not so easy. The SNP might find that, like the Labour Party at present, it would need the support of other parties to form a coalition; but none of the coalition partners (all unionist parties) would agree to a referendum on independence. Second, the Scottish Parliament has no powers to alter the constitution of the UK, and indeed no power to alter its own constitution as set out in the Scotland Act. Third, even if a legal means could be found to hold a referendum, the Scots would not necessarily vote for independence: opinion polls suggest that one-third of SNP supporters do not want independence – they vote for the SNP as the main alternative to the Labour Party. Fourth, as the Canadian Supreme Court declared in the Quebec reference case,[3] a Scottish referendum would merely provide the trigger to negotiations with the rest of the UK about independence and could not of itself constitute a declaration of independence.

Devolution, rather than being a stepping stone to secession, seems more likely to re-invigorate the existing union. That has been the experience in other large countries of Western Europe, such as Spain and Italy, which have granted devolution to parts of the territory without leading to independence. In Spain secessionist sentiment is still vigorous in the Basque country and Catalonia, but so far secessionist parties have not won mandates to negotiate independence. Indeed their support has declined. And in the first year of devolution opinion polls suggested that support for independence had declined in Scotland.

What will happen as a result of devolution is something quite familiar in federal systems. There will be much greater and more public intergovernmental bargaining between Edinburgh, Cardiff, Belfast, and London. Devolution will expose parts of the political system that have remained relatively hidden – for example, the distribution of resources to the different regions, of inward investment, and of losses and gains from European policies. This public bargaining may exacerbate tensions between different parts of the country. It may lead the Scots – spurred on by the SNP – to question how good a deal they get from the union. It may also lead the English to question whether they are being shortchanged. We will revisit the English Question later.

Northern Ireland

Until recently, Northern Ireland offered all the history there was of devolution within the UK. The fifty years of the Northern Ireland Parliament which ruled from 1922 to 1972 showed that legislative devolution was possible within the framework of the sovereignty of the Westminster Parliament; and that it was possible to have asymmetrical devolution, as devolution existed in one part of the kingdom and not in the others. Now Northern Ireland is set to make devolutionary history again, with a unique set of institutions designed to tie in both the Unionist and nationalist communities. The Assembly elected in June 1998 has 108 members elected by single transferable vote. It has legislative powers broadly similar to those exercisable by the Scottish Parliament, but in every other respect the devolution arrangements in Northern Ireland are markedly different.

The main safeguards to prevent one community from trampling on the rights of the other are a unique power-sharing executive and qualified majority voting in the Assembly. All key decisions in the Assembly must have support on a cross-community basis. Election of the first and deputy first ministers and the chair of the Assembly, the standing orders, and the annual budget allocations must be approved by a majority of both the nationalist and Unionist groups in the Assembly (parallel consent), or by 60 per cent of the Assembly and 40 per cent of both the nationalist and Unionist groups (a weighted majority). Qualified majority voting can be triggered for other decisions by a petition of concern, which can be brought by a significant minority of members of the Assembly (30 of the 108).

The executive builds on the precedent of the power-sharing executive of 1973–74 led by Brian Faulkner.[4] To be elected, the first and deputy first ministers require the support of a triple majority, as described above. Given these constraints and the distribution of parties in the first Assembly, the team of David Trimble (Ulster Unionist) and Seamus Mallon (SDLP, or moderate nationalist) was the only one that could be elected. The first and deputy first ministers have no authority to appoint or dismiss other members of the ministry, and the executive has no collective responsibility. Elections are held in the Assembly for the remaining ministers, office by office, using the d'Hondt system of proportional representation.[5] In the November 1999 elections for the ten remaining seats on the executive, this resulted in the Ulster Unionist party having three ministers, the nationalist Social Democratic and

Labour Party having three, and Sinn Fein (the political wing of the IRA) and Ian Paisley's Democratic Unionists (the DUP) having two each.

Some indication of the difficulties faced by David Trimble can be gleaned from the fact that the two DUP ministers refused to sit down with Sinn Fein and did not attend cabinet meetings during the ten weeks of devolved government before the executive was dissolved in February 2000. Another lies in the wafer-thin majority among the Unionists in the Assembly for the Belfast Agreement which underlies the power-sharing arrangements. There has been consistently more support for power-sharing among the nationalists than among the Unionists, and the Unionists are splintered into several different parties, with all the hardline Unionist parties being against the Agreement. If a majority of Assembly Unionists become opposed to sharing power with Sinn Fein, the power-sharing executive will become unworkable, as was the case for Brian Faulkner in 1974 when he still had a majority in the Assembly but could not command a majority among Assembly Unionists.

Wales

Wales has been an incorporated part of the union for much longer than Scotland or Northern Ireland, with its legal assimilation into England going back to the Tudor period. That history may explain the lesser demand for devolution in Wales: the 1979 referendum for a Welsh Assembly was defeated by four to one; and the 1997 referendum was carried by the narrowest majority, of 50.6 per cent, on a turnout of only 50.3 per cent. The opposition was able to claim that only one Welsh voter in four supported the new Welsh Assembly.

The other reason for the lack of enthusiasm may be the weak form of devolution chosen for Wales, where the Assembly has powers of secondary legislation only. It will continue to operate within a framework of primary legislation laid down by Westminster and be entirely dependent upon Westminster for its annual block grant (as are the other two devolved assemblies).[6] This weak form of devolution represented a compromise between the pro- and anti-devolution wings within the Wales Labour Party and was not supported by either of the other pro-devolution parties, Plaid Cymru and the Liberal Democrats. Lack of enthusiasm continued in the first elections for the Welsh Assembly in May 1999, when turnout was only 46 per cent. This produced a shock for the normally dominant Labour Party, which, under an electoral system similar to the one for the Scottish Parliament,[7] won only twenty-eight seats in the sixty-member Assembly and chose to form a minority government. Plaid Cymru did better than expected, tripling its share of the vote compared with the 1997 general election, by winning seventeen seats.

Wales illustrates how Tony Blair hoped to maintain control after devolution through tight control of the Labour Party. Following the surprise resignation of Ron Davies after a personal scandal in autumn 1998, Blair sought to impose his own candidate Alun Michael as the new leader of the Wales Labour Party. Michael narrowly defeated the more popular Rhodri Morgan, but only thanks to an electoral college which allowed the party membership just one-third of the votes. Labour paid a heavy price in the Assembly elections, when large numbers of Labour voters stayed home, and subsequently, as in February 2000 Alun Michael was forced to resign just before a no-confidence vote in the Assembly which he lost, twenty-seven votes to thirty-one.

Rhodri Morgan assumed the mantle that should have been his a year before, and signalled a more inclusive and open style by negotiating with the opposition parties in the Assembly. This may create more stability for the minority Labour administration, but the underlying problem remains that the Welsh Assembly has very little power. It is entirely dependent upon the degree of discretion conferred by the Westminster Parliament, where every bill is a devolution bill. A well-intentioned Westminster might confer broad delegated powers, but Parliament often leaves Wales little or no room for local discretion or choice. The Welsh Assembly risks incurring the worst of both worlds. It will create high hopes in Wales of independent action which the Assembly may not be able to fulfil, but will be a permanent supplicant in Whitehall, leading to continuous tension between London and Cardiff.

The English Regions

England still awaits its share in the devolution settlement and is thus often referred to as the hole in the centre. Regional assemblies are one of Labour's two unfulfilled promises from its 1997 manifesto. The manifesto commitment was as follows: "Demand for directly elected regional government so varies across England that it would be wrong to impose a uniform system. In time we will introduce legislation to allow the people, region by region, to decide in a referendum whether they want directly elected regional government. Only where clear popular consent is established will arrangements be made for elected regional assemblies."[8] In government it fell to Deputy Prime Minister John Prescott to implement this pledge, as the new secretary of state for the environment, transport, and the regions. He had little support from his colleagues, and none from Number 10. In the first year, the government decided to legislate for regional development agencies but not to provide a statutory basis for the eight regional chambers[9] that were created (this might have provided the first step towards regional government). There is little sign of public demand, although things are beginning to stir in the regional undergrowth.

Spring 2000 saw the launch of the Campaign for the English Regions, formed by the vanguard regional bodies of the North East, North West, the West Midlands, and Yorkshire.[10] The North East has been leading the way, and in direct imitation of Scotland, five of the eight English regions have established constitutional conventions. So far none has passed beyond sloganizing: there is none of the detailed planning for powers, functions, and composition that was part of the Scottish Constitutional Convention.[11] As to a possible referendum, the North of England Assembly will face some high hurdles. Under the evolutionary policy proposed by Labour before the 1997 election, a regional chamber would have to satisfy four conditions before it could become a directly-elected regional assembly:

- have a predominantly unitary structure instead of the existing two-tier local government (so that regional government would not create a third tier)
- receive approval by Parliament
- receive approval in a region-wide referendum
- have auditors' confirmation that there would be no additional overall public expenditure[12]

In the 2001 election, Labour referred to its 1997 pledge and repeated the commitment, but in a rather perfunctory way: "In 1997, we said that the provision should be made for directly elected regional government to go ahead in regions where people decided in a referendum to support it and where predominantly unitary local government is established. This remains our commitment." A White Paper on Regional Government is expected in spring 2002.

Elected Mayors

Since the election, a further challenge has emerged in the form of directly-elected mayors. London is the first city to have an elected mayor, and in the elections to the new Greater London Authority held in May 2000, Ken Livingstone became the city's first elected mayor. He is accountable to a twenty-five person assembly, also directly elected by proportional representation. This is a revolutionary new model for city government in the UK. Despite the mayor's limited sphere of operation and relatively small budget, Ken Livingstone and his successors will be figures of national standing simply because of their direct election by such a large electorate.

Tony Blair tried to block Livingstone's election in the same way as he tried to block Rhodri Morgan in Wales, by the device of an electoral college. Despite the setback of Livingstone's victory, elected mayors are still strongly championed by Number 10. They are not necessarily incompatible with regional assemblies, but there is an interesting tension between the two models. For at regional level there may not be room for two political leaders claiming to be the voice of the region, one as leader of the regional assembly and the other as the mayor of the largest city.[13] Which model wins may depend upon who occupies the political space first.

At present the elected mayors look likely to be the victors. The Local Government Act 2000, which provides the enabling legislation, is now in force, the government wants to see more and, since 2001, other cities can opt for elected mayors. Regional assemblies are much further from becoming a reality and must first pass through the antechamber of indirectly-elected regional chambers. Elected mayors, as the leaders of the biggest local authority in the region, may prove to be one more voice that discovers little interest in moving on to a regional assembly, once they realize that it would be a countervailing source of power over which they would have less control.

FEATURES OF THE DEVOLUTION SETTLEMENT: QUASI-FEDERALISM

Talk of a "settlement" may be misleading. It should be clear from the description of the individual elements in the devolution program that there is no coherent pattern that binds the different elements together and that devolution is unlikely to reach a steady state. But some conclusions can be offered about the nature of devolution in the UK and about the quasi-federal system that is emerging.

Differences from Classic Federalism

There is no constitutional entrenchment of the devolved institutions, although there is political entrenchment in that each was established following a referendum. The devolved assemblies continue to operate under the sovereignty of the Westminster Parliament, which can unilaterally rewrite their constitutions. They enjoy very uneven powers, with the Scottish Parliament and Northern Ireland Assembly having significant legislative power, while the Welsh Assembly has none and the English regions have no elected institutions at all.

Fiscal Imbalance

Although in many federations the central government is dominant financially, in no federation does central government retain such tight control as it will in the UK. Wales and Northern Ireland continue to be 100 per cent dependent on central government grants, while the Scottish Parliament has a marginal power to vary taxes which it is unlikely to use.[14]

A Rolling Program

Some academic experts and politicians have proposed the immediate introduction of a federal system for the UK, but the different starting points and different degrees of enthusiasm around the country suggest that a rolling program best fits the political realities. The motivations for devolution in Scotland, Wales, Northern Ireland, and the English regions are all different. A rolling program of devolution will allow different parts of the UK to move at their own speeds depending on local demand. Scotland, Wales, and Northern Ireland will set the pace; interest in the English regions may pick up as the bandwagon starts to roll.

A Long Timescale

In France and Spain it has taken twenty years to introduce a regional tier of government, and the process is still evolving. France had indirectly-elected regional chambers for over ten years before moving to directly-elected regional assemblies. In the English regions we may need to think in terms of a similar timescale. So long as the principle continues to be one of devolution upon demand, the process must be allowed to evolve at its own pace.

Never a Steady State

Devolution will never reach a perfect equilibrium. It is in the nature of territorial politics that the balance of power between the centre and the regions is being continually renegotiated: this is true even in federal systems, where the formal division of powers is laid down in the federal constitution. So it will be in the UK: the devolution settlement will be the subject of continual adjustment through intergovernmental negotiations, litigation, funding flows, and external relations (e.g., with the European Union).

Asymmetrical Devolution

Devolution need not be uniform. Other European countries live with lopsided devolution, and the UK did so for fifty years with the Northern Ireland Parliament at Stormont. Devolution will need to embrace different settlements for Scotland, Wales, Northern Ireland, and the different regions of England. The trick will be to identify and understand what items need to be held in common throughout the kingdom, as constants of UK citizenship, and what items can be allowed to vary.

A Union, Not a Unitary State

In grappling with different degrees of devolution, it is helpful to understand that the UK is a union, and not a unitary state, and one which can learn a lot from other multi-national union states, such as Canada and Spain, which allow varying degrees of asymmetry.[15]

The Risk of Leapfrog

The UK can also learn about some of the difficulties involved in trying to hold the nation-state together while allowing greater devolution to some parts than others. One is the risk of leapfrog. In Spain, a ratchet effect is observable whereby the less autonomous regions are trying to catch up to the leaders, which provokes the leaders (Catalonia and the Basque region) to seek yet further autonomy to keep one step ahead. Something similar may be at play between Quebec and the other provinces in Canada. A rolling program of devolution is likely to stimulate similar demands in the UK: from the English regions for a piece of the action granted to Scotland and Wales; from Wales for legislative powers on a par with Scotland and Northern Ireland. Will Scotland then demand more to stay one step ahead of Wales?

Demands on the Centre

In this and other respects, devolution will impose major demands on central government: to articulate a vision and give leadership to the process, to hold the ring, to lay down the basic rules, and to adapt its own structures and style. Rebalancing is required at the centre if devolution is to be built on firm foundations. Some of this work is in hand, but in a fumbling and haphazard way. The next section describes the changes taking place in the three branches of central government: at Westminster, in Whitehall, and in the courts.

THE HOLE IN THE CENTRE, PART ONE: THE IMPACT OF DEVOLUTION ON WESTMINSTER

Nowhere is the process of patchwork adaptation more evident than at Westminster. Post-devolution, it is gradually coming to terms with its new role as a quasi-federal Parliament, but in a series of unconnected initiatives and experiments. No discussions have taken place between the two houses about their different but complementary roles, and no effective lead has been offered by the government.

In the House of Commons it was left to select committees to point the way, with a 1998 inquiry by the Scottish Affairs Committee[16] and a Procedure Committee inquiry in spring 1999.[17] The government's response to both inquiries was minimalist, and the Procedure Committee's report skirted around most of the bigger questions. While wishing to undertake a full review in due course, the committee's initial recommendations were as follows:

- abolition of the Scottish, Welsh, and Northern Irish Grand Committees
- new rules restricting questions to the Scottish and Welsh Secretaries to matters relating to their reduced responsibilities
- a new procedure for bills relating exclusively to one part of the kingdom, with a special Second Reading Committee

Absent from the committee's report was any attempt to rethink the role of Scottish, Welsh, and Northern Irish MPs after devolution; to contemplate a reduction in their numbers if their role was found to have diminished; or to address the "West Lothian Question." The latter is now as often called the English Question, and refers to the anomaly that Scottish MPs at Westminster can still vote on English matters while English MPs can no longer vote on Scottish matters because they are now devolved.

Scottish MPs in particular have lost much of their sense of purpose with most of their constituency work devolved to the Scottish Parliament. Their numbers are to be reduced in the next Boundary Commission review, from seventy-two to sixty or fewer; but no one has addressed the need to make a similar reduction in the number of Welsh MPs, even though Wales is equally over-represented (with forty MPs when an equal quota would supply thirty-three). And although the government, in the person of the Lord Chancellor, Lord Irvine, says that the only answer to the West Lothian Question is to stop asking it, an answer cannot be postponed forever, because one day there will be a government at Westminster that depends for its majority on

Scottish or Welsh MPs, or both. There could then be a constitutional crisis if Scottish MPs continue to determine policy on English health and education, when English MPs can no longer vote on such issues in Scotland.

Part of the solution may lie in Westminster gradually developing its role as a proxy for an English Parliament within the wider shell of the union Parliament. Pre-devolution, it was clear when Westminster was operating in Scottish mode; post-devolution, it may need to become clearer when Westminster is operating in English mode. Over the next few years we will witness greater recognition and formalization of English business at Westminster through the work of the select committees, many of which are de facto English committees; the proposal to revive the Standing Committee on Regional Affairs (which once again could provide a forum for English regional debates, as it did in the 1970s);[18] and through the new experiment of a Main Committee sitting in the Grand Committee Room off Westminster Hall,[19] which may also provide a forum for English debates. These initiatives are part of the process of piecemeal adaptation. One interesting feature to watch is who attends these debates. Will Scottish and Welsh Members stay away from English debates and matters that are of no interest to them? And will any follow the self-denying ordinance set by Tam Dalyell and decline to vote on such issues? (Dalyell, a staunch anti-devolution Labour MP, was the originator of the West Lothian Question, which was named after his constituency). If all the MPs of Scotland, Wales, and Northern Ireland were to follow Dalyell's example, former Conservative leader William Hague's slogan of English votes on English laws would be achieved, but by a new convention rather than a new law.[20]

Just as important are the potential new roles for the House of Lords. In a quasi-federal Britain, one obvious role for the Lords would be to represent the nations and regions, as second chambers in federal systems represent the states and the provinces. As Lord Wakeham notes in his contribution to this volume, the Royal Commission he chaired came down against a full-blown federal solution, but recommended that a minority of the members of a reformed second chamber (ranging from 12 to 35 per cent) should be elected to represent the nations and regions. The proportion of elected members is too small, but the principle is right, that the second chamber could play an important role in helping to bind the newly devolved nations and regions to the centre. To strengthen this role, Wakeham also recommended that the upper house have a devolution committee and a constitutional committee, and that it generally act as a guardian of the constitution and of the devolution settlement.

THE HOLE IN THE CENTRE, PART TWO: PRESSURE ON THE COURTS

Devolution brings new pressures on all three branches of central government. The courts will play a central part in interpreting and shaping the devolution settlement and will themselves come under much greater public scrutiny. They will experience a significant increase in workload and be called upon to adjudicate in high-profile devolution disputes. Will the courts be able to take the strain?

The strain has already been evident in Scotland, with the surge of human rights cases under the Scotland Act. At the centre, the strain will be particularly great in the higher courts, the Judicial Committee of the Privy Council and the Appellate Committee in the House of Lords, where the law lords announced their intention to recruit "American style" research assistants to help ease the load. But devolution will also impose pressures of a different kind. It will require a strong legal system, and a system which commands respect on all sides, to hold the union together when the politics are strained. In this respect, the choice of the Judicial Committee of the Privy Council as the final arbiter of devolution disputes looks decidedly odd. Although the Privy Council was the ultimate arbiter of the federal-provincial distribution of powers in Canada until 1949, its work is largely unknown in the UK. It is not the final court of appeal in the UK legal system, but stands largely outside it; and its constitutional jurisdiction in the rest of the Commonwealth has declined almost to zero. It may prove to be a temporary arrangement which will be reopened when wider reform of the House of Lords opens up the question of whether we now need a supreme court which stands clearly at the apex of the legal system and outside the legislature.

THE HOLE IN THE CENTRE, PART THREE: FURTHER ADJUSTMENTS IN WHITEHALL

The third branch of central government that needs to adjust to devolution is the executive branch in Whitehall. Here, too, the adjustments have been minimalist and piecemeal. There continue to be three territorial secretaries of state, although post-devolution there is much less justification for separate representation of Scotland, Wales, and Northern Ireland in the British cabinet. The office of Scottish secretary is the most redundant, given the nature of the devolution settlement in Scotland; but in which order the posts wither away will depend more on the politics of cabinet formation than on the logic of devolution. But it is clear these posts are redundant: if in ten years' time we still have territorial secretaries of state then devolution will have failed.

The back offices of the three territorial secretaries of state may initially be merged, but in time they will fall back into the Cabinet Office, where intergovernmental relations with the devolved governments are managed by the Nations and Regions division of the Cabinet Office, which services the Nations and Regions Committee of Cabinet, chaired by John Prescott as deputy prime minister. This part of the Cabinet Office is the equivalent of the intergovernmental affairs branch of the Canadian Privy Council Office. It could in time work to a single minister, combining the roles of the territorial secretaries of state, who would be responsible for relations with all the devolved governments.

The machinery is gradually falling into place. Symptomatic of the government's piecemeal approach, the key piece of intergovernmental machinery – the Joint Ministerial Committee on devolution (JMC) – was announced late one night in the House of Lords during the committee stage of the Scotland Bill, when the government was being pressed about the need for effective liaison with the devolved administrations.[21] Further details were given in the Memorandum of Understanding between the UK, Scottish, and Welsh administrations.[22]

The JMC is the real "gearbox" of devolution, and not the British-Irish Council, which can only discuss issues with an Irish dimension. The JMC will meet in plenary form once a year, chaired by the prime minister, and in "functional" format through meetings of agriculture ministers, environment ministers, and so on as necessary. The SNP has been quick to point out that the "Joint Ministerial Committee is clearly biased in Westminster's favour since it would always be chaired by a UK Minister – including the adjudication of disputes – and ultimately by Tony Blair."[23] So far the only regular meetings have been of agriculture ministers. The machinery has also been used to consult on UK positions on EU issues. It is bound to grow as the need to consult grows on all other issues, and in time the devolved administrations may request meetings (as they are entitled to) as does the UK government. Up to now the UK government has convened meetings largely to promote its own agenda and current concerns: Gordon Brown has chaired two meetings on poverty and on the knowledge economy, to exchange information and best practices with the devolved administrations, and the prime minister has chaired a JMC on health.

Day-to-day relations between the UK government and the devolved administrations are to be governed by concordats, of which the first four were published with the Memorandum of Understanding in October 1999.[24] They cover coordination on EU policy issues, financial assistance to industry, international relations, and statistics. Since then, a dozen more agreements have been published between individual Whitehall departments and the equivalent departments in Scotland and Wales. The government has been at pains to emphasize that the agreements are not designed to create legal obligations or restrictions, but simply lay the ground rules for administrative cooperation and exchanges of information.

The Memorandum of Understanding and agreements make no provision for parliamentary scrutiny of the Joint Ministerial Committee or of any intergovernmental agreements between the UK government and the devolved governments. But that is a characteristic of intergovernmental relations in federal systems as well, where state or provincial parliaments may find themselves marginalized from negotiations conducted with the federal government; as may the federal parliament itself.

CAN THE DEVOLVED ASSEMBLIES BREAK FROM THE WESTMINSTER MODEL?

Mention of the role of provincial Parliaments leads us to the third part of this chapter, which discusses the aspirations of the devolved assemblies to be different from their creator at Westminster. The last time new Parliaments were established in the British Isles was in 1920, with the creation of the Dail Eireann in Dublin and the new Northern Ireland Parliament in Belfast. Both were miniature versions of Westminster, adopted Erskine May unthinkingly as their bible and became heavily dominated by their executives. The creators of the new Scottish Parliament, the National Assembly for Wales, and the Northern Ireland Assembly were determined that their institutions be different. In the words of the Scottish Constitutional Convention, the goal was "a way of politics that is radically different from the rituals of Westminster; more participative, more creative, less needlessly confrontational … a culture of openness."[25]

The Westminster Model

What are the characteristics of the Westminster model that the new assemblies are so determined to break? The Westminster Parliament is characterized by a largely adversarial two-party system and executive domination by the party in power, which is reflected in many of its structures and procedures:

- The government has a majority on all committees.
- Most committee chairs are held by members of the governing party (currently two-thirds of select committees in the House of Commons).
- Committee members are effectively appointed by the whips, and seldom selected because of any interest or expertise in the subject matter.[26]

- The government controls approximately 80 per cent of legislative time (depending on how many days Parliament sits) and initiates over 90 per cent of bills passed.
- Of non-legislative time, only about 12 per cent (seventeen days for the largest opposition party and three for the next largest) is allocated to the opposition.

As a consequence of these structures and procedures, the failings of Westminster are widely recognized:

- inadequate scrutiny of bills, leading to poor quality legislation
- select committees of uneven quality that do not consistently hold the executive to account
- inadequate scrutiny of public bodies and agencies
- weak ministerial accountability to Parliament
- weak financial controls, particularly over spending plans and estimates
- excessive secrecy on the part of the executive
- failure to protect against abuses of power and breaches of human rights

Devolution in the 1990s was about more than recognizing in institutional form the distinct territorial claims of Scotland, Wales, or Northern Ireland. Accompanying appeals to national identity were promises of a "new politics" that would embody inclusiveness, consensus, openness, transparency, and accountability. Scotland exemplifies this most strongly and is the case study presented here, but similar aspirations have been expressed in Wales and Northern Ireland.

Shaping Scotland's Parliament

One of the ironies in this story is that the immediate creators of the new Scottish Parliament were members of the executive who were tasked with designing a Parliament to hold themselves more effectively to account. The (non-governmental) Scottish Constitutional Convention had laid down some strong guiding principles,[27] but after the 1997 election, the torch passed to officials from the Scottish Office who were tasked with establishing the new Parliament. In November 1997 Donald Dewar, Secretary of State for Scotland, established a Consultative Steering Group to "take forward consideration of how the Scottish Parliament might operate." The Steering Group had a wide membership. It worked on a range of projects to do with the operation of the Scottish Parliament, including the standing orders, financial scrutiny, information and communication technologies, and relations with the media. In addition, there were expert panels and outside consultants: the Constitution Unit, for example, was commissioned to do a comparative study of the checks and balances required in small single-chamber Parliaments (one of the nine Parliaments the Unit looked at was British Columbia's).[28] The Consultative Steering Group published "Shaping Scotland's Parliament" in January 1999. It identified the following key principles for the Parliament:

- The Parliament should embody and reflect the *sharing of power* between the Scottish people, the Parliament and the Scottish Executive.
- The executive should be *accountable* to the Parliament, and the Parliament and executive should be accountable to the Scottish people.
- The Parliament should be *accessible, open* and *responsive*, and should develop procedures which make possible a *participative approach* to the development, consideration, and scrutiny of policy and legislation.
- The Parliament, in its operation and its appointments, should recognize the need to promote *equal opportunities* for all.

These principles should be of interest not just in Scotland, but for any Parliament seeking to increase its responsiveness to the public and its effectiveness in scrutinizing the executive. Canadian provincial Parliaments are known for their subordination to the executive and might have a particular interest in the success or failure of the Scottish Parliament as it struggles to be free. In a further research project, the Constitution Unit carried out an audit of the devolved assemblies relative to the aims and objectives set for them, to assess to what extent they succeed in breaking from the Westminster model. Thus, in the case of the Scottish Parliament, the Unit tried to assess to what extent it manages to live up to the brave principles set out above, and to what extent the realities of politics and the business of government dictate otherwise. To make the study more precise, we broke down the functions of the Parliament into the following classic functions of legislatures:

- representation
- legislation
- deliberation
- scrutiny
- budget setting

- making and breaking governments
- redress of grievances

In relation to each of these functions, the Unit's researchers aimed to assess to what extent each of the devolved assemblies realizes its ambitions to be:

- democratic, inclusive, and power-sharing
- accessible, open, and participatory
- responsive and accountable
- efficient, effective, and modern
- promotive of human rights and equal opportunities

It is worth mentioning a few of the initial findings. This is inevitably a selective list, but already certain features are markedly different from the Westminster Parliament.[29]

No Government Majority

Because of the proportional voting system, no single party has a majority in any of the devolved assemblies. Under the traditional system of first-past-the-post, Labour won a majority of the constituency seats in Scotland and Wales, but the proportionality supplied by the additional member system denied Labour an overall majority. In Wales, Labour first chose to govern as a minority administration but then entered a coalition with the Liberal Democrats in October 2000. In Scotland, Labour entered a coalition with the Liberal Democrats at the start. In Northern Ireland, there is a power-sharing executive of four political parties. The result is that the assemblies are much less subject to executive domination than Westminster is. The executive is not able to assume it will have its way: in May 2000, for example, the executive in Scotland failed to kill a private member's bill by the Scottish Socialist MP, Tommy Sheridan, which had received support from three of the parliament's committees.

Higher Representation of Women

Another difference from Westminster (which had 18 per cent female MPs in 1997) is the higher proportion of women. In Scotland forty-eight women were elected in 1999, 38 per cent of the Parliament; and in Wales twenty-four women, 40 per cent of the total. Following the October 2000 reshuffle in Wales, over half the Welsh cabinet was female, the only such cabinet in Europe. The increase in women's representation owes more to Labour's attempts to select more female candidates than to the proportional voting system itself. Women's influence is felt in such developments as more family-friendly working hours.

Powerful Subject Committees

The committees in Scotland are beginning to play a central role in influencing policy-making and in scrutinizing the executive. In committee debates it is often not possible to tell which party a member belongs to. But there has been tension where a committee convenor is also the opposition party spokesperson. Some committees are struggling under the workload of the executive's heavy legislative program and feel frustrated about having so little time to scrutinize the actions of the executive through their own inquiries. The presiding officer recently authorized a doubling of research staff for the committees in Scotland.

Leadership of the Presiding Officer

The presiding officer is more hands-on in managing the business of the Parliament than the speaker at Westminster. In Scotland, Sir David Steel chairs the Parliamentary Bureau which decides the forthcoming business and includes representatives from all the parties. At Westminster, the business is announced by the leader of the House, after negotiation through "the usual channels" (i.e., the business managers and the whips). In the Welsh Assembly, the presiding officer is also emerging as a defender of the Assembly's rights, for example in resisting pressure in February 2000 over the timing of the no-confidence motion in Alun Michael.

Scrutiny of the Budget

At Westminster scrutiny of the annual estimates is widely recognized as a charade.[30] In Scotland, the Consultative Steering Group sought expert advice on how to introduce more effective scrutiny of the government's spending plans, and one of the first measures passed by the Scottish Parliament was the Public Finance and Accountability (Scotland) Act 2000. There is to be a three-stage budget process, starting with discussion of the overall strategy and spending priorities, with input from all the subject committees. It is too early to say whether the measures will have any real impact, because the process has only just begun. Stage two will involve detailed consideration by the Parliament of ministers' spending plans, and stage three is the passage of the annual budget bill.

Increasing Public Participation

Both the Scottish Parliament and the Northern Ireland Assembly have a Civic Forum which includes representatives from a wide range of civic organizations as an additional sounding board and source of ideas. The Scottish Parliament has an active Petitions Committee to be an additional channel for public concerns and grievances. Some of the committees of the Scottish Parliament have appointed one of their number to be a reporter, to reach out and seek views from those likely to be affected. When scrutinizing legislation, the committees receive evidence directly from a wide range of organizations and interested parties, in a manner denied to standing committees debating bills at Westminster. But it is still proving hard to reach disadvantaged and disaffected groups who find it hard to engage with the political process.

CONCLUSION: HOW TO MEASURE THE EFFECTIVENESS OF PARLIAMENTS

This selective list of some of the new practices in the devolved assemblies can give no more than a flavour of the new departures they are making. It is included at the end of this chapter to make a serious point, and to issue a cry for help. There is growing interest among governments in measuring the effectiveness of their performance and in developing performance indicators (including international benchmarking) for that purpose. I am not aware of any corresponding work being undertaken to measure the effectiveness of Parliaments. It is not easy to devise good performance measures, still less to apply them to the whole range of parliamentary activity, but in a parliamentary democracy the work is of equal importance. It may well be possible to test and develop a set of performance measures and benchmarks of wider application, not just for Westminster but for all Parliaments operating within the Westminster tradition.

NOTES

1 The electoral system is based on the German additional-member system (AMS), also known as mixed-member proportional (MMP), which combines single-member constituencies with additional members to provide proportionality. In the Scottish Parliament there are seventy-three single-member constituencies and fifty-six additional members to

provide proportionality. The latter are elected on a second vote from regional lists, with the regions corresponding to the eight European Parliament constituencies in Scotland, and each region supplying seven additional members. The latter are allocated to parties on the basis of each elector's second vote, using the d'Hondt formula (see note 5).

2 *House of Commons Debates*, 4 March 1998, col. 1081.

3 *Reference re Secession of Quebec* [1998] 2 SCR.

4 Leader of the Unionist Party, who lost the support of the Unionist (Protestant) community for making too many concessions to the (Catholic) nationalists. The power-sharing executive was brought down by a Unionist-led strike.

5 The d'Hondt formula, named after its Belgian inventor Viktor d'Hondt, is a list-based system of proportional representation that requires the number of votes cast for each party to be divided by successive ascending divisors. See A. Blais and L. Massicotte, "Electoral Systems," in *Comparing Democracies: Elections and Voting in Global Perspective,* ed. L. LeDuc, R.G. Niemi, and P. Norris (Thousand Oaks California: Sage Publications, 1996).

6 The Scottish Parliament has power to vary the basic rate of income tax in Scotland by plus or minus threepence in the pound. At the maximum this would increase the Scottish budget by around 5 per cent. Because the tax variation would be expensive to administer and would yield little by way of extra revenue, the power is most unlikely to be used: see Robert Hazell, ed., *Constitutional Futures* (Oxford: Oxford University Press, 1999), 207–8.

7 There are forty constituency members and twenty additional members to provide proportionality, four from each of five regions; the latter are elected on the basis of the same rules as in Scotland.

8 Labour Party, *New Labour: Because Britain Deserves Better* (1997), chap. 9 (on politics and government).

9 Each chamber comprises 70 per cent local authority members and 30 per cent from other sectors, including the Confederation of British Industry, the Trades Union Congress, higher education, parish and town councils, the national Health Service, voluntary organizations, rural and environmental groups, and other regional stakeholders.

10 It was launched in March 2000, with its first newsletter issued in April: Campaign for the English Regions, 150 Pilgrim Street, Newcastle NE1 6TH.

11 The Scottish Constitutional Convention was launched in 1989 and produced several draft reports and working papers before issuing its final report *Scotland's Parliament; Scotland's Right* in November 1995.

12 Labour Party, *A New Voice for England's Regions* (1996). The key elements of the policy were confirmed in Labour's 1997 election manifesto.

13 Although in countries such as France and Spain high-profile mayors co-exist with a regional tier of government.

14 Blais et al., *Comparing Democracies.*

15 See Michael Keating, "What's Wrong with Asymmetrical Government?", *Regional and Federal Studies*, 8, no. 1, (1998): 195–218.

16 United Kingdom, Scottish Affairs Select Committee, *Multi-Layer Democracy,* (HC 460, November 1998).

17 United Kingdom, Procedure Committee, *Procedural Consequences of Devolution*, (HC 185, May 1999).

18 This is an issue on which the government has given a lead. Despite a lukewarm response from the Modernisation Committee when she first floated the idea in February 1999, Margaret Beckett has persisted with her proposal to revive the Standing Committee on Regional Affairs, as a forum open only to English MPs. (House of Commons Debates, 11 April 2000).

19 Modernisation Committee, *Sittings of the House in Westminster Hall* (House of Commons 194, April 1999) cols 291–3.

20 Tam Dalyell first drew attention to "The West Lothian Question" (now increasingly referred to as "The English Question") when he was MP for that constituency during the 1970s.

21 *House of Lords Debates*, 28 July 1998, col. 1487.

22 *Memorandum of Understanding between the UK Government and the Devolved Administrations*, Cm 4444, October 1999, Pt. II.

23 Scottish National Party Press Notice, "Publication of Concordats: SNP criticise London-biased documents." 1 October 1999

24 *Memorandum of Understanding between the UK Government and the Devolved Administrations,* Cm 4444, October 1999.

25 *Scotland's Parliament; Scotland's Right* (November 1995).

26 This was the subject of an unprecedented protest by the Select Committee chairmen. See the First Report of the Liaison Committee, *Shifting the Balance: Select Committees and the Executive* (House of Commons 300, March 2000) and the Government's dismissive *Response to the First Report from the Liaison Committee* (Cm 4737, May 2000).

27 Scotland's Parliament; Scotland's Right.

28 *Single Chamber Parliaments: A Comparative Study* (1998), The Constitution Unit, School of Public Policy, University College London, London WC1H 9EZ; e-mail: <constitution@ucl.ac.uk>.

29 For the full reports of the Constitution Unit's audit, see *A Democratic Design? The political style of the Northern Ireland Assembly* (2001); and on the Scottish Parliament, *Realising the Vision: A Parliament with a Purpose* (2001). Both are available from the Constitution Unit (see note 28).

30 See the Sixth Report from the Procedure Committee, *Procedure for Debate on the Government's Expenditure Plans* (House of Commons 295, July 1999).

Designing Parliament for Cooperative Federalism: South Africa's National Council of Provinces

CHRISTINA MURRAY

Most federations have bicameral legislatures but, as with the other elements of federal systems, there is huge variation in the design of second chambers and their powers. South Africa's second chamber, the National Council of Provinces (NCOP) established under the 1996 constitution, adds yet another model to the list. The NCOP is designed to be both a legislature and a forum for intergovernmental relations, and it reflects the strong desire of the dominant group in the constitution-writing process that decentralisation not be accompanied by a fragmentation of the state. The intention is for South Africa's nine provinces to be represented at the central level through the NCOP, but in significant ways this representation simply compensates for the limited nature of devolution in the country.

It is far too early for any reliable prognosis on the future of the NCOP or to speculate about its value as a model for other countries. For instance, the overwhelming dominance of one party in the system – the African National Congress (ANC), which is the national governing party that governs either in coalition or on its own in all nine provinces – means that the notion of developing provincial interests is weak. In addition, the new provinces' severe lack of capacity to develop policy or administer their affairs suggests to many that the nation needs to focus on the general development of capacity rather than on issues concerning individual provinces.

Thus, this chapter is at most a description of a work-in-progress. It provides an account of the process of establishing the new institution and of initial attempts to clarify its role and integrate it into the political life of the country. Because the NCOP is a complicated institution (too complicated according to some critics), the first part of the chapter provides a description of how it is intended to work. The subsequent shorter sections discuss the problems that South Africa has encountered in establishing the NCOP and speculate on its future. As should be clear, the future of the NCOP is closely tied to the fortunes of devolution in the country and to the gradual development of the political system.

BACKGROUND

It is well known that South Africa's constitutional negotiations led to the establishment of a form of federalism. However, the deep aversion of the new ANC government to any form of government that might divide the country is clearly reflected in the constitutional design. Divisions between the three "spheres"[1] of government (national, provincial, and local) have been described as "soft" because the constitution allows infringements of provincial and municipal integrity by the national executive in the name of effective government. In addition, most important provincial powers are to be exercised concurrently by the national and provincial governments; the list of exclusive provincial powers includes only matters that are relatively unimportant. This cautious approach to decentralization is perhaps summed up in chapter 3 of the constitution. Entitled "Cooperative Government," this chapter sets out principles which state that the national government and provinces (and municipalities) should not enter into competitive relationships with each other but, instead, should "cooperate with one another in mutual trust and good faith." Cooperative government thus means that national policy, rather than ignoring, or riding roughshod over the provinces, must be sensitive to provincial needs and concerns. It also means that provinces do not act alone or in isolation; they must be deeply integrated into the national political process.

The NCOP gives concrete expression to the principles of cooperative government. Its role is to represent the provincial perspective within the national Parliament. By giving the nine provinces a collective say in national legislation, it provides them with an avenue into national policy-making. Thus, the NCOP is a bridge between the provincial and national governments. In an important way it is also the quid pro quo for the provinces' limited power.

A variety of problems have plagued the NCOP since its inception. Outside observers have tended to ascribe problems to the complexity of its design – it is modelled on the German Bundesrat, with certain adjustments in response to South African concerns. These adjustments, it is suggested, introduce an undesirable level of complexity that is particularly problematic in a country with a weak democratic tradition. In addition, as in Canada, the second chamber in South Africa suffers both from problems of internal credibility, with South African politicians paying little attention to it, and external legitimacy, as citizens do not see it as performing a useful public role.

FROM SENATE TO COUNCIL OF PROVINCES

South Africa's interim constitution, adopted in 1993 as a bridge between apartheid and democracy, reintroduced a Senate to Parliament. In many ways this was a surprise, as the history of the second house of South Africa's Parliament at union in 1910 was a miserable one. It was soon subject to blatant political manipulation, the high-point of which was reached in the 1950s when it was packed in order to ensure the passage of racist laws disenfranchising black South Africans.[2] Its abolition in 1980[3] caused certain technical problems but gave rise to virtually no political opposition and did not make a significant difference to political processes in Parliament.[4]

Thus, the reintroduction of a Senate modelled on traditional lines in the first democratic constitution in 1993 was unexpected. Presumably the federal elements in the 1993 constitution prompted the decision to incorporate a second chamber in the newly-constituted Parliament,[5] but they do not explain the new Senate's design – although the 1993 Senate was to represent provinces in the sense that each of the provinces was entitled to an equal number of representatives (ten), and senators were nominated by parties represented in the provincial legislature on a proportional basis. No further link with the provinces was made and, on the type of bill most important to provinces, deadlocks between the two houses could be broken by a majority vote at a joint sitting. The lower house of 400 members could easily overwhelm the Senate in such sittings. Predictably, the Senate once again became a body which merely confirmed decisions taken in the lower house.

Negotiations for a "final" constitution started in 1995. The "constitution-makers," as they were called, were constrained by thirty-four "Constitutional Principles" agreed to two years earlier. Negotiated before the first democratic elections of 1994, these principles required government in South Africa to be divided into three parts – national, provincial, and local. But the governing ANC had long feared federalism, partly because of the historical balkanization of South Africa under the Bantustan system and partly because it feared that a decentralized system would inhibit the kind of radical transformation that was necessary to undo apartheid's legacy of poverty and discrimination. In addition, many ANC politicians were sceptical of the provincial system and viewed it as an imposition by other parties in the multi-party negotiating process – a compromise necessitated by the need to find a system that allowed political space for minority groupings, such as the Inkatha Freedom Party (IFP) in KwaZulu-Natal and the National Party.

Accordingly, when drafting the 1996 constitution, the majority party was quite concerned about building on the foundations laid in the interim constitution and about devising a decentralized system of government that would avoid the perceived dangers of federalism. In the interim constitution, the compromise for regions established extensive power-sharing between the centre and provinces, and relied on a broadly-worded set of principles to manage the boundaries. In the final constitution, the concept of cooperative government was introduced to provide the main protection against competitive federalism.

The final constitution provides a weak form of federation, listing in two schedules the areas in which provinces may legislate but reserving concurrent legislative power for the national government in the more significant areas that appear in the lists.[6] Thus, the most important matters for the transformation and development of the country (such as health, education, welfare, and housing) fall under the concurrent authority of the provincial and national governments. Generally speaking, the need for the central government to be able to ensure effective government determines the division of power in the concurrent areas. For instance, the national government can establish "frameworks" and national "norms and standards,"[7] and provincial governments may be left merely to fine-tune delivery. Provincial administrative competence follows legislative competence, and the constitution stipulates that provinces will also administer national legislation that deals with any matter listed in the schedules. Nevertheless, the constitution gives the national government ample power to intervene in provincial affairs if the delivery of services is threatened in any way.

By late 1995, when the form of devolution in South Africa was becoming clear, the view of the majority ANC government was that if South Africa was to retain a bicameral legislature (and the vested interests of senators made any other choice difficult), the second house should serve as a means of building unity and binding the new provinces to the centre. The Bundesrat model was attractive to South Africans because it made the second house an integral part of the system. But the Bundesrat had something special to offer those South Africans who feared federalism (who were in the majority in the negotiating process). It provided the model for a system in which a limited grant of legislative power to individual provinces could be compensated by giving the provinces substantial collective power in the national Parliament. Of course, for many the provinces were more than a compromise in the negotiating process, and the NCOP was not just a device to centralize provincial power. To a significant number of people, provinces offered another point of democratic engagement with the people of South Africa and the NCOP provided an opportunity to draw those contributions into the national legislative process.[8] Overall, the NCOP allows provinces to enrich the national legislative process and prevents them from becoming excessively parochial. The participation of a non-voting delegation representing local government is a tentative first move to bind local government into national politics in a similar way.

HOW DOES THE NCOP WORK? INSTITUTIONALIZING COOPERATIVE GOVERNMENT

The National Council of Provinces represents the provinces to ensure their interests are taken into account in the national sphere of government. It does this mainly by participating in the national legislative process and by providing a national forum for public consideration of issues affecting the provinces.[9]

The NCOP's role in developing cooperative government is reflected in its powers, membership, and expected mode of operation. It must debate and pass legislation alongside the National Assembly, but it is to do so from a distinctly provincial perspective. Hence its powers are much greater with legislation that directly affects the provinces, including constitutional amendments, than with matters that do not affect the provinces. For areas not affecting the provinces, therefore, the NCOP is primarily an advisor to the National Assembly, an arena of "sober second thoughts." In other areas it speaks more definitively for the provinces, and the National Assembly needs a two-thirds majority to override it.

In addition to passing legislation, the NCOP must oversee the relationship between the national executive and provinces (and the relationship between provincial executives and municipalities). Here it is expected to guard provincial and municipal integrity and to check abuse by the national executive. But, as a national institution comprised of provincial and local delegations, it does this with local, provincial, and national interests in mind and can ensure that basic values of cooperative government – respect for the integrity of the spheres of government and effective government – are realized.

Membership and Voting

Membership of the NCOP is based on nine ten-member delegations, one for each province. Each delegation consists of six "permanent" members and four "special" members, and must reflect in a proportional way the representation of parties in the provincial legislature. The permanent members are appointed by the provincial legislature to serve until the next provincial election and are based in Cape Town. The four special members consist of the premier or her or his nominee (thus, at least in principle, formally involving the provincial executive in the national legislative process) and three other members of the provincial legislature who are designated from time to time by the provincial legislature to represent it on a specific matter.

On matters affecting the provinces, the members of the delegation vote as a single unit and each delegation has one vote. Voting is done on the instruction ("mandate") of the provincial legislature. Thus a fundamental premise of the NCOP is that its members are selected by, and accountable to, provincial legislatures. Again this reflects a fundamental purpose of the constitution: to bind the provinces into national government by making them spheres within a single whole rather than autonomous, independent entities. Only on matters not affecting the provinces do the members of the NCOP vote as individuals or, more accurately, as members of political parties.[10]

The role of opposition politicians in NCOP delegations is much less clear and is almost certainly the result of bargaining in the constitution-making process rather than careful design. Nevertheless, it contributes to the capacity of the NCOP to provide a real forum for democratic engagement by provinces on national policy issues. On most matters, delegations have one vote, a vote which will be determined by the majority party in a province. But, the NCOP committee-system, which is modelled on the vigorous committee system in the National Assembly, gives opposition politicians ample space to contribute to debate.

The third sphere, local government, is represented in the NCOP by a delegation of ten members. Local government's role in the NCOP is different from that of the provinces. It is a junior partner, with the right to participate in debates "when necessary" but without the right to vote.[11]

The NCOP *as Legislature*

The NCOP must consider all national bills but its influence varies according to the subject matter of the bill. First, although the NCOP debates all constitutional amendments, its approval is required only for amendments that deal with provincial matters,[12] the bill of rights, or section 1 of the constitution which sets out certain principles fundamental to the South African constitutional order.

As to other legislation, the constitution distinguishes two types, commonly referred to as section 75 legislation and section 76 legislation. The distinction follows the broader constitutional division of functions into those that are purely national and those in which provinces play a role. Generally speaking, section 76 legislation is any legislation concerning a matter listed in Schedule 4 of the constitution and for which the national and provincial governments share responsibility (for example, health, welfare, and housing). Section 75 legislation is that which falls outside the provinces' constitutional ambit. The significance of the distinction is that the NCOP has real influence on section 76 matters but much less influence on section 75 matters.

So-called section 76 legislation covers bills "affecting" the provinces and must usually be passed by the NCOP. The supporting vote of five provinces is sufficient. If the NCOP and the National Assembly cannot agree on such a bill, it must be sent to the Mediation Committee established under section 78 of the constitution (along the lines of the German model).[13] If, in spite of attempted mediation, the two chambers cannot come to an agreement, a bill first introduced in the National Assembly may nevertheless become law if it is passed by a two-thirds majority in the National Assembly.

Section 75 legislation (or bills not affecting provinces) must also be considered by the NCOP. Voting procedures are different for section 75 matters, reflecting their limited significance for provinces. On section 75 matters each delegate has a vote. If such a bill is not passed by the NCOP, it may nevertheless become law if the National Assembly passes the bill again with an ordinary majority.[14]

Most bills start life in a national ministry. If a proposed bill falls into a "concurrent" area of responsibility, the ministry will usually convene a meeting between the national minister and the relevant members of the provincial executive committees. Here the proposals will be discussed and, later, draft bills considered. From there, bills go to Parliament, including, of course, the NCOP. This marks the end of the process of executive intergovernmental relations and puts debates around the bill in the public arena.

Although executive intergovernmental relations processes should mean that provincial executives are familiar with the bill by the time it is introduced in the NCOP and that provincial legislatures may have been following the bill earlier, once it is introduced in the NCOP, provinces are formally and openly engaged in the process. First, delegations are briefed on the background and purposes of the bill; then the provincial legislatures take over and prepare initial (and at this stage usually fairly general) mandates for their delegations. A week of negotiations in the NCOP follows and delegations share any concerns they may have about the bill. A week later, back in the provinces, the initial mandate may be revised to accommodate issues raised by other provinces. Finally, a vote is taken in the NCOP.

The legislative process clearly demands that provinces become fully and openly involved in national debates on major issues -- most notably those relating to transformation. Doing so establishes the NCOP as the central institution for the realization of the cooperative form of federalism to which the constitution commits South Africa. The NCOP is the linking mechanism that acts simultaneously to involve the provinces in national purposes and to ensure the responsiveness of national government to provincial interests. Many national bills place substantial burdens on provincial executives, burdens that often relate directly to provincial budgets (such as setting standards for pensions) and demand particular administrative capacity from provinces (such as facilities for paying out pensions in a particular way). From this perspective, the NCOP process can protect the provinces from unrealistic expectations by the national government. Through the NCOP, national government is sensitized to provincial interests and its processes are enriched accordingly. Equally, the NCOP engages provinces and provincial legislatures in the formulation of national policy and prevents them from becoming excessively parochial.

The NCOP process is enormously demanding on provinces. Small provincial legislatures must have the time and understanding to make decisions on major issues of national policy; this obviously displaces other legislative activities. The most obvious question raised by this aspect of NCOP procedures is why executive engagement with draft legislation is not considered sufficient. Why does the South African process differ so dramatically from its German counterpart in this regard? Certainly, if the goal is to ensure effective government in a decentralized system, the involvement of provincial executives at the national level is most valuable. The explanation for the direct involvement of provincial legislatures in the NCOP process must lie in the new South Africa's passionate commitment to democracy. Criticism of intergovernmental relations as highly bureaucratized and obscure struck a chord with South Africans intent on building institutions that would establish a strong democracy and that offered significant opportunities for popular participation.[15] In comparing the design of the NCOP, shortly before it came into being, to that of the Bundesrat, the minister of constitutional development commented that the fact that politicians "do not play much of a role in the Bundesrat" and that civil servants essentially run the legislative process is one of its greatest weaknesses.[16]

Whether or not this characterization of the Bundesrat is correct, it led South Africans to explore other approaches. Accordingly, the South African model was intended to ensure democratic rather than bureaucratic participation from the side of provinces in the national legislative process. At the same time, citizens would be given an opportunity to participate in the national legislative process through their provincial legislatures and not only through Parliament in distant Cape Town.

The charge that the Bundesrat is run by bureaucrats may be overstated. Certainly it was resisted by all the Germans that the South African negotiators met in their visit to Germany in January 1996. Instead, the Germans insisted, officials are bound by political instructions.[17] However, it seems that South Africans' usual description of their concerns is inaccurate. It is almost certainly not merely the fact that civil servants play a significant role in Bundesrat processes that concerned South Africans but the fact that the process is executive driven. South Africa's history has created a deep fear of executive domination in government, not fully laid to rest by the ANC's assumption of power. The involvement of provincial legislatures in the NCOP is primarily an attempt to limit the power of executives and ensure greater legislative control of the process. Ronald Watts has suggested that this refinement of the Bundesrat model may have been misplaced. He points out that the logic of the Bundesrat is that the *Land* executives that execute laws should participate in making them to ensure that they can be implemented.[18] Moreover, South Africa's parliamentary system, like its counterparts in many other Commonwealth countries, is dominated by the executive. The demand implicit in the design of the NCOP that legislatures should play a more prominent role may be naïve.

Nevertheless, whether or not it is based on an appropriate criticism of the German system or a proper understanding of the balance of power in parliamentary systems, in its demand for direct involvement in the NCOP by provincial legislatures, the South African model has added a layer of complexity. This burdens the country's young and fragile democratic process.

BALANCING EFFECTIVE GOVERNMENT AND PROVINCIAL AND MUNICIPAL INTEGRITY

Passing laws has dominated the NCOP's agenda thus far, but this is only one of its constitutional roles. Complementing its legislative function is a supervisory function: under the constitution, the NCOP is to play a central role in maintaining the integrity of the three spheres of government.

In the weak form of federalism that the constitution establishes, the national government is expected to ensure effective government at all levels and is authorized (perhaps even required) by the constitution to intervene if this does not occur. For example, section 100 permits the national executive to intervene in a province if the latter fails to fulfil obligations placed on it by legislation (either national or provincial). Such an intervention can extend to the national government actually taking over a provincial function. There are various political disincentives for such interventions by the national government, the most important of which relate to the national government's limited capacity to fulfil these tasks and concerns that provincial governments might be willingly relieved of unpopular tasks by national intervention.

Nevertheless, the possibility of an intervention into provincial affairs by the national government, such as that permitted by section 100, is accompanied by the possibility of abuse. As a provincial chamber acting in national politics, the NCOP is ideally suited to check such executive action. The NCOP may veto a section 100 intervention; its approval, together with that of the National Assembly is necessary if the national executive wishes to block the flow of funds to a province;[19] and, if a province disputes a decision by the national executive concerning that province's capacity to administer certain legislation, the NCOP must resolve the dispute.[20]

These checking provisions give the NCOP a critical role in the most sensitive area of intergovernmental relations. There is great pressure on the new government institutions to deliver and, in particular, to provide services to the many communities that have not had them in the past. However, in many cases, appropriate administrative structures are still being established; resources are severely stretched; and many municipalities are simply not viable. Complaints by the national government that provinces and municipalities are not functioning adequately are understandably met with the response that they are under-resourced. The NCOP is called upon to settle this type of dispute.

Thus far, the formal intergovernmental problems that have come before the NCOP have all concerned a provincial intervention in a municipality. Although complex political disputes and infighting have frequently accompanied the interventions, a challenge to municipal integrity is not as politically charged as a challenge to provincial integrity might be. Nevertheless, in responding to these problems, the NCOP has demonstrated the constructive role it can play in intergovernmental relations. Rather than reacting formalistically, merely checking the constitutionality of the action, it has assumed the role of mediator and worked with the parties to put in place solutions that will build the capacity of the municipalities concerned.[21] This approach, which blends a firm commitment to effective government with an understanding of the problems that the new administrations labour under at present, should serve the NCOP well when faced with more divisive matters.

Local Government

The ANC attributes the status of local government in the South African constitution to a comment made by Chancellor Kohl of Germany during an ANC visit to Bonn in the early 1990s. Kohl remarked that if there were one thing that he would like to change in the German constitution it was the status of local government. This sentiment struck a chord with South Africans. The ANC, which had long been concerned with maintaining vigorous grassroots democracy, saw the constitutionalization of local government as a way of achieving this. In addition, entrenched municipal power would dilute provincial power. The other main negotiating party, the National Party, seemed similarly committed to local government, perhaps in part because it assumed that it could retain pockets of power at the local level, and perhaps simply because strong local government was in line with its commitment to participatory democracy.[22]

In any event, South African constitution-makers took Kohl's remarks to heart. Although municipal powers and institutions are not defined in as much detail in the constitution as their provincial counterparts, local government is clearly established as a constitutionally protected sphere of government, with original powers emanating from the constitution rather than national or provincial statute. In addition, in a number of forward-looking provisions, the constitution anticipates local government's power increasing as newly-democratized municipalities become viable.

The constitution requires an act of Parliament to "provide for the recognition of national and provincial organisations representing municipalities" and to set up procedures for consultation between local, provincial, and national governments.[23] It is "organised local government" that is entitled to participate in NCOP proceedings, and delegations from the national organization representing local government have participated in the NCOP since its inception. Nevertheless, the future of local government participation in the NCOP is unclear. Thus far, much of the focus has been on ensuring that the procedures adopted by the NCOP are amenable to local government participation. In addition, representatives of organized local government have played significant roles when the NCOP exercised its supervisory powers over provincial intervention in municipalities. Local government participation is essential in the latter case, but the benefits of its participation may be less obvious in other matters.

Although the NCOP is clearly committed to making local government participation in the NCOP's processes meaningful, until now local government has typically engaged with the more influential National Assembly on legislative matters that directly effect municipalities. Unless the NCOP shows it can both provide a platform for local government that is not available elsewhere and ensure that the national sphere of government responds properly to municipal concerns, local government may prefer to use the public participation process established by the National Assembly rather than the NCOP. In short, it remains to be seen whether the institutional link between local government and the NCOP that the constitution provides will be developed in a way that makes the NCOP a more attractive forum for local government than the powerful National Assembly.

The National Assembly Override – Central Control?

The German system gives the Bundesrat the power of absolute veto over national legislation. This is missing in the South African model. Instead, as already mentioned, NCOP objections to legislation can be overruled by a two-thirds majority in the National Assembly. The South African political context explains the change. A veto would reflect an arrangement that granted much more power to provinces than was desired by the ANC. The question that does arise, however, is what difference this makes. Like so many other questions relating to the NCOP, it cannot be answered fully now. As long as the NCOP is dominated by the same party as the National Assembly and the overall system remains a "dominant single-party system," disagreements between the two houses are likely to be rare. At present, politicians will not easily countenance even a single ANC province breaking ranks; in South Africa's system of rigid and effective party discipline, an out-and-out conflict between the two chambers is unimaginable. Matters might change if the overall political configuration changed. Were four out of nine provinces to be held by opposition parties, the NCOP might seize the opportunity to flex its muscles.

But the National Assembly override does have an effect on perceptions of the NCOP and, accordingly, on its effectiveness. It is a constant reminder to the NCOP that it is the weaker house. In practice this seems to have contributed to the lack of confidence that even those politicians involved in the NCOP have in it. Thus, delegates to the NCOP often refer to the National Assembly override, commenting on its power. Of course, sometimes this may be a justification for a tendency among NCOP politicians to follow their political masters in the National Assembly. But, whatever the underlying motives, it is not conducive to the vigorous representation of provincial interests.

PUTTING THE DESIGN TO THE TEST

On paper the design of the NCOP is most elegant. It neatly marries the desire to represent provincial interests in the national sphere of government with a concern for democratic government. The carefully constructed provincial delegations draw both provincial legislatures and executives into the national legislative process. The tentative inclusion of local government in NCOP proceedings paves the way for fuller participation in the future. The dangers of central government takeovers of provinces are controlled by "peer review" in the NCOP, and the fact that provinces are given very limited taxing power is balanced by giving them a collective say in what their share of nationally-raised revenue should be. The centralized form of federalism deemed necessary to enable effective reconstruction in South Africa is thus mitigated by giving the NCOP checking power.

In practice, however, establishing the NCOP has been a slow and difficult process. Five years after its first sitting in February 1997, it had in place many of the institutions and practices necessary for its effective operation but, in fundamental ways, it was still struggling to establish itself firmly and to make the impact on the national political process that its design promises. Although the NCOP claims to make a difference to national bills, most of its interventions are more akin to those of a traditional Senate, involving error correction and fine tuning. Few NCOP contributions to legislation reflect its role of drawing provincial concerns into the national legislative process. Its most successful actions have been in fulfilling its obligation to approve provincial "takeovers" of municipalities. But here the work has largely been done through a small committee of permanent delegates to the NCOP, and, by and large, provincial legislatures have paid little attention to the process.

An obvious reason for the many teething problems of the NCOP is the complexity of its design. The NCOP demands a sophisticated bureaucracy and first-rate communication systems. Provincial legislatures need timely and ongoing information about bills in Parliament; they need up-to-date records of proceedings in the NCOP and its committees; and they need staff who can process and order this huge volume of information so it is accessible to the members of provincial legislatures. In turn, the NCOP needs to be able to distribute information to provincial legislatures rapidly and well in advance of meetings. Internet technology provides an obvious means of doing this but is less simple than it seems.[24] It requires technology and skills that are not always easy to set up and maintain in those provincial legislatures that are seated in small, underdeveloped towns. Sometimes even the smooth day-to-day operation of such systems is difficult to achieve.

The magnitude of the demands that NCOP processes make on provincial legislatures becomes more striking when one considers the size of these legislatures. Although the largest (KwaZulu-Natal) has eighty members, the three smallest (Free State, Mpumalanga, and Northern Cape) have only thirty seats each. From this number, a premier is chosen and ten other members join the provincial executive. Once the Speaker is accounted for, only eighteen members remain to carry the day-to-day work of the legislature. Thus the entire active membership of a provincial legislature may be significantly smaller than that of a single National Assembly committee.

But even if the provinces were better equipped to use the NCOP, it is not clear whether they would ensure that provincial interests were vigorously represented at the national level. The language of "spheres" rather than levels of government was intended to eradicate a sense of hierarchy and to introduce the concept of partners in government with distinctive functions appropriate to each level. Nevertheless, this conception does not inform political relationships. Instead, both in parties and in government itself, a firm sense of hierarchy remains: provincial politicians usually consider themselves to be serving their national parties, not some distinctively provincial interest.

South Africa's political parties are centrally organized. The ANC had a tradition of strong discipline as a liberation movement before entering Parliament, and in Parliament it met a similarly disciplined movement in the previously governing National Party. The prevailing parliamentary culture of strict party discipline and strong party loyalty is supported by the new electoral system. Closed-list proportional representation tends to give control over the political future of MPs to party elites. Although South African parties, and particularly the ANC, are remarkably democratic in their internal operation, national party organizations vet lists sent up from regional branches and control their content and the ranking of candidates.[25] In South Africa, the party-based electoral system is backed up by an "anti-defection clause": an MP's seat in the legislature is dependent on retaining membership of the party on whose ticket the seat is gained.

Many factors related to the party system detract from the ability of the NCOP to offer an alternative perspective in national politics to that offered by the National Assembly. In practice, provincial politicians defer to their national counterparts both in executive intergovernmental relations forums and in the NCOP.

These problems – the complexity of NCOP procedures and the strain this puts on resources, the weakness of provincial legislatures, and the grip of national political parties on provincial politicians – may be teething problems, but they are closely linked to another, more fundamental issue. This is the overall lack of enthusiasm in the ruling ANC for the provincial system and repeated rumours that it is being reconsidered.[26]

As noted at the beginning of this chapter, by the time constitutional negotiations started in 1990, the ANC had been committed for decades to a unitary state free of the balkanizing goals of apartheid ideology. Demands for federalism were quickly interpreted as self-interested proposals that would allow minority parties to entrench past divisions. Although there is some evidence that ANC party elites came to see benefits in a regionalized system, the model of regionalism adopted in the final constitution is at most a very weak form of federalism with much power concentrated in the centre. Generally speaking, the provincial system has not been enthusiastically embraced.

The lack of political commitment to the provincial system has been fed by the obvious failure of the newly established provinces to fulfil their obligation to deliver services.[27] The most important task facing South Africans is to transform their society from one in which a small section of the society was entitled to first-class services and the rest to minimal schooling, health care, and welfare to one in which services are distributed equally. This has to be done without a budget increase and in the context of limited economic growth. Needless to say, it is a massive and complex task. Under the scheme envisioned by the constitution, the national government would work out the policy and raise the money, and the provinces would administer the policy.

But provinces have been singularly unsuccessful in this role. There are many possible reasons. One is that a number of the poorest provinces are made up of fragments of different political entities inherited from apartheid South Africa. For instance, the Eastern Cape encompasses part of the old Cape Province and two (corrupt) "independent homelands," the Transkei and Ciskei. Establishing a new administration in such areas is a challenge under the best conditions. It was made doubly difficult by a dearth of skilled administrators, the extreme poverty of the regions, and the fact that the negotiated settlement of 1993 protected the jobs of former civil servants. For these and other reasons, provinces have battled to fulfil their mandates.

It is far from clear that the national government would be able to more successfully fulfil the functions presently allocated to provinces.

The limits on resources apply to it as to provinces, and the Provincial Review Commission was no less critical of administration in the national government than it was of the provincial situation. Nevertheless, it is the provinces that have failed and this has damaged what little political credibility they have.

Initially, it was conventional wisdom that the vested interests that provincial politicians were given in the decentralized system would secure the future of provincialism,[28] but this seems not to be the case. Although it is likely that some provincial politicians would fight to retain the systems in order to retain jobs and status, overall it seems that all politicians are aware of one critical need summed up in an ANC election slogan: "A better life for all." No one's political future is secure in a party that is not perceived to be successful in this way.[29] In other words, the centralizing tendency that seems to be characteristic of any government in power is intensified in the case of the ANC not only by a historic antipathy to decentralization but also by the urgent need to govern effectively.

THE FUTURE

Because the preceding section focused on impediments to the NCOP's effective functioning, it may seem to suggest that the NCOP has been a failure. That is not true. In spite of a multitude of problems, the NCOP has slowly refined administrative processes, clarified its constitutional mandate, and asserted itself in the national arena. Given the change in thinking that is required to understand its role, its successes are not inconsiderable.[30] Technical problems will be overcome in time, and the limited capacity of provincial legislatures to deal with the sheer volume of national legislation that the NCOP generates may eventually lead to some sharing among provinces of their resources – a truly cooperative solution. Nevertheless, the fortunes of the NCOP are closely linked to those of the provincial system generally. In turn, the future of that system is linked to the ANC's agenda for the future and, in particular, to decisions about how the very limited resources available to the government are best used.

Over the past couple of years, rumours about provinces have abounded. These range from assertions that the government is planning to abolish provinces altogether or at least drastically reduce their number, to claims that either the legislative aspect of the system will be dismantled, leaving provinces as executive or administrative centres, or that the legislative role of provinces will be retained but that their executive functions will be greatly reduced.

Most proposals that involve the retention of some form of provincial system would be compatible with the retention of the NCOP in some form or another. But, whatever adjustments are made, for the NCOP to work, provinces must engage in it with energy. They need to be confident that even views that are critical of national government policy do not undermine attempts to transform South Africa but are essential to its success. Conversely, the national government must accept that cooperative government cannot be a top-down affair with orders issued centrally and provinces cooperating. It demands honest and open debate among all players.

NOTES

The author acknowledges the excellent research assistance of Shaheena Karbanee.

1 As explained later in this chapter, the term *spheres* is used intentionally to indicate governments which operate as partners rather than governments which operate at different levels of a hierarchy.

2 For a description see B. Beinart, "The South African Senate," *Modern Law Review* 20: 562.

3 By the Republic of South Africa Constitution 5th Amendment Act 101 of 1980.

4 All political parties supported the abolition of the Senate. In a minority report for the Schlebusch Commission, the members of the official opposition (the Progressive Federal Party) who were members of the commission stated that the Senate "in its present form does not fulfil a useful function" (Interim Report of the Commission of Inquiry on the Constitution, RP 68/1980:10).

5 In addition, certain parties in the negotiations with regional support may have seen an opportunity to capitalize on that support in a regionally-based Senate.

6 It must be noted that in South Africa, concurrent legislative power is not understood in the same way as in all other countries. For instance, while in Germany concurrency means that *Lander* have the power to legislate in so far as the federation does not exercise its right to do so, in South Africa the existence of national legislation does not exclude provincial legislation. Instead, the field remains open and, if there is conflicting provincial and national legislation on a matter, the provincial legislation prevails unless the national legislation meets certain tests. Although never tested in court, in the light of the reluctance of courts to interfere in administrative matters and the urgent need for massive development on a national scale in South Africa, these tests seem relatively weak and the national power to legislate correspondingly strong. Nigeria's concept of concurrence is also different. The list of concurrent powers in the

1999 Nigeria constitution carefully delineates the power of the federal government and the states over certain subject matter.

7 South African Constitution, s. 146 (2)(b).

8 See Steven Friedman, "Why we need provincial governments," *Business Day,* 9 March 1998.

9 Constitution, s. 42(4).

10 The requirement that provincial legislatures confer authority on their delegations to cast votes on their behalf is at once a key provision in tying NCOP delegations to their provinces and a provision that makes NCOP processes extraordinarily complex. The Constitution simply states in section 65(2) that: "An Act of Parliament ... must provide for a uniform procedure in terms of which provincial legislatures confer authority on their delegations to cast votes on their behalf." The act of Parliament referred to in section 65(2) has not yet been passed. In the meantime, in a healthy process of experimentation, provinces have established practices suited to their particular political circumstances. Common to these practices, however, is that the authorization given to delegations is specific to each piece of legislation before the NCOP and leaves little or no leeway in voting. Some provinces allow minor deviations from mandates if every member of a delegation supports the change. Others appear to allow no deviations at all without consultation with the provincial legislature. This practice constrains NCOP procedures in significant ways. It also means that important aspects of NCOP decision-making take place in provincial legislatures.

11 Constitution, s. 67.

12 In this connection, NCOP approval is required for a bill which "(i) relates to a matter which affects the Council; (ii) alters provincial boundaries, powers, functions or institutions; or (iii) amends a provision that deals specifically with a provincial matter," Constitution, s. 74 (3)(b).

13 Along the lines of the German model, South Africa's Mediation Committee has equal representation from each house: each of the nine provinces can send a delegate and the National Assembly is represented by nine members elected in a way that reflects the representation of parties in the Assembly (s. 78[1]). But, unlike the German process, decisions of the South African Mediation Committee must be supported by a majority of the members of each house, five NCOP delegates, and five National Assembly members (s. 78[2]). This could be viewed as an unexpected deviation from a design that tends to grant final decision-making power to the National Assembly. But it is probably merely a reflection of political reality. Like the German committee, the South African committee may only make proposals. For its recommendations to become law, they must be passed by the NCOP and the National Assembly, or passed

by the National Assembly alone under the override provision. As I have suggested above, for political reasons it is unlikely that the Assembly will be able to use the override when the balance of power in the NCOP is against it. This means that Mediation Committee proposals will need the support of both houses to be effective – a reality reflected in the double majority requirement.

14 Following Bundesrat practice, the NCOP operates in cycles. Formally, the cycles operate in the following way: In week one of a cycle, legislation is tabled in the NCOP and the national department sponsoring a particular bill briefs the relevant NCOP committee. In week two, the bills are discussed in the provincial legislatures. Week three sees politicians return to the NCOP to discuss possible changes to bills and, later in the week, back in their provincial legislature seeking approval for negotiated changes. In week four, bills are voted on in the NCOP plenary. The four-week cycle is a direct result of pressure from the National Assembly and it imposes an extremely tight time frame. Moreover, a significant number of bills are labelled "urgent" and are dealt with in a contracted process. Clear time frames are necessary in this context – it would not be appropriate to give the second house the opportunity to undermine the national legislative process by delaying bills for extended periods. Nevertheless, if one considers that provinces are meant to consider bills in their legislatures and engage in public consultation, the four-week cycle seems unrealistic. It is noteworthy that the time frames imposed by the Basic Law are considerably longer although the Bundesrat process is less complicated (see Basic Law Arts 76–78). For a description of the way in which the NCOP cycles work and a discussion of their problems, see C. Murray and R. Simeon, "From Paper to Practice: the National Council of Provinces after its first year," *South African Public Law* 14: 96.

15 The constitution reflects a concern with public participation in government in many other ways as well. See, for instance, s. 1, 32, 59, 72, 118, and 160.

16 That this was the view of the South African constitution-makers is clearly seen in the *Report on Trip to Germany* (Cape Town: Constitutional Assembly, 16 February 1996) which documents the visit to Germany by key South African negotiators in January 1996. The report repeatedly records the group asking the German politicians and officials that they met whether the German system does not rely too heavily on officials (see, in particular, para. 13.6 which states "the question was raised, as it had been repeatedly over the week, … whether the German system … did not rely too heavily on officials which officials were granted political decision making power by virtue of their responsibility for the administration of the Bundesrat activities").

17 See *Report on Trip to Germany* (Cape Town: Constitutional Assembly, 16 February 1996).

18 Discussion with Ronald Watts, 16 September 1998.

19 Constitution, s. 216(3). Section 216(2) sets out a narrow set of circumstances in which provincial funds may be blocked. The process of approval (or disapproval) of a treasury decision to stop funds to a province is similar to that for the passage of section 76 legislation. This means that the National Assembly may override an NCOP veto but only by a two-thirds majority.

20 Constitution, s. 125(4).

21 See for more detail Christina M. Murray, "Municipality Integrity and Effective Government: The Butterworth intervention," *South African Public Law,* forthcoming.

22 National Party, *Constitutional Rule in a Participatory Democracy* (Pretoria: 1992).

23 Constitution, s. 163. The act is the Organised Local Government Act 52 of 1997.

24 The National Democratic Institute, an American NGO, has recently set up a sophisticated Internet-based system for the NCOP. Early reports are that this is improving the distribution of materials. See <http://www.parliament.gov.za>, which provides a link to the NCOP.

25 See, for instance, "ANC Meets to Finalize Lists," *Mail and Guardian,* 12 February 1999.

26 The NCOP's 1998 conference included a panel discussion entitled "Provincial Government – Where to Now?" The discussion was lively and two provincial premiers charged the national government with a failure to support provinces adequately. See, "The Imperative of Co-operative Government," Proceedings of the NCOP National Conference (National Democratic Institute, 1998). Prior to the June 1999 elections, discussion of provincial government by politicians was more "up-beat" with an emphasis on provincial successes rather than the failures which had been widely reported in preceding years. See for just one such example, "Provinces Praised on Fiscal Management" *Cape Argus,* 17 February 1999.

27 "Who Needs the provinces?" *Mail and Guardian,* 12 September 1996.

28 Richard Humphries, Thabo Rapoo, and Steven Friedman, "The Shape of the Country: Negotiating Regional Government" in *South African Review 7: The Small Miracle South Africa's Negotiated Settlement,* ed. Steven Friedman and Doreen Atkinson (Johannesburg: Ravan Press, 1994), 148.

29 Experience in the Eastern Cape, a province with a particularly poor record on delivery, showed this vividly in the run-up to the second (1999) elections. As far back as November 1997, it was reported that

the Eastern Cape legislature was battling to secure a quorum in meetings. The fairly widely accepted explanation was that the failure of Eastern Cape politicians to govern effectively had led to decisions in local party branches not to vote them back into office. At this point the politicians presumably had a choice. They could have tackled their jobs with renewed energy. Instead, however, they appear to have treated their legislative salaries as some form of "seed funding" which cut their losses and to have pursued other activities.

30 For a report on its first year, see Murray and Simeon, "From Paper to Practice," *National Council of Provinces 1996–1999 in Review* (Cape Town: National Democratic Institute and NCOP, 1999).

Conclusion: Can Canada Learn Some Lessons?

DAVID C. DOCHERTY

Westminster governments are in an exciting period of transformation. The history of change in these states is not one of incrementalism, but rather of long periods of stasis followed by brief flurries of experimental change. As the chapters of this volume suggest, a number of parliamentary democracies have been in a period of the latter since the late 1990s. However, on representational and institutional reform, Canada stands alone. While a number of other nations (including the Mother of Parliaments) have been open to changing what is understood to be the Westminster model, as Jennifer Smith points out in her contribution to this volume, Canada's Parliament and electoral system have yet to undergo such a major "overhaul."

Canada has been more active on other fronts. On the issue of responsiveness we have made significant strides with Aboriginal peoples. While there are still miles to go, there can be little dispute that the direction is at least correct. Other attempts to adapt multi-level governance outside the constitutional level have also met with measured success. Canada's greatest constitutional accomplishment, the patriation of the constitution and the introduction of the Charter of Rights and Freedoms in 1982, has had a significant impact on the country's public life. As Stéphane Dion suggests in his chapter, federalism is a sign of diversity, and when basic principles of fairness and respect are practised, it serves to reinforce the nation, not divide it.

On parliamentary and electoral reform, Canada does not stack up well compared to other parliamentary democracies. Other children of Westminster have moved in new directions, but Canada has not. One could be forgiven for thinking the country is clinging to apron strings that even the mother has cast aside. That said, this concluding chapter argues that, in certain respects, Canada has been more responsive than it may appear in adapting its governance processes to a diverse society and the expectations of its citizens.

PRINCIPLES OF MAJORITARIAN GOVERNMENT AND THE STRENGTHS OF WESTMINSTER SYSTEMS

Parliamentary democracies are based, to varying degress, on majoritarian principles. Arend Lijphart has described the prototypical majoritarian system of government as having these principal characteristics: a concentration of power in one-party or bare-majority governments, cabinet dominance, a two-party system, disproportionate election results, and a unitary government.[1] However, not all majoritarian governments share these characteristics.

Majoritarian systems of government have often been closely associated with Westminster-style parliamentary democracy. Indeed, Lijphart has identified New Zealand, prior to its adoption of proportional representation, as the ideal type of majoritarian system. But it stood almost alone in this regard. Australia has a bicameral federal Parliament where members of the House of Representatives are elected under the alternative-vote system; since 1949 senators have been elected by proportional representation. Great Britain has a second chamber that has consistently played a significant legislative and scrutiny role. Canada, with a decentralized federal system, asymmetrical arrangements between levels of government, an appointed national second chamber, and – for most of the twentieth century – a viable multi-party system, is far from the Lijphart vision of an ideal majoritarian state.

Nonetheless, Lijphart's work is an important reminder that the features of majoritarian systems are not limited to the electoral system and its impact. Further, public policies are affected by how closely a nation approximates a truly majoritarian system. For example, Lijphart argues that majoritarian systems are less effective than consensus models of government at providing participatory governance, gender and minority representation, and progressive public policies.[2]

Cabinet dominance and disproportionate electoral results are perhaps the least flattering distinctions of Canada's version of majoritarianism. A single-member plurality system imposed on a federal state rewards parties that encourage regionalism and thus perpetuates divisions within the country. In Canada this has resulted in political parties that see emphasizing regional differences and inequalities as the best way of assuring political success (or survival in some cases).[3] Other aspects of Canada's political system, such as a reliance on multi-level governance and the increasingly regional nature of Canada's national party system, deviate from Lijphart's pure majoritarian system.

Majoritarianism leads to concentrated authority rather than dispersal of power throughout a political system.[4] While the representativeness of legislatures may be contested (majoritarian systems favour single-party majorities that often receive less than majority support at elections), citizens focus on those individuals who hold power; there is a great deal of what Bingham Powell describes as citizen control of the state. In this sense, majoritarian systems allow citizens a clear view of who is in charge: an incumbent government faces a single major challenger and the decision of the electorate is clear and uncontested.[5]

Westminster systems, even those that do not fit the true majoritarian model, also produce what might be called effective government. Indeed, the greatest strength of the Westminster model may be its efficiency. Single-member pluralities and strong party discipline combine to create governments that can implement their programs with little opposition. The inability of government backbenchers and opposition members to introduce broad legislation (or any legislation that carries a price tag) means that alternative policies rarely move beyond discussion and rhetoric. The evolution of parliamentary government has made this dynamic appear almost an axiom of the Westminster system. Cabinet and prime minister have centralized authority, and are accountable for their actions at the next election. Budgets are passed without compromise. Legislation promised can be introduced without the need to dilute its content to gain acceptance from opposition parties. If properly managed, the winner truly can take all. In this sense, it is efficient government without equal among democratic systems.

Efficiency does not come cheaply, though the price is seldom paid by the victors. In Canada, and nationally in the United Kingdom, the cost of such efficiency is in part the quality of representation. In its most base form, citizens rarely speak with one voice and governments are elected by a minority and not a majority of voters. The move away from traditional two-party contests and declining voter turnout have exacerbated this problem. Governments are being elected by increasingly smaller percentages of the electorate. Among other things, this allows critics of governments to legitimately question any so-called "mandate from the people." In Canada, for example, we can ask why, when more people voted against than in favour of free trade and the GST in the 1988 federal election, we ended up with both. The answer is simple: our efficient system of government not only allows this to happen, it effectively encourages it.

By contrast, proportional systems are much more inclined to diffuse power among a myriad of "officials, offices and issues," and it is unclear where the buck stops.[6] Here questions of responsibility are more diffuse. There are far greater opportunities for citizens to access government, but often a myriad of methods to achieve legislative or policy results. The resulting consensus style may be more cumbersome, but it may help achieve "kinder, gentler" policy results.[7]

The fact that many states with a majoritarian history are adopting proportional electoral models suggests that Lijphart, Powell and others are not alone in their assessments. Indeed, Canada's adherence to its highly majoritarian system could be taken as a sign that questions of control and power are more central than questions of equitable representation and responsiveness. As the following sections argue, there is some support for such an interpretation. Successive Canadian governments have been loath to give up their monopoly on power. At the same time, majoritarian governments have embraced other avenues to encourage responsiveness in government that might have been more difficult to implement under a more consensual model.

REPRESENTATION

Changes to electoral representation have been most dramatic in New Zealand and the United Kingdom. From being the archetype of a majoritarian system to adopting a system of proportional representation, the transition in New Zealand's electoral arrangements has been profound. In part a reaction to public disaffection with strong cabinet government and the inability of Parliament to represent the public in a fair manner, the introduction of a mixed system of proportional representation was seen as more likely to improve representation than the re-establishment of a second chamber.[8] Replacing the electoral system in New Zealand required a great deal of will on the part of government. While the government was in part responding to the significant support for reform outside the ranks of the political elite, fairer representation came at the expense of a concentration of power by one political party.

It was perhaps easier for the United Kingdom, as part of its devolution program, to institute a form of proportional representation for the new Scottish Parliament and Welsh Assembly (both are mixed systems), as well as for the restored Parliament in Northern Ireland (which is elected by the single transferable vote). In fulfilling this part of its electoral manifesto, the Labour Party was not threatening its own ability to produce lopsided majorities in Westminster.[9]

The unwillingness of Canadian leaders to contemplate changes to the country's electoral system reflects this concern over losing authority. The single-member plurality system exaggerates the strength of the winning party. In cases where there are more than two parties (Canada, Westminster) the leading party can, and usually does, win office with less than half the vote. Britain has not had a government selected by a majority of voters (let alone eligible voters) since the end of the Second World War; in Canada this has occurred only once.[10] In 1979, the Progressive Conservative Party formed a minority government with fewer votes nationally than the Liberals. At the same time, parties that win 20 per cent or so of the national vote can be left with fewer than 5 per cent of the seats in the House of Commons.

Other deviations occur at the regional and provincial levels. In 1979, 13 per cent of the vote in Quebec netted the Conservatives less than 3 per cent of that province's seats. In 1997, the Liberals took nearly one-quarter of the votes in Alberta but won only two of twenty-six seats. Entire provinces can be left out of the governing caucus, and prime ministers have sometimes turned to appointed senators to ensure that each province has a voice at the cabinet table (as Pierre Trudeau did in 1980). Provinces are represented in cabinet, but the ability of elected officials to hold such ministers to account is compromised. Further, as Louis Massicotte argues, regional skews become discriminating cycles. Governments might feel inclined to ignore regions that do not have representation in the governing party, while regions with strong cabinet and caucus representation might try to "slow down changes designed to widen support" for the party in these non-represented areas.[11]

It has been more than thirty years since Alan Cairns argued eloquently that the Canadian electoral system exacerbates regional cleavages by rewarding parties that concentrate their efforts in regions rather than nationally.[12] Since then, Canada has witnessed the decline of two national parties (the Progressive Conservatives and the New Democrats) and the rise of two regional parties (the Bloc Québécois and the Canadian Alliance). While the long-term survival of the latter two parties is a matter of conjecture, there is little doubt that the single-member plurality system eased their entry into federal politics through its tendency to "reward" regionally-focused parties.

The concentration of power within the governing party does not stop with exaggerated electoral results. Consistent with the classic Westminster model, power has long resided within the cabinet. Combined with the iron hand of party discipline, this has both merits and drawbacks. For example, as C.E.S. Franks has argued, it allows governments to sponsor pan-Canadian social policies that might not have been possible in a system of loose coalitions.[13] The Canadian constitution gives jurisdiction for most social policies to the provinces. In order to implement some level of national standards, the federal government must act decisively and with unity.[14] Majoritarian principles allow for such action in response to national interests.

A key to such action is the effectiveness of executive federalism within a system that favours government by single parties. Here we see the majoritarian principle writ large. When a government enjoys a majority, it holds free rein within its own jurisdiction. Likewise, when a number of majority governments agree on a particular issue, as first ministers and ministers often do, moving ahead on a policy or program is usually easy. Internal opposition can effectively be ignored. While such concerted action is more likely when issues have "less public salience," the principles remain true in all policy and constitutional areas.[15]

Executive federalism is, however, criticized for its lack of openness. Having learned their lessons the hard way – the failure of the Meech Lake Accord was due in part to a lack of consultation and the image of eleven men making agreements in closed meetings – governments responded by encouraging greater public consultation during the subsequent constitutional process which led to the 1982 Charlottetown Accord (it too was defeated, but in a nationwide referendum). There have also been experiments with public consultation in other policy fields where executive federalism plays a key role.[16]

The concentration of power in the Canadian system nevertheless has significant drawbacks. In his description of "court government," Donald Savoie outlines how the power of the prime minister at the national level in Canada has grown dramatically. Increased technology, stronger reliance on survey data, and a more powerful Prime Minister's Office (PMO) and Privy Council Office (PCO) have all combined to make even cabinet less important than it was a generation ago. If Parliament has lost sway, so too has cabinet. In fact, recent administrations have circled their wagons even tighter and have begun to cocoon power even further within the PMO and PCO. Savoie suggests that Jean Chrétien is no different than his predecessors in this regard and is not adverse to bypassing cabinet when it suits his purposes.[17]

The very system that encourages such a concentration of authority allows the government to maintain it, despite repeated calls for parliamentary reform. Public opinion polls have consistently demonstrated a desire among Canadians to reform our elective institutions, mostly with a view to dispersing authority both within the lower chamber and between the Commons and a reformed Senate.[18]

Parties in opposition are quick to call for such reform, yet once in power they are quicker to realize that the very distortions they decried provided them with the opportunity to win office. These parties are just as aware that the concentration of authority works to their benefit once in office. Power does not come with an incentive to embrace change, and once in office parties and leaders are loath to experiment with any reforms that might weaken their grip on the levers of power. Government House Leader Don Boudria's reaction to the 2001 report of the chief electoral officer indicated the government had no intention of even debating the officer's proposed changes (which did not concern the voting system) in the House of Commons. The reaction is perhaps the most blatant example but far from the only one of this tendency to resist change.[19]

Turning to the second chambers within the Westminster systems reviewed in this volume, it is evident that the oldest, the British House of Lords, is undergoing an extensive transformation. Yet even in its final guise, still unclear at this point, its primary purpose will not be to serve as a voice for regions. The UK government has agreed to have a minority of members elected to represent the regions, but maintains that the majority of Lords will be appointed.[20]

Although, as Lord Wakeham argues in his chapter, future Lords may represent broader societal interests than in the past, it is far from clear what these interests will be and how they will be represented. Most members of the Royal Commission favoured a model that would have members of the House of Lords elected within regions for a fifteen-year term. Yet there was little consideration in the Commission report for how these elected Lords would maintain ties with their regions, a natural concern given the length of term proposed.[21] The German model was rejected by the Wakeham Commission, which suggested that links between regional chambers and the federal upper chamber would not be institutionalized.

Representation in the Australian and Canadian Senates is based on states or provinces. Australian senators represent the interests of citizens within their jurisdiction and are not voices for the sub-national governments. Neutered politically by the fact that its members are appointed, the Canadian Senate performs valuable legislative services in fine-tuning bills and often holds important public hearings (either alone or jointly with the House of Commons). Its representative function is more questionable. Although Canadian senators represent various interests, the mere fact that they are appointed, instead of elected, mutes much of this function. The Australian Senate is more powerful than the Canadian second chamber, and although prime ministers are always members of the lower house, Australian senators are more likely to be in the cabinet than their Canadian counterparts.

Despite the Canadian Senate's acknowledged weakness, its reform has become a quagmire best avoided. The need for provincial agreement on Senate reform has ground down more than one round of constitutional discussions. Notwithstanding initial support for some changes and the success of the Reform Party in Western Canada, based in part on its call for a Triple-E Senate (equal, elected, and effective), support from provincial governments has been spotty.

This is not surprising. Ontario and Quebec, each with nearly one-quarter of the Senate's seats, have traditionally been opposed to any moves that would decrease their present Senate representation. And while smaller provinces would stand to gain, smaller provincial governments would lose dramatically. A remodeled Senate, whether a variation of Triple-E or even a house of the provinces similar to the South African second chamber, would be an instrument of intrastate federalism, as discussed below. It is doubtful that all provincial premiers would willingly hand provincial senators their power to command the national stage.

In addition, the failure of the Meech Lake and Charlottetown Accords has made federal politicians gun-shy of reopening any serious constitutional discussions. The last attempt at large-scale constitutional reform, the Charlottetown Accord, was a high-water mark for public consultation on questions of constitutional and democratic reform. As part of the package, Ontario and Quebec agreed to equal provincial representation in an elected Senate. There were substantial moves on self-government, though some Aboriginal people were opposed to the proposal.[22] But the extraordinary effort that went into the Accord, only to be met with failure when brought before Canadians in a national referendum, extinguished any appetite among federal politicians to engage in large-scale reform for the foreseeable future. Even the Reform/Alliance party is comfortable leaving Senate reform on the policy back burner.[23] We cannot blame federal politicians for heeding public sentiment and bypassing mega-constitutional projects.

RESPONSIVENESS IN CANADA

Explaining the government's failure to address House of Commons reform leads one to a less sympathetic conclusion. First, there is every reason to believe that voters would welcome such moves. Parliament and the men and women who serve in it are held in low regard by the public. Members of Parliament are criticized for quickly losing touch with their constituents, and both houses of Parliament are seen as increasingly less relevant in the policy process.[24] In addition, renewal of Parliament is increasingly a subject for the national media. Whether in guest columns by academics[25] or regular features by reporters and columnists,[26] parliamentary reform has remained on the public agenda. However, it has been far from front and centre on the government's agenda.

The last significant set of parliamentary reforms was undertaken as a result of the McGrath committee report. Many of the report's recommendations were implemented by Brian Mulroney during his first term as prime minister (beginning in 1984).[27] Since then, parliamentary reform has been undertaken only at the margins, with committees receiving limited mandates. The House Modernization Committee struck after the 2000 general election is only the most recent example.[28]

Canada has been governed for successive generations by prime ministers with little regard for the centrality of Parliament in discussions of public policy. Pierre Trudeau came to appreciate the House of Commons only in his later years. John Turner, the individual with the shortest tenure in the top job, was the last prime minister whom other MPs saw as a parliamentarian.[29] Brian Mulroney only became a member of Parliament months prior to becoming prime minister.

The fact that Jean Chrétien is a political careerist in the truest sense should not be misinterpreted as a sign that he loves parliamentary life. In a style not dissimilar to that of the long-serving Speaker of the U.S. House of Representatives, Sam Rayburn, Jean Chrétien has become the embodiment of the mantra "In order to get along, you go along." Paul Thomas suggests that Chrétien's use of the party whip is stricter than all of his recent predecessors.[30] Liberal backbenchers believe the prime minister places loyalty to the leader above all other attributes when determining who receives promotions.[31]

Quite simply, governments are not inclined to harbour dissent from the men and women who carry their party's banner at election time. Canada's history of strong party discipline is second to none in Westminster jurisdictions, with the possible exception of the Australian lower chamber.[32]

Perhaps most frustrating for advocates of parliamentary reform is the lip service paid to the question by the prime minister. The 1993 Red Book, the document outlining the Liberal Party's governing principles, called for substantial improvements to free up backbenchers.[33] Two elections later, this campaign commitment has yet to be acted upon, though, as mentioned above, the government did create a House Modernization Committee following the 2000 election. As Jennifer Smith argues in her chapter, the majority of changes proposed by the Modernization Committee provide for greater efficiency, even if scrutiny is compromised. In this sense, at least, majoritarian principles continue to allow the federal government to maintain strong control over policy- and law-making.

Lijphart argues that majoritarian systems with alternating governments are more likely to mitigate the effects of non-responsiveness; systems with a single dominant party are less likely to feel the need to respond.[34] The Canadian experience with alternating governments has been limited. Canada has been governed by the Liberal party for thirty of the past forty years. Lijphart bases his argument on the presumption that a majoritarian system should have two major competing parties. While that was the case for most of the century in Canada, the past three elections have been fought by one national party, two regional parties, and two fractured national parties fighting for parliamentary survival. Canada does not have the first criterion for responsiveness.

Nor does Canada hold the second ameliorating condition, a homogeneous society. Canada is a nation of many regions, cultures, and peoples. New Zealand has perhaps been able to respond relatively effectively to questions of Mäori political participation. In that context, a unitary state and the absence of other cultural debates provided the government with more freedom to respond to questions of first peoples without fear of disagreement from sub-national governments or other significant minorities.

However, Canada's cultural pluralism has not fractured the country. Regional tensions often offset linguistic splits, and successful federal governments require support from both the anglophone majority outside Quebec and the francophone majority inside Quebec. Regions are more likely than linguistic communities to be left out of governments.

At the same time, the Canadian state has made few efforts at responding to calls for large-scale citizen participation. Canada has been reluctant to turn to referendums, despite calls for this from political parties and academics.[35] The last national experience with a referendum, the 1992 Charlottetown Accord, ran into many of the same problems that beset the Australians when they chose to maintain their monarchial ties. People voted "No" for different reasons, and it ended – at least for the foreseeable future – attempts at mega-constitutional change.

The Canadian government's efforts to react to concerns outside the larger constitutional arena have been more productive. In many instances, majoritarian principles have aided and not hindered responsiveness. This is particularly true on politically sensitive issues where opinions are divisive and deeply held.

The greatest area of such sensitivity remains Canada's relationship with its Aboriginal peoples. As Paul Chartrand's chapter points out, Canada has been less successful in encouraging indigenous persons' political participation than New Zealand. The constitutional "promise" contained in the 1982 amendments has, nearly twenty years later, not been realized. The legal meaning of Aboriginal rights as enunciated under section 35 of the 1982 Constitution Act has yet to be clarified by the courts. Further, as Chartrand indicates, neither the courts nor Parliament has adequately resolved the "question of identifying the Aboriginal peoples whose ancestral rights are protected in the constitution." Again, however, these problems are often weighted down with constitutional ramifications that require the agreement of multiple governments.

The Nisga'a treaty, ratified by Parliament in 2000, is an example of responsiveness that was perhaps easier to achieve through majoritarian principles. As Chartrand explains, the treaty is long, detailed, and complex. But, as the first of its kind, it will serve as the model for any future treaties for First Nations in British Columbia. Highly contentious throughout its negotiation, the treaty had to pass legislative muster in both the British Columbia and federal legislatures. In both arenas, majority governments and strong party discipline were essential. It is of course impossible to prove "what might have been" under different circumstances. However, had the provincial government not been able to shield itself from public reaction by relying on its majority, the treaty might never have made it through the first legislative stage.

Similarly, the creation of the Territory of Nunavut, while perhaps less controversial than the Nisga'a treaty, required government leadership at each level. This suggests governments are not stagnant and can react effectively when required. In both cases, responsiveness has led to better representation. In the case of Nunavut, with close to 80 per cent of the population being of Aboriginal origin, the vast majority of elected and senior administrative positions are held by Aboriginal people. The link between better representation and responsiveness is self-evident in both the Nunavut and Nisga'a cases. Less in the spotlight than larger constitutional questions, such successes suggest that majoritarian governments can be responsive to changing conditions. It is also a good reminder that Canada, while failing to embrace reform at the core of its Westminster system, is amenable to evolving conceptions of citizenship and society.

MULTI-LEVEL GOVERNANCE

As Lijphart suggests, federalism is the most "typical and drastic" method of dividing power in a state.[36] Federalism posses a challenge to pure majoritarian principles simply by dividing power beyond the national and sub-national governments. The latter provide both an additional avenue for public participation and a potential restriction on the freedom of the national government to pursue its policy objectives independently. Depending on the form of federation, national governments can be challenged from within (intrastate federalism) or by sub-national governments (interstate federalism). Institutions of intrastate federalism are usually found in the second chambers of the national government, while interstate federalism entails provincial (or state) governments competing or collaborating with a national government. Centralized federations tend to operate through a system of intrastate federalism, while decentralized systems typically have the principal characteristics of interstate federalism.

South Africa's Council of Provinces is an intrastate body. As Christina Murray points out, drawing on the German Bundesrat, the ruling African National Congress made a conscious effort to avoid giving too much power and independence to the provinces. In particular, the national government initiates and funds policies to be administered by the provinces. With provincial representation in the Council of Provinces, provincial concerns are represented. Murray suggests that it is too early to determine the success of the NCOP. Among other things, poorer provinces are left to administer a plethora of laws that they have not passed. However, by providing provinces with some power, albeit administrative, the need for continued dialogue and negotiation has developed. As Murray states, such a system demands "honest and open" debate between levels of government.

Canadian multi-level governance is decentralized and essentially interstate in nature. In terms of majoritarian principles, this provides some check on the exercise of concentrated power. Yet the same institutional arrangements at the national level are also largely in place at the provincial level. As Stéphane Dion points out, this has facilitated the development of highly productive executive federalism. He is also of the view that, to function properly, multi-level governance with competing strong governments requires a set of agreed-upon principles. In Canada, these principles include an understanding that executive federalism includes high-profile meetings among first ministers and extensive meetings and agreements between officials from various government departments. This suggests intergovernmental relations is a symbiotic relationship that requires interdependence and cooperation.

Among other successes, executive federalism has led to a national system of public health care, a publicly-funded pension plan (although Quebec has a separate regime), and, more recently, changes to the delivery of labour market programs and a national benefit program for children.[37] Multi-level governance in Canada has thus provided significant avenues for responsiveness to citizens' needs and expectations.

Lessons for Canada

There is little chance that Canada will, in the foreseeable future, move away from the central features of the classic majoritarian system. The elements that help to create majority governments also help ensure that majority governments will not move to alter them. Nor are majoritarian principles responsible for certain of the perceived ills of Canadian governance.

The Australian electoral system – the alternative vote in the House of Representatives and proportional representation in the Senate – provides incumbents with some measure of electoral security. Yet, as noted above, levels of party discipline in Canada and Australia are comparable. Members of Parliament at Westminster have far greater freedom from the party whip than their Canadian counterparts, yet are selected in precisely the same manner.

Party discipline in Canada is strong in part because successive prime ministers have been able to convince their backbench colleagues that it is in their best interests. While Jean Chrétien may seem to be the master of "court government," he is hardly the only prime minister to have adopted this style.[38] Parliament's decline has been evolutionary, though party discipline has been an enduring feature of Canada's version of the Westminster model. We have been reluctant to remove ourselves from the apron strings of Westminster simply because it serves the purpose of the government of the day to hold on to them.

Nor have Canadians immersed themselves in any serious discussion of the future of the monarchy. While the Queen (or the monarch's representative) is a constitutional figure in parliamentary government, little time has been spent debating the role of the Crown in our modern democracy. Perhaps due to the merits of certain governors general or the difficulty of amending the constitution in this regard, Canada has not been tempted to replicate the Australian experience of holding a nationwide vote on the merits of republicanism.

What Canada has engaged in, earlier than many of the other nations examined in this volume, is massive constitutional reform in other areas. The Charter of Rights and Freedoms stands as the biggest single transformation of post-war Canadian democracy. The impact of patriation of the constitution and the entrenchment of fundamental rights will continue into the distant future. There can be little denying the arguments of those who suggest that it has increased the role of the courts in Canadian society. But it is less clear that this in itself has meant a diminution in the role of Parliament (and provincial legislatures). Many of the ills of Parliament have been created from within and can likewise be cured from within.

It is worth noting that systems of proportional representation are often commended for representing and protecting diversity in society. Systems of proportional representation generally do produce legislatures that are more representative of society than single-member plurality models. While a charter of rights cannot, in itself, represent diversity, it can and does protect groups and individuals – as has been demonstrated through judicial interpretation of Aboriginal and official language rights. Indeed, as James Kelly contends, judicial interpretation of the Charter has deepened diversity "by advancing the principle of inclusion."[39]

Successive governments, both provincially and nationally, should also be commended for embracing new styles of federal-provincial cooperation, including seeking more citizen involvement. Less in the spotlight than larger questions of constitutional reform, these experiments have been fruitful and suggest that executive federalism can adjust to changing conceptions of representation and responsiveness.

We have been less willing to engage in similar experiments within our existing parliamentary bodies. Other Westminster systems have not been afraid to move away from traditional understandings of governance. In some cases, notably in the United Kingdom as part of devolution, major changes to majoritarian government have come about by establishing new systems of representation. South Africa's move to a National Council of Provinces came out of a much larger – and critical – search for responsiveness to a highly diverse society. The success of South African democracy will depend in part on the success of its second chamber.

Measuring the success of some other changes is more difficult. It is too soon to tell if the move to proportional representation will deliver the type of government New Zealanders believed it would when they backed reform. However, the parliamentary review completed in 2001 (see Jonathan Boston's chapter) suggests there is no compelling pressure to return to the former system.

The lessons for Canada should be clear. Several other countries that share the Westminster model have experimented with different methods of providing effective representation, responsiveness, and multilevel governance. Reform of Canada's Senate, increasing the ability of members to act on behalf of electors, and moving to a non-majoritarian electoral system have remained off the agenda of most Canadian prime ministers. As the examinations of Canada and other states presented in this volume suggest, not all attempts at reform will be immediately successful. Initial changes may require some adjustments. However, the willingness to engage in the exercise of institutional reform and related changes is in itself a recognition of the responsiveness of governments to the citizens they are charged with representing. And representing citizens, it seems, should be their primary role.

NOTES

1 Arend Lijphart, *Patterns of Democracy: Government Forms and Performance in Thirty-Six Countries* (New Haven: Yale University Press, 1999), chap. 2.

2 Lijphart, *Patterns of Democracy*, 275–7.

3 See Alan C. Cairns, "The Electoral System and the Party System in Canada, 1921–1965," *Canadian Journal of Political Science* 1, no. 1 (1968): 55–80. See also Roger Gibbins, "Early Warning, No Response: Alan Cairns and Electoral Reform," (paper presented at "Rethinking Citizenship in the Canadian Federation" conference in honour of Alan Cairns, Vancouver, British Columbia, 12 October 2001).

4 The obvious exception is the United States, where power is dispersed throughout both houses of Congress and the presidency. However, American elections often lead to one-party majorities.

5 G. Bingham Powell, *Elections as Instruments of Democracy* (New Haven: Yale University Press, 2000), 5, 175.

6 Lijphart, *Patterns of Democracy*, 275.

7 Ibid., 275. It is curious that Lijphart uses this reference, coming as it does from a former president of the United States, where majoritarian principles are more apparent than consensus approaches.

8 See Jonathon Boston's chapter in this volume.

9 Northern Ireland has eighteen regions that each elect six members; there are no constituency seats. See Robert Hazell's chapter in this volume and Robert Hazell, ed., *The State and the Nations: The First Year of Devolution in the United Kingdom* (London: Imprint Academic, 2000). Following its election in 1997, the Labour government appointed a commission chaired by Lord Jenkins. Its October 1998 report recommended a mixed system: 15–20 per cent of MPs would be elected on a proportional basis through a list system; the remainder would be elected by the alternative vote; see *The Report of the Independent Commission on the Voting System* (London: The Stationery office, October 1998). Although the Labour government had promised a referendum on the Westminster electoral system, no action on this has been taken.

10 This occurred in 1984 when the Mulroney-led Progressive Conservatives received exactly 50 per cent of the vote. In 1945 the Liberal Party won the support of 49.5 per cent of the voting electorate.

11 Louis Massicotte, "Changing the Canadian Electoral System," *Choices: Strengthening Canadian Democracy* 7, no. 1 (Montreal: Institute for Research on Public Policy, February 2001): 4. Distortions in parties' regional representation have led to a number of proposals to change Canada's electoral system: see F. Leslie Seidle, "*The Canadian Electoral System and Proposals for its Reform*," in *Canadian Parties in Transition*, 2d ed., ed. A. Brian Tanguay and Alain-G. Gagnon (Scarborough: Nelson Canada, 1996), 292–4.

12 Cairns, "The Electoral System and Party System in Canada."
13 C.E.S. Franks, *The Parliament of Canada* (Toronto: University of Toronto Press, 1987), 33.
14 For example, in health care such national standards can be found in the Canada Health Act.
15 Herman Bakvis and Grace Skogstad, "Canadian Federalism: Performance, Effectiveness and Legitimacy," in *Canadian Federalism: Performance, Effectiveness and Legitimacy*, ed. Herman Bakvis and Grace Skogstad (Toronto: Oxford University Press, 2001), 14.
16 Leslie A. Pal and F. Leslie Seidle, "Constitutional Politics 1990–92: The Paradox of Participation," in *How Ottawa Spends: A More Democratic Canada?* ed. Susan D. Phillips (Ottawa: Carleton University Press, 1993), 143–202; F. Leslie Seidle, "Executive Federalism and Public Involvement: Integrating Citizen's Voices," (paper presented at the "Changing Nature of Democracy and federalism in Canada" conference, Winnipeg, Manitoba, 14 April 2000).
17 Donald Savoie, *Governing from the Centre: The Concentration of Power in Canadian Politics* (Toronto: University of Toronto Press, 1999), 191–2.
18 See, for example, R. Kenneth Carty, "Electoral reform should begin with the Senate," *Policy Options*, November (1997): 39–41.
19 Campbell Clark, "Expect to Reveal Donors Leadership Contenders Told," *The Globe and Mail*, 17 December 2001.
20 *The House of Lords – Completing the Reform* (London: The Stationery Office, November 2001).
21 Meg Russell and Robert Hazell, "Devolution and Westminster: Tentative Steps towards a more Federal Parliament," in *The State and the Nations: The First Year of Devolution in the United Kingdom,* ed. Robert Hazell (London: Imprint Academic, 2000), 214–19.
22 Pal and Seidle, "Constitutional Politics," 167.
23 See Jennifer Smith's chapter in this volume.
24 David C. Docherty, "Our Changing Concept of Representation," in *Value Change and Governance,* ed. Neil Nevitte (Toronto: University of Toronto Press, forthcoming 2002).
25 See, for example, Michael Bliss, "Seeking Renewal for a One-Party State," *National Post*, 5 May 2001. See also Jack McLeod, "What We Need is a Revival," *National Post*, 3 March 2001.
26 See, for example, Luiza Chwialkowska, "No Room for Dissent," *National Post*, 15 February 2001, and Hugh Windsor, "Saving the Enfeebled Parliamentarian," *The Globe and Mail*, 4 April 2001.
27 Franks, *The Parliament of Canada*, 136–7.
28 Canada, House of Commons, *Report of the Special Committee on the Modernization and Improvement of the Procedures of the House of Commons*, June 2001.

29 This assessment on the part of the author is based on interviews with present and former members of Parliament over the past ten years. The author found broad agreement among parliamentary veterans that John Turner maintained a stronger belief in the centrality of Parliament than previous or subsequent prime ministers.

30 Paul Thomas, "Party Caucuses: Behind Closed Doors," *Parliamentary Perspectives* 1, no. 1 (1998).

31 David C. Docherty, *Mr. Smith Goes to Ottawa: Life in the House of Commons* (Vancouver: UBC Press, 1997), chap. 6. Subsequent surveys by the author have confirmed this finding.

32 Rodney Smith, "Parliament," in *Developments in Australian Politics,* ed. Judith Brett, James Gillespie, and Murray Foot (Melbourne: Macmillan Education Australia, 1994), 106–29.

33 *Creating Opportunity: The Liberal Party Plan for Canada* (Ottawa: Liberal Party of Canada, 1993). Among the pledges in the Red Book was a commitment to give parliamentary committees "greater influence over government expenditures" and to allow for "more free votes in the House of Commons" (see p. 92).

34 Lijphart, *Patterns of Democracy,* 31–2.

35 Matthew Mendelsohn and Andrew Parkin, "Introducing Direct Democracy in Canada," *Choices: Strengthening Canadian Democracy* 7, no. 5 (Montreal: Institute for Research on Public Policy, June 2001).

36 Lijphart, *Patterns of Democracy,* 185.

37 Harvey Lazar, "The Federal Role in a New Social Union: Ottawa at the Crossroads," in *Canada: The State of the Federation 1997. Non-Constitutional Renewal*, ed. Harvey Lazar (Kingston: Institute of Intergovernmental Relations, 1998), 114–23.

38 Donald Savoie, "The Rise of Court Government in Canada," *Canadian Journal of Political Science* 32, no. 4 (1999): 635–64.

39 James B. Kelly, "The Supreme Court and the Charter: Advancing Federal Diversity," (paper presented at the conference "Managing Tensions: Evaluating the Institutions of the Federation," Kingston, 2–3 November 2001).

Notes on Contributors

JONATHAN BOSTON is professor of public policy at Victoria University of Wellington, New Zealand. He is the author/editor of fifteen books and numerous scholarly articles on public management and public sector reform, electoral reform, New Zealand politics, social policy, and tertiary education policy.

PAUL CHARTRAND, a former professor of law and native studies, is a private consultant in Victoria, British Columbia. In 1991 he was appointed a member of the Royal Commission on Aboriginal Peoples. Since November 1999, he has been a member of the Aboriginal Justice Implementation Commission of Manitoba.

STÉPHANE DION is president of the Privy Council and minister of Intergovernmental Affairs for the Canadian Government. Before being elected to the House of Commons in 1996, he taught political science and public administration at the Université de Montréal.

DAVID C. DOCHERTY is chair of the Department of Political Science at Wilfrid Laurier University and the author of *Mr Smith Goes to Ottawa: Life in the House of Commons*. He specializes in legislative and electoral issues, and is a member of the executive of the Canadian Study of Parliament Group.

MASON DURIE is professor and head of the School of Mäori Studies at Massey University. He was a member of the Royal Commission on

Social Policy and the Ministerial Advisory Committee on Mäori Health. He has written three books, *Whaiora: Mäori Health Development, Te Mana, Te Kawanatanga: The Politics of Mäori Self Determination* and *Mauri Ora: The Dynamics of Mäori Health.*

ROBERT HAZELL is professor of government and director of the Constitution Unit in the School of Public Policy at University College London. Formerly a senior civil servant in the Home Office, he was director of the Nuffield Foundation for six years. He is the editor of *Constitutional Futures* and *The State and the Nations: The First Year of Devolution in the United Kingdom.*

CHRISTINA MURRAY is professor of constitutional and human rights law at the University of Cape Town. In 1994, she advised the South African Constitutional Assembly on the drafting of the Constitution. In 1998 she completed a needs assessment of South Africa's recently established second chamber, the National Council of the Provinces.

CHERYL SAUNDERS holds a personal chair in law at the University of Melbourne where she is associate dean, Research and Graduate Studies, and director of the Centre for Comparative Constitutional Studies. Her research interests include comparative constitutional law and thoery, constitution-making and design, and intergovernmental relations.

F. LESLIE SEIDLE is senior director, National and International Research and Policy Development, at Elections Canada. He was research director (Governance) at the Institute for Research on Public Policy (1992–96) and senior research coordinator for the Royal Commission on Electoral Reform and Party Financing (1990–91). He served as vice-president of the Canadian Study of Parliament Group from 1996 to 2002.

JENNIFER SMITH is a professor in the Department of Political Science at Dalhousie University (Nova Scotia). She has written extensively about issues related to electoral democracy, Canadian government and politics, and comparative government.

LORD WAKEHAM was chairman of the Royal Commission on House of Lords Reform (1999). He was first elected to the House of Commons in 1974 and was appointed to the House of Lords in 1992. Between 1982 and 1992 he held various posts in the British government.

Index

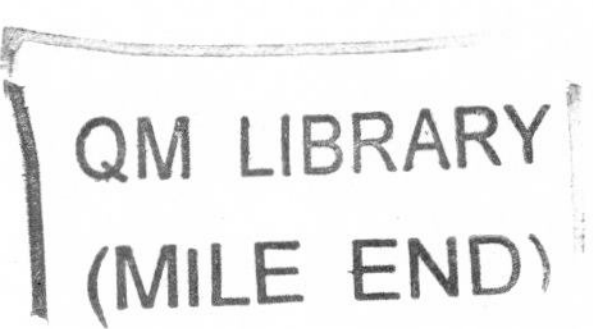

REFORMING PARLIAMENTARY DEMOCRACY